DEGREES OF DIFFERENCE

This volume investigates the dissonance between the supposed advantage held by educated women and their continued lack of economic and political power. Niemi explains the developments of the so-called "female advantage" and "boy crisis" in American higher education, setting them alongside socioeconomic and racial developments in women's and men's lives throughout the last 40 years. Exploring the relationship between higher education credentials and their utility in creating political, economic, and social success, *Degrees of Difference* identifies ways in which gender and academic achievement contribute to women's and men's power to shape their lives. This important book brings new light to the issues of power, gender identities, and the role of American higher education in creating gender equity.

Nancy S. Niemi is Director of Faculty Teaching Initiatives at the Center for Teaching and Learning at Yale University, USA.

DEGREES OF DIFFERENCE

Women, Men, and the Value
of Higher Education

Nancy S. Niemi

Routledge
Taylor & Francis Group

NEW YORK AND LONDON

First published 2017
by Routledge
711 Third Avenue, New York, NY 10017

and by Routledge
2 Park Square, Milton Park, Abingdon, Oxon, OX14 4RN

Routledge is an imprint of the Taylor & Francis Group, an informa business

© 2017 Taylor & Francis

Library of Congress Cataloging-in-Publication Data
A catalog record for this book has been requested

ISBN: 978-1-138-69742-3 (hbk)
ISBN: 978-1-138-69743-0 (pbk)
ISBN: 978-1-315-52181-7 (ebk)

Typeset in Bembo
by Apex CoVantage, LLC

For my children: Andrew, Nathaniel, and Anna

CONTENTS

FIGURES AND TABLES

Figures

Tables

PREFACE

The ideas at the center of this book began forming in 2005, as I was sweltering in a packed high school auditorium celebrating my oldest child's graduation. Pallets stacked with water bottles were being unloaded, and sweaty containers were offered to the parents and grandparents who had come to watch their be-robed children make their way across center stage. Two young women, valedictorian and salutatorian respectively, had each spoken; diplomas had been awarded. Only one more speech, mercifully, before the singing of the alma mater and the concluding "Pomp and Circumstance." T.C., senior class president and my son's good friend, got up to speak. Rising to his full 6 foot 2 inches, he smiled and began: "The two smartest people in the class may be girls . . . but look who's president." I scribbled that quote on the top of the commencement program and have hung it in every office I have had since that day. So was launched a journey of systematic research into the ways in which gender and academic achievement contribute to women's and men's power to shape their lives.

More than 10 years later, my scholarship remains rooted in investigating the ways in which the aspirations and actualities of schooling and gender impact each other. Understanding that education as a conveyor-of-equity responds to the cultural patterns in which it is situated, my work has traversed landscapes such as middle school girls' and boys' ideas of intelligence, gendered perceptions of teachers in children's literature, and multiple aspects of college students' and professors' gender identities. Schooling and the knowledge and skills it offers provides critical individual development, but absent an analysis of the ways in which its structures influence and are influenced by cultural forces, it is insufficient to create the gender equity for which so many fight.

Purpose of Book

The objective of *Degrees of Difference* is to investigate the relationship between higher education credentials and their utility in creating political, economic, and social power for women and men in the United States. Millions of people pursue college credentials believing in their power to elevate, to improve. If formal higher education is to retain its current place as a launchpad for equity and economic health, it must bear the scrutiny that such a vaunted position demands. Particularly for women across and within the racial, ethnic, and socioeconomic spectra that comprise the United States, it is imperative that relationships between school success and power be laid bare. Currently portrayed as a privileged gender—at least in arguments about academic success—women need to understand the payoffs of their investments in higher education credentials.

Further, as more people question the ways in which U.S. men come of age, it is equally important that we attempt to understand what males think higher education engagement is promising or denying them. Higher education cannot afford to become a "women's issue"; as the country's persistent, unresolved debates surrounding contraception, abortion rights, and child/family care have illustrated, so-called women's issues only stand a chance of being resolved if they are understood as *everyone's* problems, with the solutions encompassing changes in law, policy, and behavior relating to men as well as women.

Intended Audience

This book explores the relationships among gender, higher education, and power. The continuity with which these issues have been investigated has led to numerous studies, articles, books, and commentaries, appearing in a wide variety of venues. The argument I present is written primarily for scholars and students of gender and higher education policy and practice. But as a participant in higher education myself—first as student, then professor, administrator, and director who cares deeply about gender equity in and outside academia—I have attempted to write with minimal jargon in hopes of generating conversation among all who care about these issues.

Brief Overview of the Book

Degrees of Difference is about college credentials and their diminishing utility in creating political, economic, and social power for women and men in the United States. It is my contention that such credentials offer increasingly lesser advantages to individuals—particularly women—who do not have other means to shape the circumstances of their lives. Exploring how we got to this place and what we might do about it are the questions that guide this book.

Chapter 1 is an introduction to the controversies surrounding U.S. women's and men's college attendance and achievement. It explains the developments of the so-called female advantage and boy crisis in American higher education, setting them alongside socioeconomic and racial developments in women's and men's lives throughout the last 40 years. I argue that American culture and higher education are in the midst of two fundamental shifts: (1) higher education credentials are being devalued and (2) men are migrating to places other than college to gain knowledge and skills that are increasingly valued and powerful.

Chapter 2 explains the analytic lenses with which I frame this argument. Our gender identities impact the ways in which we make decisions about our lives; because they are deeply embedded in cultural norms, however, the power they have to shape such decisions is obscured. My argument focuses on the tension between beliefs about gender equity in America, the entrenched gender identities of masculinity and femininity, and the ways in which current sociopolitical contexts shape and influence the power of educational expectations for women and men.

Chapter 3 traces the struggle between American higher education and gendered cultural roles, and the continuous negotiation of male power via schooling. Examining these struggles as they connect to previous eras of educational change in the United States offers context for the current state of formal education, in which the schooling-for-all mandate serves as a foundational tenet for the American Dream. This analysis includes an exploration of the ways in which gender identities led to changes in formal high school education in America, foreshadowing some of the current shifts in higher education.

Chapter 4 offers current and often contradictory data about the "boy crisis" in the context of the "female advantage" argument, locating both in the rise of the "college for everyone" movement and what I label as "digital savior" plans. Investigation of the landscape of college access, completion, and success, as they are broken down by various kinds of institutions and students, shows that women and men still have differential access to education and that one cannot look at gender equity without also taking race and social class into account. Doing so, as others have long advocated, radically alters the picture of so-called female dominance in education.

Chapter 5 presents a detailed picture of the educational and professional sites that men are strengthening or creating in lieu of college attendance and completion. I explore ways in which some long-standing male-only spaces are retooling their claims of masculinity, while still others are newly developed in light of affordances offered by digital technologies. Additionally, I provide evidence that many of the male-only settings currently available are more racially and socioeconomically inclusive than higher education has been. Finally, I show that men, more than women, continue to have a wider range of opportunities for accessing meaningful work and accumulating social power, and that current analyses of schooling and equity ignore these realities, thus exacerbating the perception that a "boy crisis" exists.

Chapter 6 explores the ways in which women across racial and economic backgrounds still lag behind men in post-collegiate measures of gender equity. Offering data to support the claim that success in higher education does not offer evidence of an overall decrease in gender inequity, I address the gender pay gap, inequities in child care and time spent on housework, and the myth of opting out of one's career. I also examine trends in occupations where women now earn the majority of the degrees in the field, showing the professions' concomitant decline in status and value.

Chapter 7 centers on the future of formal higher education in the context of women's dominant scholastic performance. I suggest that while attaining higher education credentials is a waning strategy of advancement for men who possess racial, financial, and cultural capital, the push for greater college access for women, as well as for working and middle class men of all races, is a strategy destined to strengthen the capitalist infrastructure of education. I conclude with a reexamination of power, gender identities, and possible futures for the role of American higher education in creating gender equity.

ACKNOWLEDGMENTS

Provocative ideas offer opportunities for invigorating intellectual discussions—converting such dialogue to well-honed arguments is a job for bold (and patient) publishers and editors. To Mitch Allen at Left Coast Press, who initially said yes to this project, and to Heather Jarrow at Routledge, whose editorial stewardship carried it to completion, I offer deep thanks and gratitude. Thank you to Rebecca Collazo of Routledge as well.

I have called several institutions my home through the course of writing this book; the insights, scholarship, and support of my colleagues at Nazareth College, the University of New Haven, and now Yale University, have been invaluable. In particular, I offer thanks to Mary Skvorak, Amanda Bozack, Pat Maiorino, Susanne Murphy, Phyllis Gwatkin, Jenny Frederick, and Kaury Kucera. Julia Smith of Oakland University, who has been teacher, co-author, and friend since we first met at the University of Rochester, has been a steadfast source of intellectual challenge and unwavering support. This book is better because she has been by my side.

To my parents, Richard and Shirley Niemi, and my sisters, Patti, Jen, and Julie: The many nights you spent listening to my vociferous reflections about gender and education offered tangible evidence that you cared deeply about the completion of this project, and my well-being throughout it. Nathaniel, Anna, and Andrew: Your childhoods offered a ringside seat to my development as scholar and writer. The devotion you each bring to your life's work tells me that you observed how passion for career and family can be woven into something extraordinary.

I also offer profound thanks to Lori Reenan who has supported every professional and personal step I have taken for over 30 years. And, to my husband, Michael Morris: The hours you devoted to helping me create the best version of this text, and your forbearance at the breakfast table as the recipient of innumerable conversations about gender offer a new definition of love for which I will be eternally grateful.

1

COLLEGE CREDENTIALS AS FEMALE DISADVANTAGE?

There is good reason why Eden's apple remains the metaphor for the rewards and dangers of knowledge. The collective belief in each individual's ability to create his or her own success, undergirded by an education that is presumably offered equally to all, is so strong that it functions as the secular American religion: If you have a personal relationship with capitalism, created through sweat and school, you will be rich and successful. Formal education for all has been a foundational tenet of the American Dream, with its tantalizing promise that any*one* can be any*thing* with enough hard work and the right credentials. In this story men and women are equal: Neither is better than the other, and every one of us has a place in the future, as long as we take advantage of the opportunities given, and work very, very hard—especially in school.

The idea of American schools may be Edenic, but its daily realities have been far from it. Steeped in deeply embedded cultural beliefs about what men and women should do and be, schools and the expectations for them are simultaneously mediated by race, ethnicity, and social class. Americans of the 19th and 20th centuries loved the idea of school as the great equalizer, as long as it never stood a chance of becoming a reality. Now into the 21st century and realizing that gender equity, at least in school performance, might have been achieved, the country appears to be struggling with the results of this success. Nowhere is this more evident than in discussions of the "female advantage" in American college completion.

Women, at least as a monolithic category, now outperform men on a substantial number of indicators of college success, and Americans of different races and ethnicities attend and complete college now more than they did 20 years ago.[1] The composite successes subsequently form an unfair advantage for women, according to many analysts. I argue that the so-called female advantage in college enrollment, completion, and success is an illusion: Women are not achieving social equity with men by having college diplomas on their walls. Cultural beliefs about the power of higher education credentials and their connection to white male economic, social, and political superiority are shifting, with one result being that American culture has begun to devalue the academic enterprise altogether. In fact, it is possible that the parchment with Old English typography, pronouncing one's completion of academic requirements toward a degree, may be morphing into little more than artwork whose market value is equal to that of 19th-century reprints found in any big box store in America.

Degrees of Difference is about college credentials and their diminishing utility in creating political, economic, and social power for women and men in the United States. Media reports trumpet women's dominance in colleges and universities: They earn more degrees, are more frequently valedictorians, and more participate in extracurricular activities. At the same time, academicians parse the details of this phenomenon, studying what Buchmann and DiPrete named the *female advantage*:[2]

> This growing female advantage in higher education has attracted the attention of college administrators, policymakers, and the media, and researchers are trying to make sense of this reversal from a male advantage to a female advantage in educational attainment as it has unfolded not only in the United States but also in most industrialized societies.[3]

Christina Hoff Sommers, famous for her declaration of feminism's "war against boys," has argued that this advantage is because "as our [American] schools have become more feelings-centered, risk-averse, collaboration-oriented, and sedentary, they have moved further and further away from boys' sensibilities."[4] In other words, schools have gotten softer and so women have *naturally* begun to do better. Man it up, she implies, by utilizing boy-friendly readings with espionage, sports, and battles; letting students fight to resolve their differences; establishing more all-male classes, and supporting the continuation and development of fraternal organizations.

Her statement that "concerns about boys arose during a time of tech bubble prosperity"[5] is particularly revealing: It offers a route to topics largely missing from the "female advantage" arguments—money and power. What few have elucidated is the dissonance between this so-called advantage and the presumed socioeconomic and political power that an "advantaged" woman carries. Now that college credentials are considered the gateway degree to the revised American Dream, I want to challenge the idea that academic success in higher education offers women unequivocal benefits, and shift the conversation away from the "boy crisis" to a different interpretation of scholastic credentials and what they mean for gender equity in light of many women's academic accomplishments.

In addition to questioning the dubious relationship between female success in higher education and gender equity post-education, I pose a different explanation for white men's flattened college enrollment and completion: Men, as a group, are not opting out of college because they *cannot* achieve academically, or because they are not being offered a sufficiently male curriculum. Rather, an increasing number of men are deliberately choosing alternative and more *masculine* means to post-high school success. American cultural expectations continue to encourage men to think about their young adult lives through Western, male-defined capitalism: *Make money. Do not waste your time studying ideas that do not lead to a good job. Success is found in entrepreneurial ventures.* Now that more women have captured the academic playing field, that field has become devalued; traditional male-dominated workplaces look increasingly good to many men, and emerging female-lite spaces—like the tech industry—look even better. This thesis posits a causal mechanism at work: that more women enrolling in academia deliberately pushes men to places other than formal schooling.

Levanon, England, and Allison's analysis of U.S. Census data from 1950 through 2000 offers an introduction to this mechanism by suggesting that as occupations become female-dominated, they become devalued.[6] Beaudry and Lewis, on the other hand, argue that "the U.S. cities that saw the largest increase in the college/high school earnings premium between 1980 and 2000 also exhibited a differentially large decline in the male-female wage differential,"[7] suggesting that there is a female premium to college credentials. I am positing, however, that the male/female wage differential—otherwise known as the "pay gap"—will not be closed ultimately, or even substantially lowered, by women's overall achievement in college. Rather, women's overall college completion and achievement is part of a set of cultural shifts that are moving men away from formal higher education and toward male-dominated spaces of traditional and new educational and occupational spheres.

In some ways, Hoff Sommers was right: As women succeed academically, schools no longer feel "male." This makes sense: Norms do not become visible until they are challenged. But instead of embracing this more balanced and more *effective* means of education, it seems that men may be jumping ship, creating "bubbles" where traditional masculinity is rewarded—and where women do not often tread.[8] As this happens, higher education providers are trying to recapture men who are eschewing traditional college degrees, while at the same time trying to find new customers to fill in the places that men once occupied. Higher education's gender balance is necessary, it seems, for a healthy financial spreadsheet. As such, the market as a whole is morphing, working in conjunction with changing technologies and first-generation and lower socioeconomic college attendees, and shifting gender identities within many parts of the American populace to create new college enrollment and completion demographics that threaten the former white, financially privileged, male-dominated landscape of higher education.

To be sure, women are going to college in record numbers, earning more and higher degrees than before, and as a group they are doing better in college than the men who attend. A Pew Research 2014 analysis shows that females outpace males in college enrollment, especially among Hispanics and blacks.

Hispanic	Women	Men	% point gap, women/men
1994	**52%**	**52%**	**0**
2012	76	62	**+13 women**
Black			
1994	48	56	**+9 men**
2012	69	57	**+12 women**
White			
1994	66	62	**+4 women**
2012	72	62	**+10 women**
Asian			
1994	81	82	**+1 men**
2012	86	83	**+3 women**

FIGURE 1.1   Women Outpace Men in College Enrollment

Yet American men remain in positions of greater economic, social, and cultural power. Though the U.S. economy still rewards educational attainment and punishes the lack of it, it *more strongly* rewards accumulation of wealth and power, constraining educational accomplishments and the power that most people assume comes with academic credentials.

What I would argue is a female *disadvantage*, then, is that just as women have learned to play the higher education game very well, they are finding that the rules of the game have changed. Now that women are succeeding in greater numbers than men in college enrollment, college achievement (academic and extracurricular), and college completion, these achievements are being countered by responses in American economic and political spheres that render women's college successes less meaningful. I maintain that as women obtain more college credentials, the value of those degrees are diminishing, making the cultural call for more college attendance, particularly for those who have never attended before, a shell game with dubious rewards and significant risks.

A Crisis Created

The concept of formal education as female disadvantage may be radical, even if the focus on men's and women's differential academic accomplishments is neither radical nor new. The past 20 years, in particular, have seen academics and popular cultural commentators alike opine about women's growing advantages, in light of their robust academic performance in institutions of American higher education. In 1986, Garibaldi published one of the earliest scholarly articles documenting the racial and gender gaps in American higher education in *The Journal of Negro Education*.[9] It took another decade, however, before the media and other researchers took note of the trend in a significant way. In 1999, for example, Goucher College held a conference devoted to *Fewer Men on Campus*, at which "an array of education experts put forth a variety of gloomy explanations"— from boys' greater physicality to social taboos on male expressivity. Attendee Tom Mortenson of the Pell Institute for the Study of Opportunity in Higher Education, and the "torchbearer for the issue" of women's increasing college success, blamed single-parent families and increasing disengagement of men from family, work, and civic life,[10] stating that his objective at the conference was to "start a national dialogue on the future of men."[11]

Mortenson, as did Garibaldi before him, noted that the trends in women's college enrollment had changed the higher education gender landscape, stating that nearly all of the educational attainment over the last 30 years has been achieved by females.[12] His address to the *Goucher99* conference attendees included attention to racial, ethnic, and socioeconomic differences in U.S. males' college attendance, as well as a state-by-state analysis of college attendance trends according to gender. Commending the Conference for its vision in addressing differential rates of college attendance, he stated that the data he was presenting were the "canary in the coal mine" and that "someday, we may come to point to *Goucher99* as the time and place when the issue [of male decline in college attendance] emerged on the radar screen of public interest and policy."[13]

By this time, others were paying attention to this issue as well. "Where have the men gone?" asked the *Chronicle of Higher Education* during the same period, highlighting growing female enrollments at private liberal arts colleges.[14] Presidents, admissions deans, and professors speculated about the reasons for this shift—using largely anecdotal evidence—and many publicly worried about what these changing demographics might mean for things like alumni giving patterns and dating opportunities. "Another ladies' night, and not by choice," declared Alex Williams in the *New York Times*.

> After midnight on a rainy night . . . in Chapel Hill, NC, a large group of sorority women at the University of North Carolina squeezed into the corner booth of a gritty basement bar. . . . As a night out, it had everything— except guys.[15]

Headlines like "Worries Grow as More Women than Men Enroll in College" and "At Colleges, Women Are Leaving Men in the Dust" began appearing on the front pages of more major newspapers.[16] Online college discussion boards offered the same concerns behind the scenes, with participants revealing worries that maybe men were increasingly discouraged by having to deal with so many female registrars and administrators, or simply too many feminists.[17]

Some took issue with what they felt was a disingenuous hue and cry: Why were concerns about college participation of women, and men and women of color, just now rising feverishly? Where had these arguments been when women were the minority of college completers? King, for example, took issue with both Mortenson's analysis of gender enrollment trends, as well as that of the National Center for Education Statistics (NCES) in 2000, presenting disaggregated indicators of academic achievement by race, ethnicity, and socioeconomic status as well as gender. "There is not a generalized educational crisis among men," she concluded, "but there are pockets of real problems. In particular, African-American, Hispanic, and low-income males lag behind their female peers. . . . These conditions," she continued, "are not new. . . . There is little evidence to suggest that white, middle-class males are falling behind their peers."[18] King and the American Council on Education (ACE) supported their counter-assertion with clear evidence: Overall college enrollment was *increasing*. The number of bachelor's degrees awarded to men was rising—just not as fast as the number awarded to women.[19]

The unsexy reality was that "older men of all races, ethnicities, and incomes— and younger men of all races and ethnicities from low and middle income backgrounds (with the important exceptions of Asian Americans)" were not enrolling and completing as quickly as women of all races, ethnicities, and incomes.[20] King stated: "The fact that degree attainment is rising for both women *and men* [italics original] should remind everyone concerned about male achievement that education is not a zero-sum game in which women's success results in losses for men."[21]

Neither lack of evidence about middle class, white males' supposed diminishing academic achievements, nor reaffirmation of a growing disparity in overall college enrollment and completion between white students and black, Hispanic, and low-income students, stopped public perseveration and alarm about the perceived disparities between *all* men and women. Researchers kept pace with public hand-wringing, putting data behind the drama that Hoff Sommers declared was now a fully fledged *War on Boys*:

> [I]t has [become] fashionable to pathologize the behavior of millions of healthy male children. We have turned against boys and forgotten a simple truth: the energy, competitiveness, and corporal daring of normal males are responsible for much of what is right in the world. No one denies that boys' aggressive tendencies must be mitigated and channeled toward constructive ends. Boys need (and crave) discipline, respect, and moral guidance. Boys need love and tolerant understanding. But being a boy is not a social disease.[22]

Not a social disease perhaps, but judging from the reactions to Mortenson, Sommers, and others, the "boy crisis" may just as well have been the Battle of

Gettysburg. In 2009, Australian researcher David Zyngier found over 54,000 separate website results for "boys' education," over 2,000 academic articles listed in Google Scholar on the topic, and, in a search across Australian libraries, over 500 academic titles on the same subject, subsequently asking, "Do we really need more books telling us there is a problem with boys' underachievement in education?"[23] Only six years later, a 2014 WorldCat search offered an astounding 95,000 titles on the subject, while a 2016 Google Scholar search offered 5,500 academic articles on the same. The time and money invested in questions of gender and education has been enormous.

Major American research and public policy organizations synthesized many of the academic studies in this cavalcade of information, trying to counter the "crisis" and "war" with empiricism. Colleges wanted to know if the focus on boys' behavior at the K–12 level, and the shift that seemed to be occurring in white male college attendance in particular, was a trend that was going to need sustained attention. At roughly the same time Goucher College was asking questions about trends in male college attendance, the American Association of University Women (AAUW) investigated the issue from an intersectional perspective. At their *Beyond the Gender Wars* symposium in 2001, gender and education scholars from K–12 and higher education shared their most recent findings, including:

1.   the impact of racial, ethnic, and socioeconomic differences on gender equity in school;
2.   how the definition of success influences what counts as equity, and
3.   that cultural perceptions and values regarding gender substantially influence academic success at all levels of formal education.[24]

Researchers' recommendations for continued study highlighted the need for collaboration among gender researchers across the elementary school–college spectrum, and the importance of disaggregating educational data in order to tease out the interplay of race and ethnicity, social class, and gender. A particularly important set of voices in scholars' gender and education discussions were Spencer, Porche, and Tolman who poignantly framed the theme of the empirical work that continued throughout the decade:

> [T]he current conception of gender equity as equal rights, equal access, and fairness, though having served the crucial purpose of providing equal opportunities for girls and boys, may be too limited. We were struck by . . . the ready-made explanation of "that's just the way things are." But to reveal and challenge the covert gender ideologies that underpin them can be an incendiary process, as it taps into each of our notions of, and values associated with, not only how things are but how they ought to be with regard to gender. These beliefs, like those associated with race and

other forms of diversity, are deeply rooted in social histories that are filled with marking and using difference as a justification for subordination.

The school context, and the learning environments produced therein, are themselves influenced by a greater social context as are school personnel, who bring with them an added layer of familial and cultural background. Mandated changes in one domain can move progress along only so much. School is but one possible venue in which socialization of gender ideologies occurs, and research investigating the effects of gender equity should consider these other influences in order to accurately assess the impact of gender equity efforts.[25]

In the same year, Weaver-Hightower characterized the growth of popular, theoretical, and practical research on gender as "the boy turn" in research on gender and education[26] and the Ms. Foundation, identifying the tension between nuanced but data-laden academic reports and more hyperbolic public reports, published *Supporting Boys' Resilience: A Dialogue with Researchers, Practitioners, and the Media*[27] in the hope of ameliorating the perspectives. But the torrent of semi-academic reports, symposia, and panels that framed educational gender disparities as "problems with the way schools treat boys" kept coming. Each crisis-oriented report seemed to be countered with a more balanced investigation of the issues. The Educational Equity Center at the Academy for Educational Development, for example, reported the "growing crisis in boys' education"[28] in 2005, while Mead of the Education Sector wrote *The Truth About Boys and Girls* in 2006, and in the same year, the American Council on Education (ACE) once again weighed in. King, the ACE report's author, noted that

> The most striking change [in the college gender gap] since 2000 is the widening gender gap among white and Hispanic traditional-age undergraduates (aged 24 or younger), due primarily to a larger female share among low-income whites and low- and middle-income Hispanics.[29]

King noted that these changes led to an overall decline in the male share of traditional-age students by 3 percentage points between 1995–96 and 2003–04. Among the undergraduates aged 25 or older, she noted, women outnumbered men by almost a two-to-one margin.

By this point, there were enough data to support comprehensive studies that engaged the boy crisis conversation in earnest. Klein and colleagues, for example, published the second edition of *Handbook for Achieving Gender Equity through Education*, while Corbett, Hill, and St. Rose issued the *Facts About Gender Equity*, refuting the notion of a "boys' crisis in education" and, using National Assessment of Educational Progress (NAEP) data, produced a "comprehensive picture of [then] recent achievements by boys and girls in the U.S. educational system,"[30] corroborating King's 2006 conclusions that there was a rise in college attendance

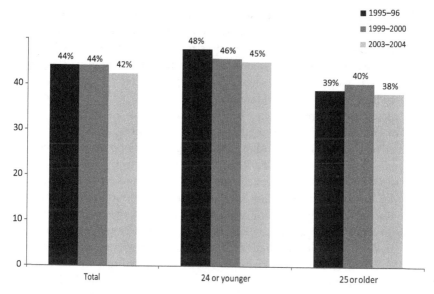

FIGURE 1.2 Percentage of All Undergraduates Who Are Male, by Age—1995–96, 1999–2000, 2003–04

for women and men in most racial, ethnic, and socioeconomic groups. In a parallel stream of research, Noguera, in 2009, and Harper and Harris, in 2010, used earlier researchers' findings on black male high school performance and subsequent college attendance to investigate the ways in which young black boys' masculinities are often contradictory to the culture of American schooling.[31] And the AAUW again contributed to the conversation with its 2012 report on gender equity in education, celebrating the 40th anniversary of Title IX.

In this period, for every empirical study or research report, journalists and public commentators countered with their own versions of the gender crisis and what it meant for American economics, culture, marriage, and most of all, education. Martino, Kehler, and Weaver-Hightower correctly noted that debates on boys' education in the United States have been and continue to be largely the province of the popular press, even as researchers have pushed back. The debate focused public attention on individual solutions rather than nuanced, systemic, and policy-focused answers,[32] and most popular writers used data selectively and sparsely in order to fan the flames of a color-blind gender war in schools. Pollack, for example, argued that a "boy code" trapped boys behind a mask of masculine power. Kindlon and Thompson were among many who argued that the organizational structure of K–12 schools was insensitive to the needs of elementary-aged boys. Leonard Sax, meanwhile, jumped on the neuroscientific bandwagon, arguing without evidence that boys and girls had biological gender differences that directly implicated how boys and girls should be taught, thus engaging in what Cordelia Fine referred to as "neuro-nonsense."[33] Fine, an Australian neuroscientist, suggested that the reason Sax and others' conflations of brain science with gender-specific educational practices received an unprecedented level of popular attention was due to "the implicit hierarchy of *scientificness*."[34] By making claims about gendered behavior and its supposed "natural" site in the brain, Sax and his explanations of (and solutions for) gender inequity in education garnered scientific credibility, even when there was none to be had.

The lack of hard evidence of a biological or wholesale sociocultural problem with *all* boys and their relationship to schooling did not stop writers for popular audiences from continuing to harness data selectively and claim otherwise. Tyre, in *The Trouble with Boys*, suggested that schools needed to change dramatically in order to serve what she maintained were the special learning needs of boys. Tyre was subsequently joined by Whitmire, who asked that we "save our sons from an educational system that's leaving them behind,"[35] and suggested that the ways to do so included changing the "gynocentric curriculum" to include more textbooks that focus on boys and men. He also suggested that schools revert to teaching reading via phonics instead of using literature that focused on text connections and feelings, which he and others thought were "too female" to be of use to men, despite evidence that teaching reading via whole language methods was more effective than phonics alone.[36]

Throughout the first decade of the 21st century, public worry about boys and schooling tacked between K–12 and college students, and public concern about college admissions, costs, access, and completion rose. More students than in the 1980s and 90s were being encouraged to consider attending college, at the same time the cost of college was soaring. Anthony Carnevale, Director of the Global Institute for Education and the Economy at Georgetown University, called this new national commitment to college a "populist promise to put a bookish chicken in every pot," stemming from the maintenance of the American culture of individualism that equates success with one's singular hard work—in this case, college homework.[37] At some point in the middle of these mixed market and academic signals, women's growing achievements in college were deemed a "female advantage," shifting the boy crisis in K–12 and higher education to what many saw as a women's takeover of college education altogether. Buchmann, DiPrete, and Powell may have been the first researchers to phrase women's increasing college achievements as an "advantage," and respected public journalists, who had already been noting these shifts in college attendance, joined the research community in making concerns about higher education, gender balance, and "the female advantage in college completion" front-page issues.

The language of many popular writers evoked a feeling that strange forces were overcoming men: Magic, mystery, and war suffused the articles about women, men, and college, just as the war on boys was being fought at the K–12 level. Writers in *Business Week*, for example, likened gender and college enrollment to the arms race, noting that men were falling behind in the "degree race,"[38] and in *The Washington Post*, writers stated that "colleges and universities across the country are grappling with the case of the mysteriously vanishing male."[39] Analyses of a female advantage in college also revealed another cultural worry, presumably created by 21st-century feminism: a lack of eligible bachelors for potential marriage partners.

With colleges being "the country's most effective marriage brokers," fewer men on campus meant fewer opportunities for women to find husbands; according to Caldwell, "dating culture [on campuses with more women] is skewed."[40] Williams agreed: "Women are paying a social price for success and to a degree, being victimized by men [by not being dated by them] precisely because they have outperformed them."[41] "Once you become decidedly female in enrollment, fewer males and, as it turns out, fewer females find your campus attractive," chimed the dean of Admissions and Financial Aid at Kenyon College, Jennifer Delahunty Britz. "Beyond the availability of dance partners for the winter formal," she continued, "gender balance matters in ways both large and small on a residential college campus."[42] In other words, the gender imbalance at some colleges offered heterosexual men more dating choices because there were now more heterosexual college women to choose from; straight women, apparently, had to come to terms with the reality that they had made it to college, but had fewer men to date.

The dating implications of the female advantage seemed clear: College dating culture was unequivocally heterosexual; it was a problem caused by women's increased enrollment (the dating culture was not a public issue when men dominated campuses; presumably, men found women to date *some*where), and women at colleges where they were the majority gender were going to be hurt if they left college without at least the prospect of having a long-term boyfriend after graduation. The digital and public debate that followed these articles was intense and prolonged, but ultimately a whisper compared to the outcry following "Princeton Mom" Susan Patton's 2013 letter to the editor in *The Daily Princetonian*, which gave gender equity in higher education—and maybe gender equity in its entirety—a slap backwards to Victorian America. She was unapologetic in her *Advice to the Daughters I Never Had*:

> Find a husband on campus before you graduate. . . . For most of you, the cornerstone of your future and happiness will be inextricably linked to the man you marry, and you will never again have this concentration of men who are worthy of you.[43]

Patton went on to say that men do not have this problem—one son had the "good sense" to marry a Princeton woman before he left school, and the other could anticipate having "any woman he wanted." The advantages of gender and social class (race goes unmentioned) were in her view indisputable: Princeton men can choose whomever they want to marry. Princeton women had better "cash in" their youth and privilege before the marriage market no longer wanted them.

Although many in public and academic spheres were outraged by Patton's sexist and classist assertions, her ideas about men, women, and availability in college were nonetheless partly based in empirical evidence within the last 30 years that demonstrates that higher education has been an important dating market. Holland and Eisenhart were early researchers of the interplay between romance, gender, and the influence of peer culture in college life; their 1990 study, *Educated in Romance*, found that many young women in the Southern colleges they studied chose to subvert their academic endeavors in order to find a potential husband, often choosing majors that did not lead easily to careers because they were planning to follow their boyfriends post-graduation. The researchers described the "sexual auction block" in which the young women participated, documenting how both black and white women came to accept the fact that their sexual attractiveness was more important than their scholastic achievement. A college woman's value, they concluded, was determined by her attractiveness and proximity to high-status men; as graduation came closer, career ambitions in many cases diminished. The researchers noted an important distinction between women at the predominantly black university and women at the predominantly white university, however: Black women, they found, were more realistic about their need to become economically independent due to racial inequities and economic instability experienced by black men and women.

Kerr built on this work with inquiry about differences between college men's and women's perceptions of their futures, finding that many of her participants' views of their prospective lives were built on stereotypical gender arrangements of work and home. A majority of men in Kerr's study envisioned a future where their wives were at home with children; many of the women, however, envisioned that the *nanny* would be home with their children while they and their husbands both pursued careers. Kerr reported that college men in her study saw a future in which:

> I wake up and get in my car—a really nice, rebuilt '67 Mustang—and then I go to work—I think I'm some kind of a manager of a computer firm—and then I go home, and when I get there, my wife is there at the door (she has a really nice figure), she has a drink for me, and she's made a great meal. We watch TV or maybe play with the kids.

The college women in her study saw their futures a bit differently:

> I wake up, and my husband and I get in our twin Jettas, and I go to the law firm where I work. Then after work, I go home, and he's pulling up in the driveway at the same time. We go in and have a glass of wine, and we make an omelet together and eat by candlelight. Then the nanny brings the children in, and we play with them until bedtime.[44]

Kerr did not claim that all participants in her study articulated these futures, but that because so many of them did, the composite scenarios she described remained virtually unchanged over 20 years of research.

Five years later, Montgomery added detail to the ways in which college women and men developed the pathways into gendered futures that looked little different from their parents' lives. Through her 2004 investigation of college students' choices of majors, she found persistent patterns of gender stratification in their post-college life choices. Just like Holland and Eisenhart's students, the women in Montgomery's study chose college majors without concern for a particular major's income potential because they planned to have traditional relationships consisting of a stay-at-home mother and a full-time, working father. Drawing on a white, middle class American discourse that calls on the necessity of mothers to be at home with their young children—often referred to as "intensive mothering"—Montgomery's female participants framed their choice of major as an individual preference—"I mean, it's just interesting to me. . . . I like the classes, and so that is what appeals to me"—even though those majors did not necessarily lead to clear career paths or post-graduate study. The women channeled cultural expectations of mothering, reiterating the special role they felt mothers of young children had: "I wouldn't want to work probably during the first five years," stated one young woman, "especially since that affects so much of their patterns of behavior for the future."[45]

Men in Montgomery's study, on the other hand, focused their future career decisions on their potential earning power, and less on their personal interest in the field. When discussing their futures, they also cited gendered patterns of child care. As one participant stated,

> If she (his future wife) *would like to work* (emphasis added), I think that's wonderful until there's kids. And at that time, I really think that the actual, proper place would be at home raising kids because the truth is they can do a better job, actually.[46]

The belief that women were naturally more able than men to care for children was persistent across a majority of Montgomery's participants, though in cases where they were raised by single parents, both women and men indicated the necessity of needing majors that would lead to jobs that could maintain their future families.

In 2012, just a few years after Montgomery's study, Goldberg and colleagues reported on their investigation of the interplay of gender with college students' future plans, having studied almost 1,000 college students at a large Midwestern university. The authors contended that the tension for U.S. women between paid work and child care had diminished significantly, and they hypothesized that current college students would create greater opportunities for sustaining dual commitments to career and family. However, they, too, found that current college students, both female and male, still held traditional gender beliefs regarding the impact of maternal employment on young children. That is, their participants believed that children were much better served if their mothers took care of them full time instead of working in the paid labor force. These results were mediated by ethnicity and culture, with Asian American students displaying the most traditional and European American students the least traditional gender role attitudes. Male Asian American students were particularly likely to believe that maternal employment led to adverse effects on their children's development. European American and Hispanic female students were least likely to see costs of maternal employment for children. As in Montgomery's study, students of both genders whose mothers stayed employed or returned to employment during their own childhood tended to have less stereotypical gender role beliefs about work and child rearing. Goldberg and colleagues concluded that

> If college students' ambivalence about mothers working when their children are young persists, we may continue to see delays in starting families, smaller family size, more part-time paid work for mothers, and more pressure on men to be breadwinners.[47]

DiPrete and Buchmann's studies of gender and college enrollment and completion, culminating in their 2013 book *The Rise of Women*, offer the most recent and by far the most complete investigation of the gender gap in American college enrollment. Their findings both confirmed and challenged what researchers and popular writers before them had asserted:

1. Men's and women's rates of bachelor's degree completion grew between 1970 and 2010, but women's grew much faster.
2. The civil and women's rights movements of the 1960s and 70s created cultural changes that allowed and encouraged more women and underrepresented minorities to attend college and use their education in the paid labor force.
3. Men's underperformance in school has little or nothing to do with their hormones, brain structure, or anatomy and much to do with American social norms about masculinity.[48]

DiPrete and Buchmann's analyses indicated that a female advantage is neither uniformly true for all women, nor an indication of how greater enrollment numbers influence gender equity outside college. Their work is measured and thorough, though their argument that women's successes and higher enrollment in college indicated a "female advantage" contributes to the current cultural zeitgeist that women are somehow in competition with, and doing better than, men.

In much of the male disadvantage/female advantage literature, discussions of race and social class have been muted, but DiPrete and Buchmann do not make this mistake. Using IPUMS (Integrated Public Use Microdata Series), they conclude that Americans of Hispanic and Asian ethnicities follow the same gendered pattern of college enrollment and completion as Americans who identify as white; that is, women complete college at rates higher than men, and now equal or exceed men in obtaining master's, doctoral, and professional degrees.[49] For Americans who are black, DiPrete and Buchmann note that while black women have long led black men in college completion—a gap that is larger now, just as it is for men and women in other racial and ethnic groups—black men have made greater progress in closing the racial gap in college completion rates than black women have in the last 50 years, though they note that racial progress for both groups has slowed recently.[50] (See Figure 1.1.)

DiPrete and Buchmann conclude that white working and middle class men, who are no longer able to use college as a lever of economic power, social power, and de facto superiority in ways that they used to, are the source of the so-called boy crisis. They posit that middle class girls' conceptions of femininity have shifted enough to accommodate having families and careers, whereas middle class boys' conceptions of masculinity remain mired in a "lingering intergenerational memory of (white male) working-class affluence, which colors their conception of masculinity as well as their concrete strategies to transition into adulthood."[51] Their recommendations for school policy include making clear the links between academic work and job opportunities, especially for boys, who demonstrate less understanding of that connection; creating college cultures that expect, value, and reward academic effort, and enhancing students' understanding of the persistence and effort needed to complete college degrees, as well as the level of achievement needed to make a return on investment in obtaining it.

The central weakness in this analysis is the lack of acknowledgment that the college enrollment gap, which was not a problem when white men dominated colleges, has now become one. In a sense, many men in the middle economy are experiencing what women and racial/ethnic minorities have always wrestled with: how to fit into a landscape that was not designed for their worldviews, their race, or for their accustomed ways of working in the world. Of course, attendance and achievement in higher education are not compulsory, and fewer men of all races, ethnicities, and social classes, relative to women, are choosing to attend college. Further, there are colleges where the working class, poor, and non-white less frequently set foot: many top-tier and private schools throughout the country. But in the wake of more college choices for students, a declining number of traditional college-age students, and more college success for *women*, the cry over the lack of adequate numbers of college men is reaching its zenith, making the always-present racial, ethnic, and social class disparities in college attendance for everyone oddly more—and less—visible.

Female College Advantage: A Shell Game?

What is missing from the female advantage argument is consideration of the powerful cultural context within which American higher education resides. Changes in numbers do not always represent a change in underlying attitudes, nor do they indicate, by default, a decrease in bias; school policy and curricular changes do not unequivocally indicate shifts in the gender ideologies held by those who work in and shape education.[52] It is imperative that we continue to investigate the gendered worlds outside of higher education as well as those inside it. Sitting quietly amidst female advantage/boy-crisis debates is the question of impact: *do the changes in higher education enrollment and completion affect overall measures of gender equity?* Does it matter how many women are Phi Beta Kappa if being the smartest in the class no longer holds the cultural capital it once did? Does it matter if women have more master's degrees if they do not pursue ambitious careers because of imagined future children? To put it another way: Now that a majority of women across race, ethnicity, and social class are perceived by men to be "winning" the academic contest, are men abandoning the game?

There have been hints throughout the past century that such a massive shift in the value of educational credentials was possible. Even as the 1990s bore witness to concerns about males and education, and about women's overall college enrollment and completion rates, there have been signs that women's participation in higher education could be a false signal of gender equity. In 1996, for example, Jacobs began noting that gender inequity persisted despite high levels of education for women.[53] Drawing an early connection between the rise in women's college enrollment and the decrease of women entering male-dominated professions, he wrote that

> Most observers view the large and growing number of women in colleges and universities as yet another indication of how far women have come. But this welcome development may also have a darker side, as it reflects in part the continued obstacles women face in obtaining high-paying jobs that require no diploma. In other words, until we see more women wearing mechanic's overalls, we can expect to see more and more women marching in caps and gowns at graduation.[54]

Shortly thereafter, Weaver-Hightower also noted that women's academic achievements were not translating into superior social or economic status; indeed, he stated, certain practices like reading fiction could be rewarded in school but ultimately be self-defeating if engaging in them leads women to adopting traditional feminine identities, such as being rescued by or subordinate to men.[55]

Even college presidents within the last decade noticed that women's higher enrollments in college were not unqualified evidence of growing gender equity. MaryAnn Baenninger, President of the College of St. Benedict, suggested that women's and men's "gender-laden" experiences have unintended consequences in their own lives and in larger society. She observed that female students underestimated their abilities and had less self-confidence in themselves than those abilities warranted.[56] Male students, on the other hand, tended to overestimate their abilities, assuming they had skills—or potential for them—even if none were immediately evident. Further, she concluded that the male college students' work ethic, at least on her campus, was less stringent than those of the college's women; male students spent less time studying and more time playing games, sports, and relaxing, while women spent more time studying, running clubs, and preparing for future work activities through activities such as internships and community projects. Baenninger worried that college women were learning to define success as overachievement while men may have already accepted the idea that college work did not directly relate to success after graduation, foreshadowing DiPrete and Buchmann's conclusions that men less realistically understood the connection between working hard academically and success than women did. Put another way, the male students at the College of St. Benedict seemed to feel that they could afford to invest less energy in their higher educational pursuits than their female peers because they had received the message that the post-college market would award them bonuses simply for being male.

Some speculate that males' disconnect between academic hard work and future life accomplishment signals the continuing existence of a belief in what Connell termed the "patriarchal dividend"—a kind of "affirmative action for men" in which they are relatively assured that women will be excluded from the best jobs, the highest positions of power in their field, and from authoritative decision-making about their families' future trajectories.[57] Social class, race, and ethnicity alter the size of this dividend to be sure. But in most arenas of life, it has been understood that men benefitted simply by being men. The presumed causal links between school achievement and gender equity did not need to be challenged as long as men could usually cash in on their dividend. As long as the investment in a college education acted like a sensible and primarily male return on investment, male college attendance remained a fait accompli for many white, socioeconomically stable young men and their families.

However, the last 40 years have witnessed significant changes in women's legal and economic rights and in the American sociocultural landscape, and in their gendered wake, the causal link between schooling success and socioeconomic success was highlighted in a way that it was not when men's socioeconomic and cultural superiority went unquestioned. As the cultural context changed, women's academic achievement was recast as an "advantage over" men rather than as a needed counterbalance to the prior 200 years of male academic dominance. With the advantage argument in place, and with no clear alternative to higher education to which men could now turn, the assumption was that women's dominance in school success signaled an end to overall male social dominance. The hyperbole that created the "boys' crisis" in American (and British and Australian) K–12 schools matured into a "female advantage" crisis in higher education; this argument, in turn, has been used as the basis for speculation that not only has gender equity been achieved, but that it is boys and men who now suffer academically and culturally.

Socioeconomic reality suggests otherwise. More than 50 years after the passage of the 1963 Equal Pay Act, women still make less money than men across virtually all occupations, despite their success in higher education.[58] Even after controlling for college major, occupation, and employment sector, pay gaps between men and women remain, no matter what college women attended, or what grades they earned, or in what extracurricular activities they participated. Even one year out of college, women who were working full time were paid, on average, just 82 percent of what men working full time were making.[59] Further, the gender wage gap grows as women's careers advance. Women will make less than men in almost any line of work they pursue and even if they gain highly advanced degrees, they will still make less than a man with the same credential. In the top 25 percent of the earnings distribution, women lead men by 13 percent in graduation rates—in other words, women need an education credential much more than men in order to be a high-wage earner; overall, women with advanced degrees make just 66 percent of what men do with the same degrees.[60]

Women of color experience daunting challenges. They have alarmingly low high school graduation rates: Over 45 percent of Native American female students fail to graduate on time, if at all; the same is true for 38 percent of female black and 39 percent of female Hispanic students, which translates to still fewer women of color pursuing college degrees of any kind. The gender wage gap for women of color is subsequently more striking: not only do black and Hispanic women make just 88 cents for every dollar that black and Hispanic men earn, but they make 83 and 69 cents, respectively, for every dollar that their white female counterparts earn, regardless of the level of schooling obtained (see figure 1.3).

Beyond income and career opportunities, from lack of paid maternity leave to rising levels of cosmetic surgery, from sexual violence to full access to health decisions and reproductive rights, from lack of political representation to lack of laws protecting them from abuse through unpaid and domestic labor,[61] American women do not experience equity with American men. Their rise in higher

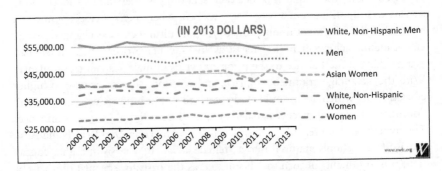

FIGURE 1.3   Median Earnings for Full-Time, Year-Round Workers

Source: Census Bureau, Current Population Survey.

education achievement may be notable, but a "female advantage" in schooling may not be so advantageous if more and better college degrees do not change the lives of women significantly for the better.

Going Elsewhere

Still, American women, no matter what their race, ethnicity, or social class, *are* finding more academic success than men. That is, they exist in a scholastic world where their gender is the majority and where they can be fairly certain that, with varying levels according to their race, ethnicity, and economic status, they will attain in college the things they seek: top grades, multiple majors, field experience in their areas of study, and extracurricular opportunities that allow them to practice their skills. They are valedictorians, salutatorians, and degree holders. In 40 short years, they have gone from low application and admission rates and separate-and-mostly-not-equal facilities to *being* the college admission standard against which others are measured. Although racial, ethnic, and social class equity among women in college is still not yet achieved, American women, writ large, define the college experience, creating a scholastic déjà vu from the previous century when they dominated American high school attendance and performance.

In contrast to the "boy crisis" analysts, particularly those who recommend affirmative action for *some* (mostly white) men while offering scientifically spurious claims about the nature of boys' brains and their incompatibility with female teaching,[62] I argue that American culture and its regard for higher education is in the midst of two fundamental shifts:

1. Higher education credentials, now that women excel at achieving them, are being devalued to the point of being economically and socially neutered.
2. Men are migrating to places other than college to gain credentials and skills—places that are increasingly culturally valued by American society— that promise to restore the male positional advantage that higher education traditionally conferred.

The last two American centuries have allowed boys and young men to push and shape the structure of formal schooling and for a while, with every female breach of the schoolhouse door, they were able to create new, largely woman-free spaces. After girls were allowed to attend grammar school, men went to high school; then girls entered high school, and men went to college or to work, both in places where women, again, were largely absent. Each time females entered the clubhouse-disguised-as-schoolhouse, earning excellent grades, insisting on wanting the same opportunities that males had—such as locker rooms, harassment-free classes, and access to labs, social clubs, and internships—men could move on, creating new spaces and new opportunities for themselves. For a while, separate educational spheres for men of different races and ethnicities muted racial tensions, and white women from families of means created colleges of their own. But these spheres eventually merged, and American women have not only proven their ability to succeed in gaining higher education, but they have excelled at doing so. And so, as with the turn of the 20th century, men 100 years later are turning to new settings for their knowledge and skill development—this time, not only where there are no female students, but also no female teachers. In fact, they are gravitating to places where higher education as we have known it is no longer relevant.

Enmeshed in the female advantage/boy crisis discussion is the current debate about the necessity of a college education—what, the current national conversation asks, does a college education *buy*? Most elected officials, for example, maintain that everyone needs a college education, or at least access to some form of postsecondary education or training. "Everyone needs a postsecondary education," states the 2006 Report by the U.S. Commission on the Future of Higher Education. "Indeed we have seen ample evidence that access to postsecondary education and training is increasingly vital to an individual's economic security."[63] Many governors have agreed, making millions of dollars available for community college students and other nontraditional learners.[64]

However, other political and business leaders question whether college is necessary at all, renewing an argument that waxes and wanes with economic trends: "Who in his right mind," asked recent Georgia Governor George Zell, "would want to go into debt for the privilege of reading Beowulf when he could make $30,000 a year in air-conditioner maintenance straight out of high school?"[65] Samuelson opined in *The Washington Post* that it is time to "ditch" the "college-for-all crusade," which "looms as the largest mistake in educational policy since World War II."[66] And, *The Public Agenda* reported in Fall 2016 that Americans are increasingly uncertain of the necessity of a college education as an indicator of success in "today's work world."[67] These opinions and findings offer as many questions as they do answers: Does college buy a credential that indicates potential as opposed to actual skills or knowledge developed? Does it buy prestige by association? Opportunity? And, if fewer men are attending, do any of these carry as much value as whatever the non-attending men are doing? Is it a coincidence that the power of the college degree may be declining just as more women and minorities attend? Finally, the proliferation of for-profit colleges and online degrees also calls into question the egalitarian-sounding message of "college for all." Is the availability of higher education coming in conjunction with proportionally fewer men attending and completing it merely a coincidence? Or, is it the case that when everyone can have it, fewer men want it?

About Power

My argument that the value of higher education credentials is declining in conjunction with men's steady pursuit of female-free domains of learning is only applicable to postindustrial Western society, and in the confines of this book,

only to the United States, as that is where I have access to the data and cor
support it. What I am **not** arguing is that formal education for girls is ii
or meaningless; nowhere is this more evident than in the places around the world
where girls and women are denied access to formal education. The Clinton and
Gates Foundations 2015 report, *No Ceilings: The Full Participation Project*, offers
ample data on the ways and means by which girls' and women's access to schooling in many world regions continues to be a significant challenge, particularly
at the secondary education level.[68] Nicholas Kristof highlighted the threat that
educated women and girls represent in many parts of the world when he asked,
"What's so scary about smart girls?"[69] elaborating on the changes in age of girls'
marriage (it rises), the birthrate (it declines), and the improvement of economic
development and general well-being of a society that formally educates women.

Kristof also acknowledges this truth: Girls' education is not a magic wand for
creating gender equity. "Girls' education is no silver bullet," he writes. "Iran and
Saudi Arabia have both educated girls but refused to empower them, so both
remain mired in the past. But when a country educates and unleashes women,
those educated women often become force multipliers for good."[70] Ultimately,
however, it may be that education credentials—any credentials, actually—are
a signifier of power only in a cultural context where men hold more of that
credential. It makes sense, then, that in places where gaining degrees suggests a
female encroachment on men's monopoly, girls and women who pursue them are
resisted through law, violence, and seemingly impenetrable cultural traditions.
When finally, and in what seems to be the case in American society, women gain
full access to the highest credentials available and obtain them in numbers and in
rates higher than men, then the value of that credential declines.

Formal education in the United States has been the primary gateway to gaining skills, knowledge, and the means and power to control one's life and well-
being. But as barriers to these academic mechanisms of power have continued
to fall, mechanisms of patriarchy may be creating new educational settings that
will once again hinder women's access to equity. In the absence of another level
of schooling—or the perceived necessity for it—American patriarchy's answer to
this latest gender breach is to shift the locus of power and value to somewhere
other than higher education. If women have entered the clubhouse, men are
no longer going to play in it. The locus of the development of American social
equity seems to be leaving its century-old place in schools, and this movement of
privileged men out of such a democratic space strips the façade from the secular
religion that American educational opportunity signifies.

The shift in site of patriarchy does not seem to take race or social class into
account; in fact, I hope to show that social class is almost flippantly dismissed
and race is ignored as men move into locations that hold no allegiance to the
egalitarian principles to which schooling is held. Although it has long been the
case that black and Hispanic boys and men have not achieved at the same educational level of white, black, and Hispanic women and white men, the American

communal belief that schooling was *supposed to* help achieve racial, socioeconomic, and gender equity kept some portion of the American electorate and educational communities focused on trying to achieve this goal. A faction of educational researchers, social scientists, and cultural commentators has examined this dynamic in myriad ways for the last century (see, for example, Linda Darling-Hammond, Stan Karp, Jonathan Kozol, and Gloria Ladson-Billings). Now, as more working and middle class women and men have access to the very system in which Americans have put their belief as a mechanism of social equity, those credentials are being diminished and no new structure seems to be taking their place.

It is likely that elite institutions of higher education will remain as places where men continue to enroll, insofar as they are places of power and of the "right" kind of women. It is also likely that new forms of higher education will continue to proliferate, offering degrees, credentials, and certificates to virtually anyone who wants them. However, if my thesis is correct—that the value of higher education credentials is diminishing in relation to women's higher education success while at the same time white men are creating and strengthening a number of dominant, all-male exclusionary spaces—it will matter much less what credentials women earn, and how well they earn them.

American higher education is at a critical juncture, and gender equity continues to be highly contested. The intersection of the two brings advantage, privilege, and power into bright relief; how American women and men respond to these collisions is, as Martin Luther King Jr. stated, the subject of "legitimate and unavoidable impatience" if we value them both equally.[71]

Notes

1. Pew Research Center. (2014). Retrieved from www.pewresearch.org/fact-tank/2014/04/24/more-hispanics-blacks-enrolling-in-college
2. Buchmann, C., & DiPrete, T. A. (2006). The growing female advantage in college completion: The role of family background and academic achievement. *American Sociological Review, 71*(4), 515–541.
3. DiPrete, T. A., & Buchmann, C. (2013). *The rise of women: The growing gender gap in education and what it means for American schools.* New York: Russell Sage Foundation, p. 1.
4. Hoff Sommers, C. (2013, February 3). The boys at the back. *The New York Times,* Sunday Review, pp. 1, 6.
5. Ibid., p. 1.
6. Levanon, A., England, P., & Allison, P. (2009). Occupational feminization and pay: Assessing causal dynamics using 1950–2000 US census data. *Social Forces, 88*(2), 865–892.
7. Beaudry, P., & Lewis, E. (2012). *Do male-female wage differentials reflect differences in return to skill?,* NBER Working Paper 18159.
8. See, for example, Hacker, S. L. (1989). *Pleasure, power and technology: Some tales of gender, engineering, and the cooperative workplace.* Boston: Unwin Hyman.
9. Garibaldi, A. M. (1986). The expanding gender and racial gap in American higher education. *The Journal of Negro Education, 83*(3), 371–384. DOI: 10.7709/jnegroeducation.83.3.0371

10. Pollitt, K. (1999, December 27). Subject to debate: Affirmative action for men? *The Nation, 269*(22), p. 10.
11. Mortenson, T. (1999). *The changing gender balance: An overview. Fewer men on campus a puzzle for liberal arts colleges and universities.* Postsecondary Education Opportunity. November 15–16, Goucher College, Baltimore, MD.
12. Mortenson, T. (2003). *The Mortenson research letter on public policy analysis of opportunity for postsecondary education.* Retrieved from www.postsecondary.org/
13. Ibid., p. 4.
14. Gose, B. (1997). Liberal-arts colleges ask: Where have the men gone? *Chronicle of Higher Education, 43*(39), A35–A36.
15. Williams, A. (2010, February 7). The new math on campus: When women outnumber men at a college, dating culture is skewed. *New York Times*, Sunday Styles, pp. 1, 9.
16. *Rochester Democrat & Chronicle*, 8.24.03; *New York Times*, 7.9.06.
17. Pollitt, K. (1999, December 27). Subject to debate: Affirmative action for men? *The Nation, 269*(22), p. 10.
18. King, J. E. (2000). *Gender equity in higher education: Are male students at a disadvantage?* Washington, DC: American Council on Education, p. 2.
19. King, J. E. (2006). *Gender equity in higher education: 2006.* Washington, DC: American Council on Higher Education, p. v.
20. Ibid., p. 21.
21. Ibid.
22. Sommers, C. H. (2001). *The war against boys: How misguided feminism is harming our young men.* New York: Simon & Schuster Paperbacks.
23. Zyngier, D. (2009). Doing it to (for) boys (again): Do we really need more books telling us there is a problem with boys' underachievement in education? *Gender and Education, 21*(1), 111–112.
24. Dyer, S. K. (Ed.). (2001). *Beyond the gender wars: A conversation about girls, boys, and education.* Washington, DC: American Association of University Women Educational Foundation, p. 14.
25. Spencer, R., Porche, M., & Tolman, D. (2003). We've come a long way—maybe: New challenges for gender equity in education. *The Teachers College Record, 105*(9), 1801–1803.
26. Weaver-Hightower, M. (2003). The "boy turn" in research on gender and education. *Review of Educational Research, 73*(4), 471–498.
27. Pimentel, A. (2004). *Supporting boys' resilience: A dialogue with researchers, practitioners, and the media.* New York: Ms. Foundation for Women.
28. Froschl, M., & Sprung, B. (2005). *Raising and educating healthy boys: A report on the growing crisis in boys' education.* New York: Educational Equity Center at the Academy for Educational Development.
29. King, J. E. (2006), p. v.
30. Corbett, C., Hill, C., & St. Rose, A. (2008). *Where the girls are: The facts about gender equity in education.* Washington, DC: American Association of University Women Educational Foundation.
31. Noguera, P. A. (2009). *The trouble with black boys: And other reflections on race, equity, and the future of public education.* San Francisco, CA: John Wiley & Sons; Harper, S. R., & Harris, F. III. (2010). *College men and masculinities: Theory, research, and implications for practice.* San Francisco, CA: John Wiley & Sons.
32. Martino, W., Kehler, M. D., & Weaver-Hightower, M. B. (Eds.). (2009). *The problem with boys' education: Beyond the backlash.* New York: Routledge.
33. Fine, C. (2010). *Delusions of gender: How our minds, society, and neurosexism create difference.* New York: W. W. Norton & Company.
34. Ibid., p. 169.
35. Whitmire, R. (2010). *Why boys fail: Saving our sons from an educational system that's leaving them behind.* New York: American Management Association.

36. Newkirk, T. (2002). *Misreading masculinity: Boys, literacy, and popular culture.* Portsmouth, NH: Heinemann.
37. Carnevale, A. (2008, January/February). College for all? *Change,* pp. 23–29.
38. Farrell, C. (2001, March 16). Men are falling behind in the degree race. *Business Week Online.* Retrieved from www.businessweek.com
39. Gurian, M. (2005, December 4). Disappearing act. *The Washington Post.* Retrieved from www.washingtonpost.com/wpdyn/content/article/2005/12/02/AR2005120201334.html
40. Caldwell, C. (2007, February 25). The way we live now: What a college education buys. *The New York Times Magazine,* pp. 15–16.
41. Williams, A. (2010), pp. ST1, 8.
42. Lewin, T. (2006, July 9). At colleges, women are leaving men in the dust. *The New York Times,* pp. A1, A16.
43. Patton, S. (2013, March 29). Advice to the young women of Princeton: The daughters I never had. *The Daily Princetonian.*
44. Kerr, B. (1999, March 5). When dreams differ: Male-female relations on campuses. *The Chronicle of Higher Education,* pp. B7–B8.
45. Montgomery, L. M. (2004). "It's just what I like": Explaining persistent patterns of gender stratification in the life choices of college students. *International Journal of Qualitative Studies in Education, 17*(6), 785–802.
46. Ibid., p. 788.
47. Goldberg, W. A., Kelly, E., Matthews, N. L., Kang, H., Li, W., & Sumaroka, M. (2012). The more things change, the more they stay the same: Gender, culture, and college students' views about work and family. *Journal of Social Issues, 68*(4), 833.
48. DiPrete & Buchmann, 2013, p. 14.
49. Ibid., p. 51.
50. Ibid., p. 52.
51. Ibid., p. 210.
52. Moss-Racusin, C. A., Dovidio, J. F., Brescoll, V. L., Graham, M. J., & Handelsman, J. (2012). Science faculty's subtle gender biases favor male students. *Proceedings of the National Academy of Sciences, 109*(41), 16474–16479.
53. Jacobs, J. A. (1996). Gender inequality and higher education. *Annual Review of Sociology, 22*(1), 153–185.
54. Jacobs, J. A. (2003). Detours on the road to equality: Women, work and higher education. *Contexts, 2*(1), 32–41.
55. Weaver-Hightower, M. B. (2003). Crossing the divide: Bridging the disjunctures between theoretically oriented and practice-oriented literature about masculinity and boys at school. *Gender and Education, 15*(4), 407–423.
56. Baenninger, M. (2011). For women on campuses, access doesn't equal success. *Chronicle of Higher Education.* Retrieved from www.chronicle.com/article/for-women-on-campuses-access/129242
57. Connell, R. W. (2005). *Masculinities.* Berkeley, CA: University of California Press.
58. Bureau of Labor Statistics, U.S. Department of Labor, *The Economics Daily,* Median weekly earnings, 2004–2014 on the Internet at https://www.bls.gov/opub/ted/2014/ted_20141028.htm
59. Corbett, C., & Hill, C. (2012). *Graduating to a pay gap: The earnings of women and men one year after college graduation.* Washington, DC: American Association of University Women.
60. Ewert, S., & Kominski, R. (2014, January). *Measuring alternative educational credentials: 2012.* Household economic studies (U.S. Census Bureau Report No. P70–138). Retrieved from www.census.gov
61. The Clinton Foundation and the Bill and Melinda Gates Foundation. (2015, March). *No ceilings: The full participation report.* Retrieved from www.noceilings.org

62. See, for example, Gurian, 2005; Sax, L. (2006). *Why gender matters: What parents and teachers need to know about the emerging science of sex differences.* New York: Broadway Books.
63. United States Department of Education. (2006). *A test of leadership: Charting the future of U.S. higher education.* A report of the commission appointed by Secretary of Education Margaret Spellings. ED-06-C0–0013U.S.
64. No ceilings: The full participation report.
65. Pollitt, 1999, December 27, p. 10.
66. Samuelson, R. J. (2012, May 27). It's time to drop the college-for-all crusade. *The Washington Post.* Retrieved from www.washingtonpost.com/opinions/its-time-to-drop-the-college-for-all crusade/2012/05/27/gJQAzcUGvU_story.html
67. Public Opinion on Higher Education. (2016, September 12). Retrieved from www.publicagenda.org/pages/public-opinion-higher-education-2016
68. No Ceilings: The Full Participation Report.
69. Kristof, N. D. (2010, March 27). The boys have fallen behind. *The New York Times.* Retrieved from www.nytimes.com
70. Kristof, N. D. (2014, May 10). What's so scary about smart girls? *The New York Times.* Retrieved from www.nytimes.com
71. King Jr., Martin Luther (1963, April 16). "Letter from a Birmingham Jail." Retrieved from African Studies Center, University of Pennsylvania (Philadelphia, PA). www.africa.upenn.edu/Articles_Gen/Letter_Birmingham.html

2
POWER, PATRIARCHY, AND GENDER IDENTITY IN HIGHER EDUCATION

All the learning in the world, all the good grades and high test scores . . . don't mean a thing when people have no power.

Thomas Frank[1]

Researchers, journalists, and cultural analysts from many fields offer wide-ranging explanations for the causes of women's and men's varying commitments to and success in academia. The theoretical frameworks on which these analyses have been built often result in a baroque combination of neurobiological,[2] socio-cultural,[3] and structural[4] debates. These arguments continue, in part, because no matter what their disposition, they mask a cultural theology that lies at the heart of the issues surrounding gender and schooling: educational success is the gateway to the attainment of the American Dream. The belief system on which virtually all viewpoints on gender equity and schooling is based is that working hard and completing school successfully is the portal by which men and women can transcend their circumstances of birth—including the expectations that come with one's gender.

Boys' crisis and female advantage debates address this tension between individualism, the pursuit of gender equity, and patriarchal gender norms delicately. The majority of Americans persist in the belief that each person has the opportunity to be anything she or he aspires to be, with school success—now understood as the attainment of some kind of college degree—as the primary means to achieve their aspirations, even as they maintain ambivalence about gendered life expectations for women and men. Powerful and entrenched cultural beliefs about what constitute natural roles for men and women shape individual and collective gender identities; gender ideologies, in turn, undermine efforts aimed at equity by making uneven outcomes of schooling to seem natural and even necessary. With this mindset, it is possible for people to maintain their belief that schooling is a conduit for equal opportunity for women and men, while at the same time stay blind to the ways in which gendered forces direct educational pathways back into the gendered patterns that participants believe education was helping to ameliorate. People also translate the gender differentiation they see in much of their lives outside of school as normal and equitable by attributing gender differences to individuals' personal choices. Equity potentially exists for other people, even if not for those directly in one's view.

This chapter begins by offering the concept of *patriarchal equilibrium* as a theoretical framework for understanding how women's successes in higher education can be perceived as threats to the "natural" gender order, which are then countered by shifts in other institutional arenas, effectively diminishing or even nullifying the impact of educational successes. Essential to understanding these shifts is an exploration of Americans' sustained, yet oppositional beliefs: Schooling is a primary mechanism for creating social equity *and* schooling is an appropriate conveyor of accepted gender identity norms. Understanding why and how these beliefs comfortably co-exist is critical to the future of higher education and gender equity in the United States.

Patriarchal Equilibrium

Understanding, much less counteracting, the ways in which power works has never been simple, of course; the apparatuses by which individuals, markets, behaviors, and beliefs change in relation to each other are almost always hidden by seemingly normal or natural explanations, making dominance—male dominance in this case—opaque and difficult to counter head-on. This describes the concept of *patriarchal equilibrium*. Ironically, a long-standing symbol of manliness—beer—offers a window into how this concept works to explain subtle and subversive cultural shifts in power. Through the evolution of the brewing industry in Medieval England, one can observe patriarchal equilibrium in action: By seeing how changes that threatened 14th- through 16th-century patriarchy in one sector were countered by responses in other medieval business and cultural sectors, it is possible to understand how cultural explanations of "normalcy" and "nature" conceal shifts in gendered power and education in 20th- and 21st-century America.

Brewing was a "home-based trade" in late Medieval England, one of many small moneymaking ventures available to women of the time, not unlike the businesses of Etsy in the 21st century.[5] According to Bennett, brewing was "low skilled, low profit, low status"—a job that along with selling eggs, baking, and caring for people in their homes was considered appropriate for women.[6] However, economic changes such as centralized manufacturing processes, the professionalization of workers, and growing organizational monopolies transformed beer-making into the brewing industry between 1300 and 1600, making it a large-scale operation in which men could and did eventually dominate. Bennett's concept of patriarchal equilibrium illustrates how this happened. She writes,

> At every turn, brewsters found themselves unable to respond as effectively as men to new opportunities. They encountered historical circumstances that discouraged them from brewing and encouraged men to take up the trade: household economies that required wives to assist husbands at their trades (rather than the other way around); laws that limited the contractual powers and economic autonomy of women; economic powers that limited women's access to capital and credit; local and national governments that sought to control brewsters through their husbands; and ideological principles that made it difficult for brewsters to establish themselves as reliable and trustworthy tradespeople.[7]

Fourteenth-century media began characterizing brewsters as dirty and untrustworthy; civic leaders claimed that women disrupted the trade; new regulations limited single women's work, arguing that it took such work away from married men and threatened husbands' authority over their wives. "Put more abstractly," Bennett concluded, "what happened is this: an economic change that might have advantaged women was countered effectively by responses rooted in ideology, law, politics, and family."[8] That religion, business, and law are not institutions inherently designed to subordinate women is a further confounding factor of patriarchal equilibrium, Bennett argues; that is, law and family structures have the wherewithal to advantage women as well. It is the combination of societal beliefs about women's and men's appropriate roles, religious dogma, and the weight of tradition that shapes these institutions into gendered structures. Therefore, any changes that happen (for example, to women in medieval brewing) can be viewed as supporting a presumably natural state of men's and women's being; it becomes virtually impossible to point a causal finger to any one structure, process, or group of persons.

In medieval times and now, dominance resides in multiple sites and is enacted through exclusion, segregation, and division, obfuscating power. Consequently, as the metaphorical dance steps of patriarchy evolve, women are asked to follow them only after changes that reestablish dominance have been made.[9] Because privileging men's lives is the norm, such changes do not seem strange until questions of gender equity begin to be applied to the new "dance" as well. Patriarchal equilibrium, then, allows for change, and sometimes radical change, in the ways in which women are involved in sociocultural, family, and economic structures, but also accounts for the simultaneous and strategic alignment of counteractions that keep male privilege sovereign. Change does not necessarily mean transformation.

Julia Adams supports Bennett's analysis, but questions how far the concept of patriarchal equilibrium can be extended in modern economic and political systems, as she sees the mechanisms that work within each as potentially dis-aggregated.[10] She also wonders whether the gains in gender equity, evident in some systems in Western societies, are evidence of the concept's obsolescence: "Would Bennett argue that such a change has happened," Adams asks, "but is in the process of being re-enfolded in continuing subordination, in a sequence of slightly remodeled patriarchies? If so, why? What would be the explanation, or even the materials for an analysis?"[11] The higher education conversation over the last several decades provides one answer, and such materials. The gains that women have made in higher education are being re-enfolded into subordination.

Boys and men, in proportion to women, are engaging in fewer college expe-riences and taking formal learning opportunities less seriously than women are; women, on the other hand, are succeeding in higher education at unprecedented rates. They earn more college degrees overall, their academic performance is better, and they get into prestigious schools at the same or better rates than men. At the same time, "college for all" has been a bipartisan national commitment.[12] Just as women's college participation and success rates overall are increasing faster than men's, black, Hispanic, and working class women are participating in higher education at even higher rates; their participation is evidence of success, even to a country that has not effectively addressed race and its relationships to poverty.[13] Black and Hispanic men's academic success is sadly still so unexpected that their participation in college, when it occurs, is not considered evidence of a disruption to the social order.

Simultaneously, college costs are rising disproportionately to inflation and income, the gender pay gap has remained static, and occupational gender seg-regation has widened.[14] Further, a number of indicators suggest that young Americans across gender, racial, and socioeconomic lines believe that women are naturally suited to stay home with young children. Meanwhile, many sci-ence, technology-intensive, and financial fields are remaining or becoming more male-dominated; abortion rights laws are being repealed and access to reproduc-tive care is diminishing. Cosmetic surgery rates continue to rise.[15] These oppos-ing forces suggest that a new wave of patriarchal equilibrium may be in motion: Potential major economic and intellectual shifts that could advantage women (success in achieving higher education credentials, combined with rising work-force participation and accomplishment) are being countered by responses rooted in other arenas that seem natural, including continued reverence for maternal instincts, political conservatism representing an ideologically more "traditional" state of being, and what seems to be a slow, male disengagement from higher education.

The last of these—male disengagement of from higher education, either through slower new enrollments or opting out altogether—suggests that Ameri-can men may be creating new places or enhancing traditional ones, where on the one hand they gain or improve their knowledge and skills post-high school, and on the other, where the end-credential is not connected to school performance and where nontraditional displays of knowledge are rewarded. As men gravitate to these and other settings, they become economically and culturally more valuable vocational sites, at the same time ushering in a resurgence of traditional definitions of masculinity, along with renewed economic and political power.

These shifts signal the diminishing primacy of higher education and threaten the democratic ideal if not the actuality of schooling as the great American equalizer; it seems possible that women's successes in higher education may in fact signal a weakening of the common belief in the importance of schooling for everyone. If the national conversation urges working class and lower income families to consider higher education as a necessary investment in their future success, the weakened belief is hidden, and the slow abdication from schooling of white, middle and upper class men is placated. The centrality of schooling is maintained, and male dominance, as America has known it, restored. The diminishing value of higher education would also signify the waning of whatever advantages women may have gained via their current successes in higher education; indeed, the occupation with costly and time-consuming academic endeavors that offer prestigious credentials but little in the way of power may turn out to be a *dis*advantage for American women.

Higher Education as Secular Religion

Meyer suggests that Americans' belief in the power of schooling is so strong that it can be thought of as a secular religion. He argues that the current disconnections between societal gender inequity and the seemingly equitable gender practices of formal schooling can be understood only if we see schooling as akin to a "sacred canopy."[16] That is, Americans have an overarching depiction of schooling-for-all as a guiding doctrine of their lives—a cosmological view of a universalized larger environment to which all humans and their activities are linked.[17] According to Meyer,

> [M]any features of the American school system make much more sense if one sees schooling as constituting a religious system rather than an instrument of social functioning. Features where this is evident include: universalism of rules of participation, the universalistic rationalism of its core content, the standardization of forms and content, the cosmological character of the knowledge involved [and most importantly for the understanding of schooling and gender], the weak linkages of educational knowledge and participation to the practical and differentiated roles of actual social life.[18]

Given the current primacy of higher education in America, such an argument can easily be transferred to postsecondary schools as well. Schooling, by this vision, does not actually have to produce equity, but to keep the social order, everyone has to *believe* that it does and act in accordance with this belief. Education as it was created in early America was seen as "essentially religious, relating initiatives to the wider cosmos"; since all children were understood to be children of God, there was no need to articulate the educational practice that extended from this design.[19] With this understanding, women can be welcomed and firmly entrenched in the process of schooling without harming the expectations of a gender-role-bound society.

Framing American schooling as a kind of secular religion, then, releases the cognitive tension created by universal rules of participation in schooling on the one hand, and unequal life circumstances between men and women on the other. And as higher education has become an expectation for the economic betterment of all, so, too, has it been co-opted by the same dissonance: a potential equalizer, but not disruptive of gendered, race, and social class norms. With universal higher education as a powerful ideal but toothless reality, U.S. culture allows for women's participation and dominance in higher education even as law, politics, and ultimately men's and women's gender role expectations continue to counter an educational female advantage that is offered as evidence of gender equity. This circular reasoning offers a near-perfect window into the conflicting paradigms that make up the female disadvantage/boy crisis argument: All are equal in the eyes of college-as-opportunity, even as this worldview accepts and expects that men and women have different life destinies.

Emerson, Smith, and Sikkink, studying white, conservative Protestants in the late 1990s, offer a glimpse into how this dissonant reasoning is constructed. In their study of black and white Evangelical Christians, participants demonstrated overwhelming belief that everyone in America was equally created by God and had equal opportunities to be socioeconomically successful; they also maintained that schooling had much to do with these opportunities.[20] And yet, over 70 percent of the same respondents cited individual culture, lack of motivation, and lack of initiative as reasons why people—and black men and women in particular—do not achieve this success to the same degree as white men and women.

The respondents' cultural worldview, developed by their version of Christianity, explains the differences. Framed by pervasive individualism, anti-structuralism, and relationalism,[21] they can hold people individually responsible for their actions, and give no berth to the underlying structural inequities. If there are no structural barriers and one's relationship with Christ matters more than everything else, then responsibility for racial, socioeconomic, and gendered disparity lies with individuals' personal unwillingness to create conditions of equity for themselves. "For a full understanding of the individualist versus structuralist hypothesis, it must be nuanced," write Emerson and his colleagues. They continue:

> White conservative Protestants tend to avoid acknowledging contemporary social structures that deny the importance of individual determination. . . .

[R]eligious identity and subculture matter. Without considering such effects of explanations of racial inequality, our understanding is incomplete, and policies and programs meant to reduce racial inequality may be stymied.[22]

Because social class and gender are inextricably linked to race, they, too, are implicated by the same reasoning. Rationalizing the troubling reality that many women are now achieving in college to a higher degree than men means casting solutions through individual means, and not structural changes in higher education itself, much less cultural changes in gender roles. If there is indeed a female disadvantage to success in higher education, this Christian-influenced view of gender and individuals' behaviors places the blame for such a state squarely on women's shoulders—women have accomplished too much at the expense of their natural roles, and men, quite naturally by this argument, are finding avenues other than schooling to restore the accepted gender balance.

Recasting education as a sacred–secular American space allows us to see how Americans are still committed to higher education's eventual ability to offer deliverance from social inequities. Across the spectrum of religious beliefs and orthodoxies that are practiced throughout America, what remains common is that salvation of some kind is understood to come in the future, though it remains at some distance; human roles within the belief system are executed in the present, and gender norms are among the most scripted among them. As such, we do not expect higher education to actually remake *at present* the social realities that we passionately believe it will help solve in the future.

With college-for-all as an accepted aspiration, the 21st century has recast higher education to play the role that the common school did a century ago: Postsecondary education is acceptable, and now even necessary, for men and women without differentiation, because all in the democracy should be entitled to receive its benefits. The institution of education remains, in its new form, the primary conveyor of access to opportunity. What students do with a college degree, as well as the ways in which different kinds of college degrees offer gateways or roadblocks, can subsequently be attributed to individual characteristics rather than structural ones, so that the institution stays sacred, but personal variations will cast graduates in varying (and unequal) places. As long as educational merit is widely believed to be equally available to all, it matters less whether it is actually realized by all.

This paradox persists in Americans' consciousness because at the same time we espouse our belief in schooling as equalizer, we still operate on the belief that men and women have gendered natural roles that lead to separate spheres, even though most women play a significant role in the country's economic, political, and public domains. Women's participation and success in higher education challenges the fiction that "natural" gender roles and the high academic success can live quietly together, however. As women's success in schooling approaches a critical mass, the institution is on the verge of being devalued through the renaming of women's academic success as an (unfair) advantage.[23]

This tension can be seen in a number of ways. Ten years ago, the "opt-out revolution"[24] became a source of heated cultural debate, whereby a number of highly educated, white, affluent women loudly claimed that opting out of work was their choice, and a good one at that. Many women of color, feminists, and middle and working class women argued that the option *not* to work was a privilege afforded to those with the right (white) color, wealth, and social status; natural feelings of womanhood or not, many women need to earn an income. Cordelia Fine's work debunking the purported neuroscientific causes of gendered behavior illustrates how women's academic success is newly devalued in the 21st century through claims that the natural state of gender is located in discoveries about human brains. She writes that

> As the barriers of a sexist society continue to fall, there seem to be fewer and fewer social scapegoats to call on to explain continuing gender inequalities. . . . When we can't pin the blame on outside forces, all eyes swivel to the internal—the differences in the structure or functioning of female and male brains.[25]

In fact, by blaming higher education for creating too *much* gender equity, we slay the institutional structure that we have most valued: We reject the very equity we claim as education's power. Recurring cultural arguments about the pay gap, child care, occupational segregation, abortion rights, access to birth control, sexual harassment—the list continues—expose the gendered tensions that lie beneath higher education, their relevance to women's power to control their lives surfacing like a giant whack-a-mole game: When earning a college degree helps to sink one of these inequities, another resurfaces. Having the degree might change the way a new problem presents itself, but it does not mitigate it. The college-for-all mantra distracts from the game, offering ostensible pathways for every student to achieve.

Schooling and Gender Identities

The metaphor of schooling as religion helps explain the last 20 years of vociferous arguments that it is boys and men who are "at risk" or "in crisis" in schooling and, in some cases, in their overall lives. Weaver-Hightower's exploration of the "boy turn" in research on gender and education offered eight causes of this 21st-century shift of attention toward boys and men:

- Media panic, popular-rhetorical books, and news events
- Feminist explanations of gender roles
- Narrow initial indicators of gender equity

- New Right and neoliberal reforms in education
- Explicit backlash politics
- Economic and workforce changes (the "crisis of masculinity")
- Parental concerns and pressure
- The "thrill of the new" for researchers and educators.[26]

Most relevant to the idea of schooling as a female disadvantage is Weaver-Hightower's underlying premise—that the eight causes of the "boy turn" are cultural responses to female successes, many of which are in school. This is evidence of patriarchal equilibrium at work. The responses Weaver-Hightower articulates are not revolutionary by themselves, but together they crystalize a collective moment for boys, men, and formal higher education, distinct in its traction in popular and academic analyses.

Interestingly, only one of Weaver-Hightower's etiologies is directly about schooling; the others have cultural, economic, political, social, or parental roots that intersect with the structure of formal education. That these elements represent the potential for women to achieve the kind of equity that schooling promises is what makes them dangerous—kindling to the female advantage bonfire. A boy crisis in response to a female advantage, then, offers a counterweight to the threat that women's educational success represents. By drawing on the religious undertones of schooling, forces of patriarchal equilibrium gain energy from unspoken cultural worry that gender identities—what defines men and women—will be shifted if females are *too* advantaged: Schooling is transforming women and men into something they are not supposed to be. And *that* was never the compact of equal access to education.

Ideal and Practiced: Masculinity and Femininity In and Out of School

Two decades ago, Jacobs noted the absence of discussion about the ways in which gender identities intersect with higher education, calling specifically for the examination of distinct aspects of higher education with regard to women. Presciently maintaining that sociologists of education must pay attention to gender in order to understand the direction of higher education, he offered three recommendations for future study:

1. A theory of when gender is likely to be consequential and when it is likely to be unimportant needs to be developed. Also necessary is a theory of what economic, social, cultural, and political trends can be expected to affect . . . gender in the educational sphere.
2. Educational decision-making processes need more attention. Attention to large-scale sets of data promotes an input–output model, which moves attention away from how education and gender are socially embedded processes.

3. College experiences need to be incorporated into a general account of educational inequity. As gender inequity in the United States is now less a matter of inequity in access and more of a matter of gender differentiation in educational experiences and outcomes, they need to be linked to access in a general analysis of the educational system.[27]

Jacobs's call for a theory that explains how economic, social, cultural, and political trends affect gender in education implicated the necessity of analyzing gender identities. As gender identities—like all identities—are enacted in accordance within context-specific conditions, the consequentiality of gender in higher education, then, can be seen in masculinity and femininity as they are perceived and practiced within and around the institutional context.

Those arguing in favor of a female advantage in higher education seem to imply that current college women have upset gender identity expectations for women by succeeding too much; perhaps higher education has pushed gender norms too far. A number of gender identity theorists have argued that when gender identities in practice deviate too much from deeply imbedded cultural norms, new settings are established so that the deviation can be "corrected," with identities thereby reconstituted into more culturally normed shapes: Is this patriarchal equilibrium by another name?[28]

School and Its Impact on Gender Identities

Although masculine and feminine identities are definitively influenced by college experiences, students enter higher education already deeply affected by American expectations of men and women. Defining identity, for the purposes of this analysis, as "social categories in which an individual claims membership as well as the personal meaning associated with those categories,"[29] culturally mediated definitions of masculinity and femininity have shaped students' entire lives, intermingling and becoming part of their ethnicity, social class, sexual orientation, and a host of other intersectional selves. College students' gender identity work is impacted further by a conflicting multitude of motives and functions embedded within institutions themselves,[30] making the interplay of gender identity work and institutional shape-shifting feel a lot like academic science fiction. In fact, Walkerdine claims that masculinities and femininities are "fictions linked to fantasies," which are so hidden from everyday interactional view that they "take on the status of fact when inscribed in powerful practices, like schooling."[31] Defining identity as the ways in which individuals are produced through language and power, she maintains that all identities are performances and that people can construct, sustain, and recreate identities through their interactions within institutions, often doing so with marginal awareness of the shifts.

Given the interplay between structure and identity, questions of how students' identities shape and are shaped by higher education become paramount when investigating the claim that higher education participation and success have become so powerful that it has fundamentally altered the definitions of being female and male. Lips's research on gender and "possible selves" offers insight into how these structures interact. Investigating the ways in which university students envision their futures, she contends that "self-views are important for understanding many behavioral choices, including the persistent tendency for male and female students to separate into different academic and career paths. . . ."[32] One especially troubling trend, she notes, is that

> in some cases, there is a large gap between students' current self-evaluations and their perceptions of what is possible for them in the future. Over and over again, the data show that, for women, *current* self-views . . . may be more comparable to those of their male counterparts than are their *possible* self-views of future. . . . It appears that, even though women and men in these samples differ somewhat in how they see their current academic selves, these self-views translate into an even more different set of possibilities envisioned by these young women and men.[33]

Lips's subsequent work built on this finding, and her analyses suggest that one reason for women's scarcity in top political, corporate, and financial positions is their inability to imagine powerful roles for their future selves while still in college.[34] Some of her female study participants rated powerful roles, like the CEO of a major corporation, political leader, and director of a major scientific research center, as a less positive choice for their futures because they were worried that such roles would make them too busy and/or stressed to have good family relationships, or may position them to be disliked at work.[35] Male study participants, on the other hand, felt the prospect of leadership as a much more possible—and desirable—choice for their futures.

If these students' views are indicative of the wider college population, then participating in higher education seems to offer to men and women what looks like the same means—college credentials—to very different ends. If the constructions of masculinity are built on traditional ideas of dominance—on what a man should be—then males' consideration of the importance of schooling is firmly related to its power to shape such futures. If, on the other hand, constructions of femininity are built first and firmly on being liked and having strong familial relationships—an enduring definition of what a woman should be—then women's consideration of the importance of schooling is firmly related to its relevance for their futures as well, albeit subordinate ones. Being praised and liked by teachers, approved by the academic system, and following the rules set before them are all part of women's academic experiences and fit well within this construction of femininity.

College students' ethnic, racial, and socioeconomic identities are implicated in gender identity developments as well; too often in advantage/crisis arguments, the unspoken color of gender is white and its given status, middle class, making many of the claims about the importance and impact of higher education on developing gender identities ring hollow for working class students and students of color. Many crisis-induced proclamations about gender and higher education offer solutions for all student futures without consideration of the ways in which membership in multiple identity categories impacts participation and therefore how someone thinks of his or her future. For girls and women of color, in particular, Gushue and Whitson argue that "valuing and integrating key aspects of the identities could lead to a stronger sense of personal agency in general."[36] Such an intersectional analysis allows for social identities to mutually constitute, reinforce, and naturalize one another,[37] broadening the ways in which college attendance, completion, and success can be differently understood by the many different kinds of students who participate in it, as well as by those who claim its importance for all.

An intersectionality perspective requires that identity categories be studied in relation to one other at the individual, interpersonal, and structural levels. As a socio-structural category, gender constructs and maintains the subordination of women to men.[38] For individuals who participate in higher education, gender is not always the most salient social identity, but within the American mindset of higher education as both keeper of gender norms as well as deliverance from them, it is virtually impossible for students *not* to be reminded that their gender is structurally relevant. Embedded within higher education's practices, policies, and pages, gender remains present. At the same time, however, individual identity categories have specific historical and contextual features that come into play as more students labeled as coming from "nontraditional backgrounds" are considered.

Higher Education, Identity, and Language

While some evidence indicates that definitions of post-college successful womanhood may be driven by identity integration (see Gushue and Whitson), successful post-college masculinity may be driven more by fragmentation. In other words, having a college degree may not influence the definition of manhood in the same way it might for womanhood.[39] The demographic complexities of college students—the fluidity of their gender, race/ethnicity, and social class identities—demand that conclusions regarding the impact of college and subsequent social equity be drawn with caution.

Central to the formation of gender identities in education is the idea that language-in-context—discourse—is a primary mechanism by which men and women understand who and how they are supposed to behave.[40] Researchers in the last decade have become increasingly aware of the ways in which social, economic, and political agendas shape and fight for attention, as seen in the language of college students' identity development, in turn offering ways in which to understand how similar college experiences can lead to quite different educational outcomes.

Tonso, for example, used classroom discourse in engineering classes to reveal the socialization processes by which engineering culture remains aligned with male identities. "Engineering students," she noted, "have well-developed masculine identities. . . . [C]lassroom and teamwork settings indicated the cultural norms of engineering talk and how this discourse reinforced traditional practices that were only rarely open to revision."[41] She argued that for women to be accepted into engineering culture, they needed not to challenge its norms. To be a successful engineer meant practicing stereotypical masculine and feminine identities, effectively discouraging women's pursuit of engineering. Tonso wrote:

> Women's experiences on student teams varied in direct relation to the extent to which their male teammates engaged high-status (academic-science-affiliated) cultural identities. The cultural model of campus life marked an intersection of academic science with a culture of romance, but virulent sexist practices flowed with and through the prestige of academic science practices. By producing hierarchical forms of womanhood and manhood appropriate to the campus system, [the University's] engineering education system produced women's subordination.[42]

Because gender identities are so interdependent with other identities, trying to reshape one identity in the context of another is met with fierce cultural resistance. Krefting argues that this phenomenon is ambivalent sexism at work: "When group stereotypes are interdependent," she states, "they become prescriptive and do not change even with substantial contrary evidence."[43] Gender stereotypes end up functioning prescriptively, ultimately serving as a dominant and seemingly inescapable ideology: *This is how it is supposed to be*, it whispers, as it is circulated and disseminated through the discourse of men and women.

Recent studies set in universities offer fresh examples of the ways in which higher education discourse continues to construct and challenge gender identity norms. Jackson and colleagues explored the discursive construction of masculinity in a British university's sports science degree program, doing so within the classroom context. Students suggested that masculinity in such contexts included "talking and generally being loud (which disrupted classes); being a joker; throwing stuff; arriving late; and being rude and disrespectful to lecturers."[44] A few women, seen by others in the program as exceptionally assertive for females, challenged men in the classroom who displayed such behaviors, including one incident in which an older female student stood up and said to the males in the class, "Will you shut the fuck up, I'm trying to learn."[45] This kind of challenge came with risks, however, and according to the researchers, it was only a few older female students who dared step out of a typical feminine discursive pattern of subordination; dynamics of age as well as gender intersected within the academic context.

Discursive examples outside the academy point to the ways in which linguistic patterns that are developed, maintained, and/or disrupted in college can manifest themselves in subsequent workplace patterns of gender equity. Such connections illustrate how equal college credentials conferred to men and women do not on their own confer equality once in practice. The *Ellen Pao v. Kleiner Perkins Caufield & Byers* case is an example. In 2012, Pao filed a gender discrimination lawsuit against her employer, the venture capital firm Kleiner Perkins Caufield & Byers. Pao, a graduate of Princeton University (1991), Harvard Law School (1994), and Harvard Business School (1998) claimed that the workplace was a culture of male entitlement, that she was ultimately denied promotion to senior partner because of her gender, and that the firm retaliated against her by firing her when she complained; the firm denied these claims and was acquitted of all counts in 2015.[46] Part of the evidence submitted to support Pao's claims was her assertion that she was punished for not speaking as assertively as the men in her company did, that she did not embrace the "interrupt-driven environment" effectively.[47] Ms. Pao was expected to use language practices that were highly assertive and, in a strongly male-dominated culture, accepted as the interactional norm. Yet the "double-bind of speaking while female"[48] also made it clear that if *she* used such assertive language, she would be punished for it. The discursive coding of language infuses many actions with gender identities that, only in aggregate and often in hindsight, become visible.

Schooling, Gender Identity, and the Economy

Finally, the mechanisms that contribute to patriarchal equilibrium as it operates between higher education and gender equity are constituted by economic forces, in conjunction with gendered norms and historical legacies. The fact that women get paid to work outside their homes is no longer questioned by mainstream society.[49] Moreover, women's wholesale participation in the workforce has not led to serious calls for men to retreat from the labor market.[50] Waged work may now be equally valorized for men and women out of economic necessity, but the nature of such work and how one becomes qualified to do it may be increasingly related to a changing relevance of higher education for men and women. Both men and women need to earn a living, but having formal higher education may be a waning rite of passage for men's membership in a neo-capital system, and an *added* requirement for women to participate in it.

Fraser hints at this possibility in her analysis of second-wave feminism and its multiple effects on culture to date. She maintains that the assumed trajectory of cultural institutions catching up with societal attitudes did not occur, but rather that societal changes in attitudes toward women (like accepting their full-time work outside the home) now obscure "a more complex, disturbing possibility: the cultural changes jump-started by the second wave [feminism], salutary in themselves, have served to legitimate a structural transformation of capitalist society that runs directly counter to feminist visions of a just society."[51] A hard look at education-as-institution supports this assertion: Generally accepted attitudes about women's equity have not made formal schooling sites of equitable practice, nor of equitable outcome—though female advantage proponents would argue otherwise. Second-wave feminism wove together three analytically distinct sites of gender injustice: political, cultural, and economic, but as these strands have separated, Fraser argues, each has been co-opted by forces that prioritize capitalism. As American capitalism, by hers and others' accounts, cannot be separated from proscribed male and female identities,[52] it follows that the capitalist co-optation of schooling also imbues the institution with a naturalized and gendered understanding of men and women. If this is the case, then the structural transformation to which Fraser alludes is evident in the devaluing of schooling for men: The institution of higher education may be morphing into a "women's structure," making it a truly ineffectual means to achieve gender equity.

Educational Credentials as Waning Economic Capital for Men

If formal education is becoming understood as something that women do, then the shifts comprising patriarchal equilibrium serve to reduce its value. As women's increasing college attendance and success raise concern, even in the face of almost-as-high rates of male college attendance (depending on race, ethnicity, and class), economic and organizational analyses allow us to unpack the impact of college degrees, investigating how new forms of socioeconomic power evolve.

The current, predominant emphasis on college degrees as work credentials, as opposed to credentials that build critical thinkers and thoughtful lives,[53] is a final piece of evidence in the case that patriarchal equilibrations may be occurring. Bennett countered the standard historical narrative of the medieval brewing, stating that:

> To be sure, many things changed in the experiences of women who sought to profit from brewing between 1300 and 1600. . . . Brewing changed, and women's access to brewing changed, but in 1600, as had been the case in 1300, women's work was low-status, low-skilled, and low-profit. There was much change in women's experiences, but no change in women's status.[54]

Likewise, in the last 200 American years, many things have changed in the experiences of women who have sought to profit from higher education credentials. Higher education continues to change in shape, form, and substance; women's— and men's—access to it is changing as well. But, as we watch these credentials, gender norms, job access, and economic inequities tumble over one another, we see little change in women's overall status. With more credentials, we seem no closer to social equity.

Educational credentials have always been, in part, a signaling device showing that the holder *could* learn, not that one actually *had* learned. Some credentialing theorists argue that "educational certification is a historical legitimation of advantages that empower degree holders in occupational and organizational recruitment."[55] In other words, having a high-status college degree allows graduates to get jobs that then become high status because of the perceived value of their degrees. According to the *human capital* interpretation of the relationship between degree and graduate, participation in education and training is a personal and social investment. An individual receives higher earnings and better career opportunities through his/her higher education credentials and society receives a highly skilled workforce.[56] In this arrangement, higher education is a shared investment between the individual and the state. By contrast, a *credentialist* views the higher education credential as an instrument of power; social groups, by this perspective, use higher education credentials to gain economic and cultural advantage. It is this latter perspective, college-as-means-to-status, that has more strongly characterized the U.S. higher education narrative; that is, until women started to attend and succeed in it.

As women have begun to equal and in many cases exceed men's college performance, the credentialist interpretation of degree-as-power may be used against them as the degree's status declines. The advantage/crisis argument may be the canary in the lecture hall. Even when analyzed in conjunction with race and ethnicity, the college-degree-as-valuable-commodity argument does not offer uncomplicated realities of higher power and status. Young women of Hispanic descent, for example, are first-time college attendees at rates much higher than their male peers.[57] Still, the gendered expectations of these women influence what majors they choose, which subsequently influence their career opportunities. The less white and more female higher education credential does not offer its recipients more status. This reality will be explored in detail in subsequent chapters.

Alternative visions of the higher education credential suggest that a college degree is becoming the single *most important* (and therefore powerful) marker of social status. Baker argues that the pervasive increase in college degree attainment in Western society signals a concomitant belief in the power of that degree; that the degrees and their use in the labor market, for most in postindustrial society, is becoming the *only* path to adult status.[58] He argues that at least four fundamental beliefs accompanied the spread of mass education (the "mass education revolution") and now construct the logic that underscores the expansion of higher education:

1. Belief in equality of opportunity as social justice rises with the value of universalism in education. . . . While educational merit is never fully realized, it is to a substantial degree, and hence is widely believed to exist and to be socially just.

2. Belief in the development of modern individuals as a collective good is a core educational idea closely aligning human development and empowerment with societal development.
3. Belief in the dominance of academic intelligence becomes not only important for school achievement, the education revolution privileges academic intelligence and positions it as the master human capability. . . . Seen this way, educational degrees become indications of individuals' cognitive ability, a now believed-in generalized ability that is widely assumed to be crucial for post-education life.
4. Belief that a diversity of academic degrees is synonymous with a diversity of specialized knowledge and expertise intensifies as academically infused credentialing stems from the institutional dominance of the university as the arbitrator and producer of valued knowledge and the chartering of degrees connected to this knowledge.[59]

Ultimately, Baker proposes that Americans will see "horizontal institutionalization" as the process by which the use of education degrees as a credential for access to jobs spreads across the population of occupations.[60] As formal education is more deeply connected to occupations, greater meaning will be attached to the degrees themselves, which more and more people will hold.

The argument supporting the existence of patriarchal equilibrium suggests the opposite: *If women and minority men and women are perceived as threatening white male power as a result of their college degree attainment, it may mean that the value of that degree will decline, so that white male power can reclaim the positional advantage, once available via college, by other means.* Women have repeatedly challenged the dominant discourses of gender, race, and social class, affecting claims of unquestioned male legitimacy, and unsettling the powerful and unspoken social contract on which gender norms have operated. These challenges are certainly not new, and schooling in America is where these challenges often unfold. Over the course of two and half centuries of higher education in the United States, boys and men have realigned their relationships to the institution to accommodate and head-off the encroachment of women and minorities. Now that women in large numbers, as well as men and women with previously little power, are cast as overtaking the highest formal educational hurdle, it may be that many men are finding alternative means to reassert their advantage.

Notes

1. Frank, T. (2014, May 8). Congratulations, Class of 2014: You're totally screwed. *Salon.com*. Retrieved from http://www.salon.com/2014/05/18/congratulations_class_of_2014_youre_totally_screwed/
2. Gurian, M., & Stevens, K. (2005, May 2). What is happening with boys in school? *Teachers College Record*. Retrieved from www.tcrecord.org ID Number: 11854; Sax, L. (2006). *Why gender matters: What parents and teachers need to know about the emerging*

science of sex differences. New York: Broadway Books; Sommers, C. H. (2001). *The war against boys: How misguided feminism is harming our young men.* New York: Simon & Schuster Paperbacks.

3. Ceci, S. J., & Williams, W. M. (2009). *The mathematics of sex: How biology and society conspire to limit talented women and girls.* New York: Oxford University Press.
4. Corbett, C., Hill, C., & St. Rose, A. (2008). *Where the girls are: The facts about gender equity in education.* Washington, DC: American Association of University Women Educational Foundation.
5. Bennett, J. M. (1997). Confronting continuity. *Journal of Women's History, 9*(3), 73–94.
6. Ibid., p. 83.
7. Ibid.
8. Ibid., p. 87.
9. Ibid., p. 88.
10. Adams, J. (2008). The persistence of patriarchy. *History matters: Patriarchy and the challenge of feminism.* Panel discussion. The Social Science History Association Conference, Miami, Florida.
11. Ibid., p. 4.
12. The White House. (2011). *Education blueprint: An economy built to last.* Retrieved from www.whitehouse.gov; Carnevale, A. (2008, January/February). College for all? *Change*, pp. 23–29.
13. Sue, D. W. (2013, November). Race talk: The psychology of racial dialogues. *American Psychologist, 68*(8), 663–671.
14. Charles, M., & Grusky, D. B. (2004). *Occupational ghettos: The worldwide segregation of women and men* (Vol. 200). Redwood City, CA: Stanford University Press.
15. Goldberg, W. A. et al. (2012). The more things change, the more they stay the same: Gender, culture, and college students' views about work and family. *Journal of Social Issues, 68*(4), 814–837; Ashcraft, C., & Blithe, S. (2009). *Women in IT: The facts.* Boulder, CO: National Center for Women in Information Technology; Nash, E., Gold, R. B., Rowan, A., Rathbun, G., & Vierboom, Y. (2014). Laws affecting reproductive health and rights: 2013 state policy review. *Guttmacher Institute. http://www.guttmacher.org/statecenter/updates/2013/statetrends42013.html.*
16. Meyer, J. (2000). Reflections on education as transcendence. In L. Cuban & D. Shipps (Eds.), *Reconstructing the common good in education* (pp. 206–222). Redwood City, CA: Stanford University Press.
17. Ibid., p. 209.
18. Ibid., p. 210.
19. Ibid., p. 212.
20. Emerson, M. O., Smith, C., & Sikkink, D. (1999). Equal in Christ, but not in the world: White conservative protestants and explanations of black-white inequality. *Social Problems, 46*(3), 398–417.
21. Bellah, R., Madsen, R., Sullivan, W., Swindler, A., & Tipton, S. (1985). *Habits of the heart: Individualism and commitment in American life.* Berkeley and Los Angeles, CA: University of California Press.
22. Emerson et al., 1999, p. 399.
23. See also Yoder, J. D. (1991). Rethinking tokenism: Looking beyond numbers. *Gender & Society, 5*(2), 178–192.
24. Belkin, L. (2008, June 15). When mom and dad share it all. *The New York Times Magazine*, pp. 44–51, 74, 78; Boushey, H. (2008). "Opting out?" The effect of children on women's employment in the United States. *Feminist Economics, 14*(1), 1–36; Mainiero, L. A., & Sullivan, S. E. (2005). Kaleidoscope careers: An alternate explanation for the "opt-out" revolution. *The Academy of Management Executive, 19*(1), 106–123; Stone, P. (2007). *Opting out? Why women really quit careers and head home.* Berkeley, CA: University of California Press.

25. Fine, C. (2010). *Delusions of gender: How our minds, society, and neurosexism create difference.* New York: W. W. Norton & Company, xxi.
26. Weaver-Hightower, M. (2003). The "boy turn" in research on gender and education. *Review of Educational Research, 73*(4), 476.
27. Jacobs, J. A. (1996). Gender inequality and higher education. *Annual Review of Sociology, 22*(1), 177–178.
28. For example, Gee, J. P. (2000). Identity as an analytic lens for research in education. *Review of Research in Education, 25,* 99–125.
29. Ashmore, R. D., Deaux, K., & McLaughlin-Volpe, T. (2004). An organizing framework for collective identity: Articulation and significance of multidimensionality. *Psychological Bulletin, 130,* 80–114.
30. Gee's concept of identity theory (Gee, 2000) is particularly illustrative for understanding this concept.
31. Walkerdine, V. (1990). *Schoolgirl fictions.* London, UK: Verso Books, xiii.
32. Lips, H. M. (2004). The gender gap in possible selves: Divergence of academic self-views among high school and university students. *Sex Roles, 50*(5–6), 357, 370.
33. Ibid., p. 370.
34. Lips, H. M. (2007). Gender and possible selves. *New Directions for Adult and Continuing Education, 2007*(114), 55.
35. See also: Brickhouse, N. W., & Potter, J. T. (2001). Young women's scientific identity formation in an urban context. *Journal of Research in Science Teaching, 38*(8), 965–980.
36. Gushue, G. V., & Whitson, M. L. (2006). The relationship of ethnic identity and gender role attitudes to the development of career choice goals among black and Latina girls. *Journal of Counseling Psychology, 53*(3), 379. Socio-cognitive career theory (Lent, 2013) offers a window into these differences as well. From an SCCT perspective, gender role and ethnic identity interact with social context. From this theoretical perspective, however, race, gender, and social context can serve as distal influences or as direct influences at the time of goal formation.
37. Shields, S. A. (2008). Gender: An intersectionality perspective. *Sex Roles, 59*(5–6), 301–311.
38. Lorber, J. (1994). *Paradoxes of gender.* New Haven, CT: Yale University Press.
39. Kimmel, M. (2006). A war against boys? *Dissent, 53*(4), 65–70.
40. Discourse is broadly defined as "a set of norms, preferences, and expectations relating linguistic structures to context which speaker-hearers draw on and modify in producing language in context" (Ochs, E. (1988). *Culture and language development.* Cambridge, UK: Cambridge University Press, p. 12), though there are many variations and strongly held opinions on this definition.
41. Tonso, K. L. (2007). *On the outskirts of engineering: Learning identity, gender, and power via engineering practice.* Rotterdam, The Netherlands: Sense Publishers, 217.
42. Tonso, K. L. (1999). Engineering gender—Gendering engineering: A cultural model for belonging. *Journal of Women and Minorities in Science and Engineering, 5*(4), 365–405.
43. Krefting, L. A. (2003). Intertwined discourses of merit and gender: Evidence from academic employment in the USA. *Gender, Work & Organization, 10*(2), 269.
44. Jackson, C., Dempster, S., & Pollard, L. (2015). "They just don't seem to really care, they just think it's cool to sit there and talk": Laddism in university teaching learning contexts. *Educational Review, 67*(3), 300–314.
45. Ibid., p. 307.
46. Streitfeld, D. (2015, March 27). Ellen Pao Loses Silicon Valley Bias Case Against Kleiner Perkins. *The New York Times.* Retrieved from www.nytimes.com/2015/03/28/technology/ellen-pao-kleiner-perkins-case-decision.html
47. Ibid.
48. Sandberg, S., & Grant, A. (2015, January 12). Speaking while female. *The New York Times.* Retrieved from www.nytimes.com/2015/01/11/opinion/sunday/speaking-while-female.html

49. Rhode, D. L. (2014). *What women want: An agenda for the women's movement.* Oxford: Oxford University Press.
50. Ibid.
51. Fraser, N. (2009). Feminism, capitalism and the cunning of history. *New Left Review, 56,* 97–117.
52. Ibid.
53. Appiah recently referred to this as "Utility U. versus Utopia U." Appiah, K. A. (2015, September 13). The college crossroads: The dream and the crisis of higher education. *The New York Times Magazine,* pp. 17–20.
54. Bennett, 1997, p. 84.
55. Brown, D. K. (2001). The social sources of educational credentialism: Status cultures, labor markets, and organizations. *Sociology of Education, 74,* 20.
56. Tomlinson, M. (2008). "The degree is not enough": Students' perceptions of the role of higher education credentials for graduate work and employability. *British Journal of Sociology of Education, 29*(1), 50.
57. Krogstad, J. M., & Fry, R. (2014, April 24). More Hispanics, blacks enrolling in college, but lag in bachelor's degrees. Retrieved from http://www.pewresearch.org/fact-tank/2014/04/24/more-hispanics-blacks-enrolling-in-college-but-lag-in-bachelors-degrees/#
58. Baker, D. P. (2011). Forward and backward, horizontal and vertical: Transformation of occupational credentialing in the schooled society. *Research in Social Stratification and Mobility, 29,* 5–29.
59. Ibid., pp. 11–13.
60. Ibid., p. 14.

3

WE'VE BEEN HERE BEFORE

Gendered Realignments Behind the Ivy

As the long-standing meeting site of aspirational community and equality, schooling has served as a particle-acceleration chamber for the economy, politics, law, and culture as they collide with entrenched beliefs about gender. When people's beliefs about women and men are in flux, debates about gender masquerade as anxieties about other cultural issues, primary among them educational policy, including the ways in which schools should sustain tradition or support new arrangements between men and women.[1] Women's recent academic successes challenge the ways in which masculinity and capitalism have been bound historically to the structure of schooling. Ironically, the possible unbinding of masculinity and economic success from academic study may serve to disadvantage women even as they succeed within it.

Necessary to understanding the current realignments of gender and power in higher education is an examination of women's past interactions with American higher education. Early patterns of advance and retreat reveal ways in which groups with little or no power—in this case women from multiple social classes and racial and ethnic groups—used the knowledge and credentials associated with formal education to try to gain economic, social, and political advantage. With each encroachment, cultural sectors generally acquiesced, more or less accepting changes until it looked as though such gains might mean real disruption of what many saw as the natural order—the power differential—between white and non-white, between wealthy and working class, and above all, between men and women. A parallel focus to the development of women in higher education, then, is necessarily on the counter forces to the threat they posed: What aspects of the cultural power structure shifted each time women's relationships to higher education changed, so that gender norms could remain stable?

Early Tensions Between Gender Roles, Postsecondary Schooling, and Equitable Futures

With the tacit understanding that schooling functioned as secular religion, supporting the gendered norms that Christianity clearly espoused, 19th-century America began building limited opportunities for girls of race and class privilege to become college educated; doing so, under these conditions, would not fundamentally change society. A new definition of woman was emerging during this time: Women were equal to men in their souls and now also in their civic responsibilities, but still decidedly different and separate from men with regard to their abilities to exercise power over their own lives.

Nonetheless, a vigorous debate around schooling emerged: If girls gained an education similar to that of boys, could they not be tempted to challenge the gender order of adult society? Would not a rigorous education "unfit" young women for their separate destinies? Opponents and proponents of full rights for women agreed that education had the potential to disrupt the separate gender spheres, although the former condemned the change and the latter welcomed it. What was clear, according to this mindset, is that the future of America depended on individual women making the "right" choices. "Yours it is to determine," offered a 19th-century reverend to his female parishioners, "whether the beautiful order of society . . . shall continue as it has been [or whether] society shall break up and become a chaos of disjointed and unsightly elements."[2] It was the duty of middle and upper class white women to protect their souls—and by extension the country's—by prioritizing their duties as wives and mothers over the demands of developing their intellectual lives.

Privileged men were also woven into the argument that higher education was an appropriate battleground on which to defend traditional gendered norms and ideologies.[3] During the early to mid-19th century, as the white "cult of womanhood" developed, women of all races were barred from attending most colleges; higher education was the singular province of white, wealthy men. The first bachelor's degree awarded to a woman in the United States was not conferred until 1841 at Oberlin College.[4] Vassar College opened in 1865, and postsecondary coeducation was also encouraged by the passage of the 1862 Morrill Act funding university growth.[5] Still, there was no clear mandate that women should spend their adolescence studying instead of scrubbing; middle and upper middle class white parents tried to ensure that the effects of education on their daughters did not deter them from their proper roles as wives and mothers.[6]

Progressive women of the era themselves reassured worried parents that education would not make their daughters less marriageable. Whether women such as Emma Willard, who established the Troy Female Seminary, or Catharine Beecher, creator of Hartford Female Seminary, actually believed this to be true, or largely co-opted this reasoning to gain support for their educational institutions, is unascertainable. The reality was that "the public's conviction that marriage and motherhood should be women's ultimate destiny was so powerful that Beecher and others insisted that teaching was an ideal preparation for motherhood and that teacher-training programs were not seminaries for producing celibates."[7] This tension presented itself in black American communities as well, though with added pressures to preserve racial communities as well as gendered structures. Black scholars of the early 20th century argued that black women "must not be educated away from being a mother. . . . The race is dependent upon her giving her best to her children";[8] this "best" included a woman's pursuit of a formal education in order to educate "superior sons."[9]

Some black female leaders of the same time period saw the situation differently, "believing their role was to ameliorate the effects of racism, seeing the future of the race as residing squarely in the realm of women."[10] Focusing on formal study had the potential to threaten this pursuit. These tensions constrained the professional aspirations of black women: Too much success, such as earning advanced degrees, contested the line between caring for one's self and caring for others. Just like white women, regardless of their abilities and potential for achievement, black women were still "subject to the scrutiny of 'what a woman ought to be and to do.'"[11] Women, regardless of color, were subject to universal laws as keepers of children and community, even as the communities themselves had vastly different amounts of power to control their destinies.

Still, the necessity for educating women to be teachers grew in black and white populations, as did the popularity of doing so; as more opportunities for work in industrial America grew for men, more women were needed to educate domestic and immigrant children.[12] The tête-à-tête between women's schooling and gendered cultural expectations intensified; as the numbers of women attending postsecondary school increased, the topic of women and higher education became controversial and the subject of great public interest. By 1890, women graduated from high school at twice the rate of boys, and women's undergraduate enrollment in the last third of the 19th century increased substantially: In coeducational institutions, there was a threefold increase in the number of male students from 1875 to 1900, and a sixfold increase in the number of female students.[13]

This success of women in high school and the expansion of female college attendance did not go unnoticed. New college curricula and programs were established in reaction to their presence, designed to attract males to higher education, and keep them separate from females. May writes:

> At Northwestern University, for example, engineering courses were added to stem the dangerous tide. At the University of Nebraska, growing numbers of female students provided the Regents with a rationale for creating a school of commerce to retain male students. And when the number of women students at Stanford rose from 25 percent in 1892 to 40 percent in 1899, the university adopted a limit on the number of women students to "preserve the college from an unwanted change in character."[14]

Further, girls' high school performance was simultaneously downplayed as irrelevant to their futures, as some educational figures highlighted the disconnect between success in educational pursuit and the realities of their lives-to-be. Those who offered this rationale justified boys' disdain for and poor performance in schools (where it existed) by asserting that public schools must be defective if girls' achievement was greater than boys'. There was a great gender disparity between success in school and success in later life, observed James Armstrong in 1910:

> The valedictorians of high school graduating classes are almost always girls; but in after-life, whether in universities or in life occupations, boys have not shown themselves wanting. [It is striking that] . . . [T]he Great Business College of Life has conferred its highest degrees upon many a boy who has been marked a failure in high school when compared with the average girl.[15]

As long as schooling was considered largely irrelevant to future life success, the narrative that boys could do poorly in school, or go without it altogether, without much damage, could hold sway. But economic and social conditions would allow this reasoning to continue for only a little while longer.

The Progressive Era and the Precursor to the First "Boy Crisis"

What was it that compelled young women to attend high school and college, knowing that their life trajectories were not likely to be altered by taking this action? The Progressive Era (1890–1920) saw a confluence of the conditions that would affect, for the first of several times in the next century, women's and men's responses to formal schooling in pronounced ways. While the era witnessed forward movement in social causes, economic equity, and political progress, it also set in motion the first wave of boys and men finding pathways away from formal schooling, in what would become in retrospect the first "boy crisis."

The U.S. economy during the late 19th and early 20th centuries needed workers to support rapid urbanization and industrialization, and men did not need much formal schooling to get a job; places other than schooling offered chances for economic and social betterment. Meanwhile, with socioeconomically privileged women's life choices more their own than in previous decades, and with slowly changing ideas of what women could do, many attended college. Black women's higher education enrollment and graduation rates during this time period display that they, as much as white women, were ready to take advantage of greater educational opportunity. In 1920, 18.9 percent of bachelor's degrees awarded by historically black colleges were granted to women.[16] Women who could afford to do so could go to college at this time and succeed without threatening the gender or racial social order.

Almost all men, on the other hand, could skip the step—with the ironic exception of men of high privilege, who often used formal higher education as a pathway to even greater economic and political power. Both wealthy and working class white men had gender expectations, but no matter what the route, these expectations involved contributing to an expansive and powerful American economy and world presence. Young men learned vocational skills largely on the job, or through apprenticeships and mentoring through their father's occupations; schooling was only loosely coupled to careers. The economic conditions of the time improved after the Panic of 1893 subsided, largely by 1897, when unemployment rates of up to 43 percent began to diminish,[17] making the way for more job creation. Labor unions grew rapidly, as did immigration, until the start of World War I in 1914. In short, there was work to be done, and jobs were easy to obtain. Black men had significantly more opportunities for better paying employment relative to black women, and so also entered the workforce instead of school. Schools offered formalized knowledge, but in reality working class children across the racial spectrum, especially males, were depended upon to start working; they were considered family breadwinners.

There were, of course, those who continued to argue that schooling for women could lead them to futures other than being wives and mothers; early women's movement leaders such as Elizabeth Cady Stanton, Susan B. Anthony, and other activists offered the radical idea that schooling should lead women to any occupations available to men. Henrietta Rodman and Crystal Eastman argued that coeducation could lead to the elimination of gender distinctions altogether. Meanwhile, the National American Woman Suffrage Association (NAWSA) was formed in 1890, and, led by Carrie Chapman Catt in the early 20th century, it became the primary promoter of women's right to vote.[18] Intersecting with potentially socially disruptive changes proposed by the NAWSA and other organizations were women who invoked traditional ideas of their roles as wives and mothers to work in their communities; using motherhood as the entry to community activism, they employed oppositional tactics that would be reignited to fight the passage of the Equal Rights Amendment later the same century. Many women also fought continuously for the cause of Prohibition, noting that alcohol distracted men from their roles as wage earners, fathers, and husbands. Birth control for women was becoming more freely available during this time as well, expanding women's sexual and reproductive choices,[19] even as they were beginning to take advantage of their academic and political choices.

The First "Boy"

When it became clear that formal higher education was not only useful but necessary to differentiate a growing American middle class population from the growing immigrant population, attitudes about high school and higher education in general began to change. Whereas a decade earlier, boys' lack of school success or attendance was largely dismissed, the second decade of the 20th century began to see what in retrospect became the first "boy problem."[20] In fact, Tyack and Hansot claim that "much of progressive education can be understood as a campaign to fit schooling to boys."[21] This shift in the importance of American high school education offers the most direct parallel to the position in which colleges currently find themselves: It has again become a general social problem that middle class white men do not academically succeed in or attend schooling with vigor and numbers equal to or greater than those of white, middle class women.

High school attendance at the turn of the 20th century was still not compulsory, and its success as an institution of male progress hinged on convincing the small population of middle class white parents that high school was a way to pass along advantages without seeming to appear as part of an elite group. "The rhetoric of the high school," Tyack and Hansot argue,

> gave the appearance of a meritocratic system of performance-based evaluations, whereby the talented succeeded. This clearly carried great appeal to middle-class urbanites, who instinctively eschewed the open display of social advantage or favoritism based on anything but ability and accomplishment.[22]

As the connection between the credentials conferred by schooling and middle class employment became more evident to parents and graduates, high school and then college became acceptable places for middle class boys to invest their energy.

With women's encroachment and success in the previously male territory of high school and college education, however, came the backlash. Combined with awareness that educated women were also demanding social and political changes, prominent representatives of schooling responded to increased social anxiety about gender roles by reinforcing the connections between girls' education and their gender-normed futures. Researchers in the nascent discipline of psychology, as well as many physicians, argued that women's physiology would be harmed if they participated in too much education.[23] In particular, eminent biological determinist Edward H. Clarke's book, *Sex in Education: Or a Fair Chance for Girls*, helped rationalize women's exclusion from higher education, arguing that as women went through puberty, their energies were needed for the development of their reproductive capacities. An education for young women, equal to that of young men, called for sustained and continuous effort, which he argued was "out of harmony with the rhythmical periodicity of the female organization."[24] Presaging 21st-century neuroscience arguments like those of Leonard Sax and others,[25] Clarke and like-minded physicians argued in the face of women's rising academic prowess that women's bodies were not fit to handle the rigors of study and higher education.

Despite these contentions, girls' enrollment in schools did not decline.[26] However, the success of girls and women in school raised uneasy questions that just several decades earlier had been ignored, most central among them: Why educate girls if they were just going to become mothers? Americans demonstrated tolerance for women's temporary employment prior to motherhood, but not for fully fledged careers, especially if such aspirations threatened men's positions in the workplace. High school and college education was becoming a strange kind of finishing school, or even a holding tank: Women could obtain knowledge and skills, even as they were expected to do so with an eye toward their accepted destinies of motherhood and family care.

The incongruity between women's education and future expected roles was only part of the issue; women's proficiency in educational tasks was, simply put, upstaging men. The problem of boys not attending or liking school only fully materialized into a boy "problem," however, when compulsory attendance laws allowed comparisons of large numbers of boys and girls. When women continued to enroll in higher education, their success became part of the newly named problem as well. In response, policy makers and school reformers offered evidence that purported to show how boys were simply uninterested in sitting still and reading rather than not being able to learn, and they began to criticize the predominance and practices of female teachers. In other words, practices that required obedience such as standing in lines and the general requirement that boys needed to do what they were told by their (female) teachers were presented as the cause of their poorer performance, rather than the boys themselves.[27] (Interestingly, the requirement of obedience to teachers was not seen as a problem with girls' behavior. The literature of the time also does not reveal acknowledgment by "boy problem" critics that the same practices they decried as being too restrictive for boys in common school were those that the armed forces and other all-men's groups insisted upon.) The prevailing social order that depended on young people's adherence to gender norms was being disrupted by women's success in high school and college, and it needed to be corrected.

One such correction was a change in the American high school curriculum: Home economics and typing courses were created and instituted, designed to channel women into specific lines of nonthreatening work, just as engineering and business majors were added to college curricula several decades earlier in order to channel men into fields where women did not gravitate. Concurrently, the National Women's Trade Union League (NWTUL) supported egalitarian education in the skilled trades for women. Their leadership advocated the idea that being skilled in a high-paying trade, in combination with protective legislation, suffrage, and unionization, could improve working women's lives. If their advocacy had been successful in shifting gender norms, women might have developed a set of well-paid and respected vocational choices equaling that of men's, so that their post-high school choices were not so limited.[28] But, attitudes about women's "natural" place at home, as well as union resistance to women's presence in male trades made the idea of equal coeducation in skilled blue-collar jobs largely untenable.[29] Differentiation of academic skill acquisition was one strategy used to channel women's educational success away from impacting male dominance in some occupational fields.

Another way in which society-at-large countered female encroachment in male educational territory at this time was to create gender-exclusive social settings outside of school. Extracurricular sports, fraternal lodges, and social organizations like the Boy Scouts (formed in 1910) and the Dude Ranchers' Association (1926) were spaces that reinforced a traditional masculine identity, characterized by physical strength, a connection with the outdoors, and male bonding in general. The American Girl Scout program was also organized during this era (1912), but its difference from the male-centric nature of boy scouting was clearly articulated:

> If character, training, and learning citizenship are necessary for boys, how much more important it is that these principles should be instilled into the minds of girls who are destined to be the mothers and guides of the next generation. . . . The Scout movement, so popular among boys, is unfitted for the needs of girls, but on something the same lines has been devised . . . giving a more womanly training for both mind and body.[30]

At the college level, fraternities during this period became almost aggressively masculine.[31] Part of American university life since 1825, fraternities' place as keepers of a particular type of masculinity—rugged, athletic, strong, white, and wealthy—had been long-established, even if closed to all but a privileged few. However, as women entered higher education in greater numbers, and as women's roles in society began to change, more fraternities were formed, and they were more often defined by men who participated in exploitative sex, used their wealth conspicuously, and drank alcohol in large quantities.[32] Intercollegiate sports, while also a long-standing tradition in university life, gained status and financial backing from alumni during the first decades of the 20th century, again coinciding with increases in women's collegiate attendance.[33] Also characterized by increased violence, hyper-masculinity, and conspicuous alcohol consumption, college sports became a "symbolic litmus test of regional and/or ethnic esteem and assimilation,"[34] as attempts to separate middle class white men from women and immigrants became further encouraged by university administrators and alumni.

Women's college attendance in the Depression Era is characterized in what little scholarship exists as a "time of retrenchment for women, both in and outside of academia, following the heady gains of the 1920s."[35] Some scholars of women's participation in higher education between 1930 and the beginning of the U.S. involvement in World War II argue that the concept of "good citizenship" was used as a reason for and against women's participation in further scholarship. On one hand, people speculated, participation in higher education could postpone childbearing, which then would negatively affect birth rates; on the other, educated women might gain the wherewithal to produce healthier future children. In the black community, college-educated women were also considered more likely to have the skills to create "racial uplift,"[36] necessary to help the entire community's circumstances rise. The discourses on higher education for women during this time focused on formal study as community development, rather than individual enhancement. To some extent, discussions of boys' postsecondary educations were informed by community enhancement as well, though this was strongly mediated by individuals' social class positions.

In the years in between the Depression and World War II, in communities where manufacturing jobs were largely filled and there were lower numbers of immigrants, it was easier to convince boys and their families of the merits of high school attendance; the connection between employment and schooling was more evident and seemed more reasonable in places where jobs were not as easily obtained.[37] But growth in attendance was slow; by the 1940s, only 50 percent of the country's young adults had graduated from high school even though by this time every state had compulsory attendance laws.[38] Gender identity lines were still clear—men and women stayed relatively safely in their traditional social spaces, and the political upheaval that some expected in the wake of universal women's suffrage had not occurred.[39] Although white women in particular had made inroads in political representation, college attendance, and control of their reproductive lives, they still largely stayed at home, focusing on their families and communities, where social expectations directed them. Black women were participating in the paid workforce at higher rates than white women, but their energies were expected to return to family and community as well.

The Development of the Second "Boy Problem" in Schools

In the Progressive Era, broad objective and ideological changes in gender patterns in American society as a whole prompted activists to generate an agenda for social reform, and women's attendance in formal schooling grew in this wake.[40] The second wave of anxiety about males and education would find its height during the Civil Rights Era, when again the gendered expectations of men and women were at odds with new developments. Sociopolitical realities and gender expectations began to diverge, as women began demanding more power over their futures. When job prospects grew more uncertain for men, and when racial identities of men and women were being challenged, the question of the importance of higher education returned.

World War II and its aftermath had provided a temporary suspension of gender norms for women in particular; in an all-hands-on-deck atmosphere, the bonds of social expectations for women were loosened before being forcefully reasserted in post-war America. During the late 1940s and 1950s, college attendance, fueled by the GI Bill, was at a century-long high, adding tens of thousands of students to college campuses.[41] Women went back home—only temporarily—as veterans went to college in larger numbers; between 1948 and 1949, women's representation of college attendance was at 29 percent, its lowest level in the 20th century.[42] Beginning in the 1950s, though, women's rate of enrollment in college began to outpace men's and by 1960, women constituted 36 percent of the college population.[43]

Also growing at this time was women's participation in paid employment, particularly married, college-educated women, who had in previous decades been expected to stay at home. The 1960 census found that 55.2 percent of the U.S. female labor force was "married, husband present,"[44] with college-educated white and black women among the most likely to be part of that labor force.[45] These changes worked in tandem with the maintenance of social expectations for women however. Americans' religious beliefs and long-standing cultural mores continued to shape most people's understanding of women's primary destinies as wives and mothers, in separate spheres from men. Further, the male-centric organizational structure of higher education yet again changed to accommodate these traditional beliefs. For example, many colleges, particularly selective ones, began to place quotas on women's admissions, some overtly, and some by establishing covert barriers.[46] Colleges and universities also began creating or channeling their female students to what amounted to a "women's curriculum": Parenting and cooking classes were not uncommon, even at elite universities like Wellesley and the University of Chicago, and nursing and teaching majors were recommended as family-friendly occupations.[47]

Equally if not more powerful than organizational changes in many colleges was what the president of Radcliffe College, Mary I. Bunting, referred to as the "climate of unexpectation"[48] for women: They could go to college, albeit with the silent understanding that they would repurpose their degrees as household instruction manuals thereafter. Most college-educated women complied[49] and the M.R.S. degree was born. Cultural observers and college administrators did not foresee significant changes in the ways in which women's participation in higher education would influence marriage or financial markets. Highly skilled jobs remained available for men, and women continued to be considered out of sync with gender norms if they wanted to do something with their college degrees.[50] The status quo of men in college was not threatened, and neither was their place in the economy. Through the late 1960s, white men still dominated higher education by number, access, and major.

Not surprisingly, black women's and men's access to college at this time differed from that of white women and men, though the same patterns remained. Even as the last of the legal barriers to college entry fell via the Civil Rights Act of 1964, the Higher Education Rights Act of 1965, and other historic legal actions,[51] it was not immediately apparent that the changes affecting the lives of black Americans were directly applicable to black women. Unjust laws governed slavery and its aftereffects, evident in the Jim Crow Era laws, voting rights, employment laws, and education. The legal changes of the Civil Rights Era spoke to the ways in which white Americans were beginning to come to terms with its past and present treatment of black Americans. But, as historian Stacey Jones wrote, "In higher education, opposition to racial discrimination did not guarantee opposition to sexual discrimination."[52] In other words, challenges to racial oppression were not often accompanied by challenges to gender oppression. These battles were fought largely separately; the visibility of economic opportunities for women coupled with sustained and organized legal complaints to higher education policies were in many ways the levers for women's successful participation in higher education.

The "Boy Problem" a Third Time

During this time, a growing tension was developing between women's participation in higher education, market work, and a changing cultural understanding of what Americans thought educated women should be doing with their lives. The artifacts of these frictions ultimately resulted in what would become the third and present "boy problem." With women's expectations for their lives changing radically and rapidly throughout the 1970s and 80s, coupled with economic changes that necessitated their sustained participation in the workforce, their altered expectations of careers brought the necessity and desire to have more college degrees in broader majors.[53] Hewitt writes:

> Contemporary observers remarked on the obsession of college students in the 1970s, both men and women, with preparing for careers, since it was a vivid contrast to the rebellious college students of the 1960s. . . . The difference was attributed to the worsening economic climate of the 1970s. The epidemic of workaholism on campus . . . stems from the economic realities of the present. The number of job opportunities is dwindling while the number of seekers, including women in unprecedented numbers, is increasing.[54]

In fact, the numbers *were* as unprecedented. Jones argues that the critical mass of women entering law and medical schools removed the isolation and informal barriers that women had previously experienced, and increased the protests by women over blatant discriminatory practices throughout academia. Her claim that "the importance of group pressures and externalities in driving social change" explains why men's professional school applications stagnated during this time, even as women's kept growing, offers another part of the cultural shift that contributed to the third installment of the boy crisis.[55]

Shifts in the acceptability of women's graduate and professional training and consequent career pursuits affected, in turn, their pursuit of early marriage and childbearing. The average age of marriage began rising for women and men, particularly college-educated women,[56] the development of the pill offered more freedom regarding reproductive choices, and women's participation in the work-force was now increasingly supported by changes in law—blatant gender discrimination was no longer legally sanctioned. Brewing together, these changes in and out of academe came within 40 short years: In 1970, 58 percent of all college students were men; by 1980 men and women attended in roughly the same proportions. By 2010, it was women who constituted 57 percent of all college students.[57] The transformation of women's participation in higher education came swiftly, and with it, a fully flowered recurrence of the worry about boys.

Garibaldi argues that the current version of the boy crisis is different, growing "primarily because the disproportionality between white males and white females enrolled in college is rapidly widening."[58] He correctly points out that writers and researchers were not, until recently, lamenting black males' absence from college. The monolithic call that "something was wrong with our [white] boys" was sounded, and, as with the first and second boy problems, human biology was implicated.

Interestingly, during this version of the boy problem/crisis, it is boys' biology that was blamed first, as people searched for explanations regarding the changes that many saw in white boys' college enrollment and behavior, both in and out of the classroom. Some researchers argued, for example, that the reversal of the gender gap in college enrollment and completion may be due largely to persistent behavioral and developmental differences between men and women. Some centered on boys' later maturity and their higher incidence of behavioral problems. Goldin, Katz, and Kuziemko concluded that,

> [B]ehavioral factors [school disciplinary and behavioral problems, and fewer hours completing homework], after adjusting for family background, test scores, and high school achievement, can explain virtually the entire female advantage in getting into college for the high school graduating class of 1992.[59]

Essentially, they argued, boys will be boys, a claim consistent with 100 years of explanation for male and female differences in school performance: Boys and men do not see the need for formal education, and their maleness—their biology—is simply not suited for school. They have other places in which to succeed. Goldin, Katz, and Kuziemko state as much:

> Another possible reason for the reversal of the college gender gap is that girls may have lower nonpecuniary (or effort) costs of college preparation and attendance than boys. After all, girls have exceeded boys in secondary school performance and attainment at various times during the last century even when the labor market barriers faced by women meant substantially lower expected labor market returns to schooling for girls than boys.[60]

In other words, females' seeming ability to "play school" well allowed them to enroll and excel in formal education, even when there was—and still is—less opportunity for this academic excellence to convert to financial and social advantage. Developmental causes and explanations remain in vogue, however, and they have been joined by newly developed arguments implicating women's and men's biology.[61]

As in the past, in a patriarchal culture when boys and men find themselves losing economic, political, or cultural ground—in this case, in higher education—cultural messages urging males to shift their behaviors will once again be in sync with normed gender expectations.

Importance of Education as Virtue

Finally, it is important to note that throughout the nation's prior two centuries, formal educational attainment has not only been about obtaining credentials and status, but also about virtuousness. As Meyer states, "[E]ducation-based meritocratic assignment is generally, in the modern cultural system, taken to be virtuous and proper—clearly more highly legitimated than other forms of status transmission and allocation."[62] Yet merit assignment via educational status was legitimated in a context when men were the dominant participants; as women have increasingly engaged with and succeeded in formal education, the belief that educational success merits assignment into a privileged world is challenged.

Cultural understandings of virtue and propriety for women have been traditionally defined in terms of home and family; women have merited their place in the social order by adhering to these roles. For men of wealth, their higher status in a male-centered society was assigned at birth; school performance increasingly offered similar status to those in the middle class. As schooling became more common for women, though, merit and virtue began to deviate from each other, leaving the definition of virtue open for subtle reassignment: If merit were offered in exchange for academic prowess, virtue was then free to become associated with the propriety of women in particular. Schooling could become a channel to reassert virtue—now named "appropriate behavior"—made all the more important as education credentials for women became permanent indicators for their potential success in the economic market place. If the credentials no longer differentiated men and women—or increasingly favored women—the propriety of appropriate behavior salvaged some measure of female virtue.

If formal education continues to function as a secular American religion in the 21st century, then the proximity and assignment of women to formal schooling—and by opposition, men as distant from it—offers a way for women to maintain the cultural expectations of gender, even as they dominate in school success. In other words, women can dominate and still maintain propriety, winning the educational contest even as they stagnate in economic and political realms. This perspective offers troubling implications for girls' and women's educational attainment, further complicated by racial, ethnic, and social status.

Although arguments about women's dominance or advantage in higher education suggest that women are winning in their pursuit of successful and equitable lives, the relevance of formal schooling remains dependent on the economic status of men, and on the resolution of the cultural discomfort of women's power in political and social domains. The latest wave of boy worry combined with girl fear, now fully blossomed, is explored in Chapter 4.

Notes

1. Tyack, D., & Hansot, E. (1992). *Learning together: A history of coeducation in American public schools.* New York: Russell Sage Foundation, p. 2.
2. Welter, B. (1966). "The cult of true womanhood: 1820–1860." *American Quarterly, 18*(2), 151–174.
3. Harper, S. R., & Harris III, F. (2010). *College men and masculinities: Theory, research, and implications for practice.* San Francisco, CA: John Wiley & Sons.
4. Oberlin College. (2016). Oberlin College Early History. Retrieved from https://new. oberlin.edu/about/history.dot
5. May, A. M. (2006, October). "Sweeping the heavens for a comet": Women, the language of political economy, and higher education in the United States. *Feminist Economics, 12*(4), 625–640.
6. Even Horace Mann, though perhaps the greatest proponent of common school during this time, did not necessarily think that women's schooling should be the same as men's or than women ought to aspire to male roles in adult society (Rury, J. (2013). *Education and social change: Contours in the history of American schooling* (4th Ed.). New York: Routledge, p. 76).
7. Tyack & Hansot, 1992, p. 43.
8. Gaines, K. (1996). *Uplifting the race: Black leadership, politics and culture in the twentieth century.* Chapel Hill, NC: University of North Carolina Press, p. 140.
9. Ibid.
10. Crocco, M. S., & Waite, C. L. (2007). Education and marginality: Race and gender in higher education, 1940–1955. *History of Education Quarterly, 47*(1), p. 73.
11. Ibid.
12. Tyack & Hansot, 1992.
13. Rudolph, F. (1962). *The American college and university: A history.* New York, NY: Alfred A. Knopf; Solomon, B. M. (1985). *In the company of educated women: A history of women and higher education in America.* New Haven, CT: Yale University Press.
14. May, 2006, p. 629.
15. Armstrong, J. E. (1910). The advantages of limited sex segregation in the high school. *School Review, 18*, 337.
16. Bertaux, N. E., & Anderson, M. C. (2001). An emerging tradition of educational achievement: African American women in college and the professions, 1920–1950. *Equity and Excellence in Education, 34*(2), p. 18.
17. Parshall, G. (1992). The Great Panic of '93. *U.S. News & World Report, 113*(17), p. 70.
18. Flexner, E., & Fitzpatrick, E. (1996). *Century of struggle: The women's rights movement in the United States.* Cambridge, MA: Harvard University Press, pp. 208–217.
19. Tone, A. (2001). *Devices and desires: A history of contraceptives in America.* New York, NY: Hill and Wang.
20. Kimmel, M. S., & Holler, J. Z. (2000). *The gendered society.* New York: Oxford University Press.

21. Tyack & Hansot, 1992, p. 166.
22. Ibid., pp. 85–86.
23. Ibid.
24. Clarke, E. H. (1875). *Sex in education: Or, a fair chance for girls*. Boston: James R. Osgood and Company, p. 83.
25. Sax, L. (2006). *Why gender matters: What parents and teachers need to know about the emerging science of sex differences*. New York, NY: Broadway Books; Gurian, M., & Stevens, K. (2005, May 2). What is happening with boys in school? *Teachers College Record*. Retrieved from www.tcrecord.org ID Number: 11854
26. Bruder, A. (2012). Determination and resistance in women's higher education. Retrieved from http://greenfield.brynmawr.edu/items/show/; Hall, G. S. (1904, 1916). *Adolescence: Its psychology and its relations to physiology, anthropology, sociology, sex, crime, religion, and education* (2 vols.). New York, NY: D. Appleton & Company.
27. See Hall, 1904, 1916 for an early example of this connection.
28. Cantor, M., & Laurie, B. (Eds.). (1977). *Sex, class, and the woman worker*. Westport, CT: Greenwood Press.
29. Tyack & Hansot, 1992, p. 211.
30. Rothschild, M. (1981). To scout or to guide? The girl scout-boy scout controversy, 1912–1941. *Frontiers: A Journal of Women Studies*, 6(3), p. 117.
31. Syrett, N. (2009). *The company he keeps: A history of white college fraternities*. Chapel Hill: University of North Carolina Press.
32. Ibid.
33. Bell, R. C. (2008). *A history of women in sport prior to Title IX*. Retrieved from http://thesportjournal.org/article/a-history-of-women-in-sport-prior-to-title-ix
34. *The role and cope of intercollegiate athletics in U.S. colleges and universities*. http://education.stateuniversity.com/pages/1846/College-Athletics-HISTORY-ATHLETICS-IN-U-S-COLLEGES-UNIVERSITIES.html
35. Nash, M. A., & Romero, L. S. (2012). "Citizenship for the college girl": Challenges and opportunities in higher education for women in the United States in the 1930s. *Teachers College Record, 114*, p. 3.
36. Ibid., p. 4.
37. Goldin, C. D. (1998). America's graduation from high school: The evolution and spread of secondary schooling in the twentieth century. *Journal of Economic History, 58*(2), 345–374.
38. Tyack, D. (1974). *The one best system: A history of American urban education*. Cambridge, MA: Harvard University Press.
39. Testi, A. (1995). The gender of reform politics: Theodore Roosevelt and the culture of masculinity. *The Journal of American History, 81*(4), 1509–1533.
40. Tyack & Hansot, 1992, p. 244.
41. Smith, W., & Bender, T. (2008). Introduction. In W. Smith and T. Bender (Eds.), *American higher education transformed: 1940–2005* (pp. 1–11). Baltimore, MD: Johns Hopkins University Press.
42. U.S. Department of Education, 1948–62.
43. Ibid.
44. U.S. Bureau of the Census, 1975.
45. Jones, S. (2009). Dynamic social norms and the unexpected transformation of women's higher education, 1965–1975. *Social Science History, 33*(3), p. 260.
46. Riesman, D. (1965). Two generations. In R. J. Lifton (Ed.), *The American Woman* (pp. 72–97). Boston: Houghton-Mifflin.
47. Solomon, 1985; Kaledin, E. (1984). *Mothers and more: American women in the 1950s*. Boston, MA: Twayne.
48. Eisenmann, L. (2006). *Higher education for women in Postwar America, 1945–1965*. Baltimore, MD: Johns Hopkins University Press.

49. Solomon, 1985.
50. Eaton, J. (1997). The evolution of access policy: 1965–1990. In L. F. Goodchild, C. D. Lovell, E. R. Hines, & J. I. Gill (Eds.), *Public policy in higher education* (pp. 237–246). Needham Heights, MA: Pearson Custom Publishing.
51. Brock, T. (2010). Young adults and higher education: Barriers and breakthroughs to success. *The Future of Children, 20*(10), 109–132.
52. Jones, S. (2009). Dynamic social norms and the unexpected transformation of women's higher education, 1965–1975. *Social Science History, 33*(3), p. 267.
53. Solomon, 1985.
54. Hewitt, V. L. (2015). *A challenge to excel: Creating a new image for elite women's colleges in the 1970s.* Philadelphia, PA: University of Pennsylvania. Unpublished dissertation.
55. Jones, 2009, p. 279.
56. DiPrete & Buchmann, 2013.
57. Snyder, T. D., Dillow, S. A., & Hoffman, C. M. (2007). *Digest of education statistics 2006 (NCES 2007–017).* Washington, DC: U.S. Department of Education, Institute of Education Sciences.
58. Garibaldi, A. M. (2014). The expanding gender and racial gap in American higher education. *The Journal of Negro Education, 83*(3), p. 373.
59. Goldin, C., Katz, L. F., & Kuziemko, I. (2006). The homecoming of American college women: The reversal of the college gender gap. *The Journal of Economic Perspectives, 20*(4), p. 154.
60. Ibid., p. 153.
61. A prime example of this is former Harvard President Lawrence Summers's infamous attributions of women's lesser success in mathematics and science to innate differences between the sexes. Summers, L. H. (2005). *Remarks at NBER conference on diversifying the science & engineering workforce.* Cambridge, MA: Harvard University Office of the President.
62. Meyer, J. (2000). Reflections on education as transcendence. In L. Cuban & D. Shipps (Eds.), *Reconstructing the common good in education* (pp. 206–222). Stanford, CA: Stanford University Press.

4

THE AMBIGUOUS "FEMALE ADVANTAGE"

Why would any self-respecting boy want to attend one of America's increasingly feminized universities? Most of these institutions have flounced through the last forty years fashioning a fluffy pink playpen of feminist studies and agitprop "herstory," taught amid a green goo of ecomotherism and anti-industrial phobia. . . . Perhaps this explains why American men have taken a demographic plunge in higher education. . . . In a world where male talent in mathematics and engineering confers significant national advantages in wealth and power, [female college dominance] is portentous indeed.

George Gilder[1]

Men, according to Gilder, have become the "unschooled male underclass."[2] Truly, a vastly different educational landscape does exist for women now. Americans have witnessed a four-decade rise in women's enrollment and success in higher education due to years of changed policies and procedures in higher education, financial necessities of families, and evolving expectations for women's career pursuits, combined with strong legal pressures for equal opportunities for women and men representing racial, ethnic, and socioeconomic diversities. Many like Gilder have lamented the losses—perceived and real—of the American white male, telling the story of 21st-century higher education with a zero-sum scoreboard: advantage, women. Loser, men. Deemed a female *advantage* phenomenon, the story of women's recent successes in college comes wrapped in accounts of male decline and *crisis*, bringing with it century-old reprisals of educational incompatibility for men, while data substantiating underrepresented minorities' progress in college completion and achievement sit mostly untended.

Even when writers less extreme than Gilder discuss what they see are the impacts of changes in higher education gender demographics, many fail to acknowledge that the shifts in women's and men's college experiences themselves evidence of gender transformation and social equity. Upon tion of the economic and cultural contexts surrounding these shifts, arguments for the existence of a female advantage in college completion and success become deeply ambiguous. Once higher education attendance and completion data are examined inclusive of race and social class as well as gender, and the definition of college success dissected; once the influences of the "digital turn" and for-profit colleges are explored and the "college for all" mantra is unpacked, and once the relationship between higher education and socioeconomic equity is parsed, a female advantage is *not* evident, and the boy crisis looks more like the arrival at a new version of an old crossroads: as women begin to dominate another formerly male institution, where will men go to reestablish power?

When white, socioeconomically privileged men dominated higher education, no one considered them advantaged; having privilege means never having to admit one has it. Pratto and Stewart point out that people, researchers included, refer to problematized groups as "stigmatized" or "disadvantaged" but do not describe the contrasting group as privileged. They continue:

> The practice of marking the "problematic" group reveals that the unmarked situation of dominant groups is assumed to be normal. Such a stance is only half-blind concerning group privilege because although it focuses attention on "problematic" groups and may acknowledge group inequality, it does not acknowledge the positions of the referent group as privileged. . . . [T]he implicit assumption is that dominance is normal. By taking dominance as normal, superior social positions and greater power do not seem to be privileged.[3]

Male dominance in college attendance and completion have reflected the gendered status quo of higher education in America, therefore existing as part of culturally accepted "normalcy." Women's recent college gains challenge that constant, however; with the referent group's (men's) former privilege in education now upended, cultural rhetoric labels not only males as "in crisis" but women as "advantaged," reframing achievements that stood to make higher education more gender-equal into threats targeting white boys and men.

The creation of a boy crisis—a problem, reborn—offers an opportunity to examine the ways in which the intersections of gender, race, class, and higher education are defined and discussed. As was the case in earlier eras of American educational history examined in Chapter 3, specifically asking who is succeeding, and in what ways, offers the opportunity for nuanced depictions of the methods by which power and privilege are engaged. Such questions also offer lessons in the tenacity of cultural gender norms. By investigating the details of the case for female advantage, it is possible to see how 40 years of open college doors can lead to rooms of surprisingly retrograde ideas.

College Attendance and Completion Inclusive of Race, Ethnicity, Social Class, and Gender

Who Attends College? Who Earns Degrees?

In 2014 America, over 21 million people chose to attend over 7,000 colleges and universities.[4] In the last 50 years, more than 1,800 college campuses have been created, representing a remarkable national commitment to higher education.[5] For-profit colleges, one of the newer elements of higher education, made up an even faster-growing segment; enrollment at for-profit colleges increased by 225 percent between 1990 and 2012, while overall enrollment in degree-granting higher education institutions grew 31 percent during the same period.[6] The astronomical increase in for-profit postsecondary higher education compared to not-for-profit postsecondary growth is in part due to the low for-profit enrollment in the early 1990s.[7] Very recent evidence suggests that for-profit college growth has hit its peak and is now beginning to decline, in part due to federal investigations of such colleges' recruitment practices and concurrent return on investments for their students.[8] Nonetheless, higher education industry analysts predict that the for-profit arm of postsecondary education is permanent, even if its growth continues to level or decline.[9]

During this time of rapid growth in higher education, American women have *really* heeded the call, enrolling and completing college in unprecedented rates, so much so that by 2010, they earned roughly 60 percent of all associate's degrees, bachelor's degrees, and master's degrees awarded in the United States, as well as roughly 53 percent of doctoral degrees.[10]

TABLE 4.1 Number of Degrees Conferred to U.S. Residents by Degree-Granting Institutions, Percentage Distribution of Degrees Conferred and Percentage of Degrees Conferred to Females, by Level of Degree and Race/Ethnicity: Academic Years 1999–2000 and 2009–10

Level of degree and race/ethnicity	Number		Percentage distribution		Percent conferred to females	
	1999–2000	2009–10	1999–2000	2009–10	1999–2000	2009–10
Associate's	554,845	833,337	100.0	100.0	60.3	62.0
White	408,772	552,863	73.7	66.3	59.8	60.9
Black	60,221	113,905	10.9	13.7	65.2	68.3
Hispanic	51,573	112,211	9.3	13.5	59.4	62.4
Asian/Pacific Islander	27,782	44,021	5.0	5.3	56.8	58.5
American Indian/Alaska Native	6,497	10,337	1.2	1.2	65.8	64.9

(Continued)

TABLE 4.1 (Continued)

Level of degree and race/ethnicity	Number		Percentage distribution		Percent conferred to females	
	1999–2000	2009–10	1999–2000	2009–10	1999–2000	2009–10
Bachelor's	1,198,809	1,602,480	100.0	100.0	57.5	57.4
White	929,106	1,167,499	77.5	72.9	56.6	56.0
Black	108,013	164,844	9.0	10.3	65.7	65.9
Hispanic	75,059	140,316	6.3	8.8	59.6	60.7
Asian/Pacific Islander	77,912	117,422	6.5	7.3	54.0	54.5
American Indian/Alaska Native	8,719	12,399	0.7	0.8	60.3	60.7
Master's	406,761	611,693	100.0	100.0	60.0	62.6
White	324,981	445,038	79.9	72.8	59.6	61.8
Black	36,595	76,458	9.0	12.5	68.2	71.1
Hispanic	19,384	43,535	4.8	7.1	60.1	64.3
Asian/Pacific Islander	23,538	42,072	5.8	7.0	52.0	54.3
American Indian/Alaska Native	2,263	3,960	0.6	0.6	62.7	64.3
Doctoral	106,494	140,505	100.0	100.0	47.0	53.3
White	82,984	104,426	77.9	74.3	45.4	51.4
Black	7,080	10,417	6.6	7.4	61.0	65.2
Hispanic	5,039	8,085	4.7	5.8	48.4	55.0
Asian/Pacific Islander	10,684	16,625	10.0	11.8	48.8	56.5
American Indian/Alaska Native	707	952	0.7	0.7	52.9	54.8

National Center for Education Statistics (NCES) data from 2016 show that over 50 percent of U.S. females had completed an associate's or higher degree, compared with 41 percent of males.[11] Also according to these data, the percentage distribution of degrees conferred to each of the *non-white* racial/ethnic categories increased over this time period; only the percentage of degrees conferred to white women and men decreased in every major degree category.

Buchmann and DiPrete called the differences in degree attainment by gender a "rare example of a reversal of a once persistent pattern of stratification."[12] And at initial glance, the female advantage argument is hard to refute if "advantage" is defined as "greater numbers." For *all* American women and men, within *every* racial/ethnic group, women are now the majority of bachelor's degree holders.

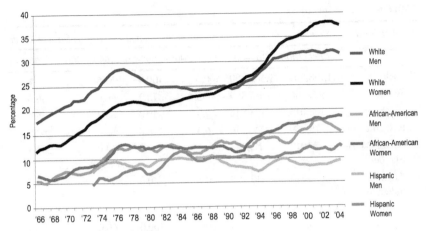

FIGURE 4.1 Percentage of Americans Aged 25–29 With a Bachelor's Degree, by Race/ Ethnicity and Gender, 1966–2004

Interestingly, and mostly unnoticed in female advantage arguments, the primacy of women's college degree earning in the case of black and Hispanic populations is a long-standing reality. As early as 1954, black U.S. women comprised the majority of students enrolled in historically black colleges and universities (HBCUs) and in 1974, when the U.S. Census Bureau began disaggregating college completion by gender and race, women earned 57 percent of all bachelor's degrees awarded to blacks, though in the early 1990s, black males enrolled in college directly from high school at rates higher than women.

Currently, black females earn between 65 and 70 percent of *all* college degrees awarded to black students in the United States.[13] The patterns are similar for Hispanic females; in 1994 they enrolled in college directly after high school at the same rates as Hispanic males, but in 2012, Hispanic women's percentage of college enrollment increased to 76 percent, whereas Hispanic men's increased to 62 percent.[14] Across most non-white populations, college enrollment at all but the doctoral level is a continuation of gender dominance, not a reversal of it.

Further, since the beginning of 2000, U.S. students of color are enrolling in degree programs at a faster rate than either male or female white students. Pew Research Center data show that in 2014, for the first time, a greater share of Hispanic recent high school graduates are enrolled in college than whites, with black students not far behind.

Cries of a "white crisis," however, remain unvoiced—at least not directly. Such silence may suggest that depictions of a female advantage in higher education foreshadow the coming of a U.S. "minority advantage" discourse. As lower-status groups demand higher education credentials, the advantage argument may be working in tandem with the female advantage discourse, quietly signaling higher education's declining value, along with shifts in acceptable professional credentials in the wider market. Indeed, greater degree attainment has hardly produced an

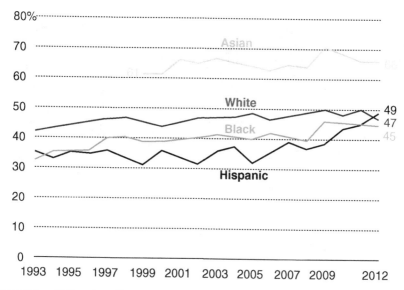

FIGURE 4.2 College Enrollment Rates Among 18–24-year-old High School Completers, by Race and Ethnicity, 2014

Notes: "White" includes only non-Hispanic whites. Starting in 2003, respondents could identify more than one race. The figures for 2003 onward refer to the white-, black- and Asian-alone populations. The data shown prior to 2003 consists of those identifying themselves as "Asian or Pacific Islanders."

Source: Pew Research Center analysis of the CPS Historical School Enrollment Time Series Table A-5a (http://www.census.gov/hhes/school/data/cps/historical/index.html)

unequivocal picture of increased female power and privilege in or outside the institution for any racial or ethnic group. Moreover, overall trends can hide the joint effects of institutional type and gender, as well as the effects that college attendance and completion confers to degree holders once outside the academy.

Elite College Differences

At elite institutions of higher education—the Ivies, research-intensive, and high-status specialized schools that do not have a single-sex history—female dominance in numbers is for the most part nonexistent: Women and men are equally represented.[15] Suggs, using both IPEDS data (Integrated Postsecondary Education Data System) and Carnegie Classification Data to investigate the relationship between college wealth and gender enrollment, found that as institutional wealth (as defined by endowment size) increased, the percentage of women enrolled decreased.

All of the categories of college classification have a higher percentage of women enrolled than men, with the exception of high-research and very-high-research institutions, where the gender enrollments are equal. Jacobs' research on elite schools' deviation from the gender pattern at other schools attributed this

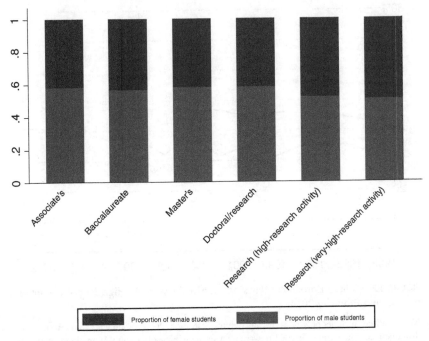

Proportion of female students   Proportion of male students

FIGURE 4.3 Gender Breakdown of 2014–15 College Student Populations, by 2010 Carnegie Classifications

pattern to the relative scarcity of women in large engineering programs (which these schools tend to have) and the greater tendency of women to enroll in school part time.[16]

Bielby and colleagues, investigating the same phenomenon, found that the equal gender attendance in elite colleges was singularly attributable to those institutions' admissions reliance on a criterion that favors men—their overall SAT scores.[17] They concluded that admissions offices at elite schools were not overtly privileging women or men, but that their reliance on SAT scores as indicator of student quality allowed for more male admittances. Since more women than men applied to elite schools overall, the final class resulted in gender balance. This reliance on SAT scores, the researchers maintained, was maintained despite the scores' unreliability for predicting college success, and can be traced both to elite institutions' efforts to preserve their rankings and possibly to gender biases in admissions offices themselves.

Both sets of researchers argue that the importance of having a degree from an elite college increases as the labor market becomes saturated with bachelor's degree recipients.[18] As more men than women intend to pursue prestigious and therefore highly paid labor, they place more value on having an elite degree. Prestigious academic institutions play critical roles in the transmission of power and privilege, particularly to those who anticipate working in, or being proximal to, high-status occupations.[19] Connections available through elite college attendance remain a strong pathway to future social and economic strata, and it makes sense, then, that privileged men and women would still use them as a means to this end.

Although it is not news that elite schools offer out-sized life advantages to its graduates, it is notable that their gender balance counters the prevailing gender trends in other kinds of higher education. As Bielby and colleagues suggested, gender may be differently taken into account in elite college admissions: more women than men apply to elite schools, but because such schools can afford to shape their classes in ways that less wealthy institutions cannot, they can accept fewer women and more men, thereby offsetting the problems that "too many women" on campus purportedly creates. In a 1992 study of elite college admission, Persell, Catsambis, and Cookson found that young women's economic, cultural, and educational assets broadly resulted in lower admissions to elite schools compared to men. Even after controlling for race and social class, the researchers found that women need to be smarter and more accomplished than men in order to be accepted to an elite school. The one group of women who were able to override this hurdle, however, were young women who attended elite boarding schools: in other words, girls who signaled "rich." Subsequent researchers have corroborated these findings, adding that colleges likely accept girls in this category for reasons of school ranking and other possible "outward-facing" effects,[20] such as having a balanced number of datable men and women.

Attention to outside constituents' perceptions of an elite school is likely always at play, according to these researchers. No matter what the inclinations of admissions officers and college administrators might be, the influence of external gatekeepers remains. Persell and colleagues report that the elite schools they studied were often "unwilling to reduce the [60:40 male/female] gender ratio . . . because the university did not believe that alumnae would be able to contribute as much as would alumni, as long as they faced barriers in the occupational world."[21] The institutional status of Ivies and similar highly elite academic institutions may be still too powerful a brand to be potentially diminished by the dominance of women, who might still be seen as deficient, as Armstrong said in 1910, in "the great business college of life."[22]

College Majors and Gender

Another signal that increased female engagement may indicate a concurrent diminishing of the college credential is the persistence of gender patterns in college majors. In the early 1960s, more than 70 percent of female undergraduates majored in only six fields: education, English, fine arts, nursing, history, and home economics.[23] "From the late 1950s to the early 1970s," state Goldin, Katz, and Kuziemko, "female college attendees [chose to] pursue various female-intensive occupations, such as teaching and social work, to major in fields such as education, English, and literature, and to find suitable mates."[24] Goldin independently argued that this trend changed in the 1970s as women became more career oriented; their college majors broadened as they invested more in professional pursuits.[25] Gender segregation in majors reflects this pattern, with segregation declining dramatically during the 1970s and then slowing from the mid-1980s onward.[26]

Data from the last five years suggest that the decline in college major gender stratification may have been temporary. Major disciplines remain sharply divided by gender and in fact now largely mirror the stratification of 40 years ago: A 2011 study found that women earned 85 percent of the degrees in nursing and health professions, 80 percent in education, and 77 percent in psychology, but only 30 percent in economics, 29 percent in philosophy, and 19 percent in physics and engineering.[27] But science, technology, engineering, and mathematics (STEM) fields offer a more complicated picture. On the one hand, female undergraduates in science and engineering majors have increased consistently since 1966; by 2001, women garnered slightly more than half of all bachelor's degrees in science and engineering (as a whole),[28] and by 2004, women constituted the clear majority of students in the biological sciences and in the social sciences, with the exception of economics.[29] On the other hand, despite the increase in enrollment numbers overall, the proportion of women in computer science, mathematics, statistics, and physics majors has *declined*, and women's participation remains well below that of men at all degree levels and subfields of engineering.[30]

Beede and colleagues observed this phenomenon, noting that in 2009, almost half (48 percent) of all male STEM majors chose engineering degrees, which is two and a half times the rate that women chose them (18 percent).[31] Analysts in the 1980s hoped that the growing field of computer science might offer a way to even the STEM gender imbalance.[32] It had no male-dominated history to overcome, and women had proven adept in computer data entry. Yet in 2011, only 18 percent of all bachelor's degrees in computer science were granted to females, a number that has declined in the last decade (see figure 4.4).[33]

Consequently, there are more women majoring in STEM fields overall, but the STEM fields have become gender stratified. The majority of women's STEM degrees are in fields that connect them to low-prestige, lower-paying niches within science, while men gravitate to higher paid science professions; identifying exactly when and where the tipping point of female abundance/lower pay occurs within STEM majors has been elusive.

Research on possible reasons for gender differences in major choices has focused on possible gendered differences in skill, individual differences in subject preferences, and cultural socialization. For example, Turner and Bowen investigated the degree to which gender differences in college major are associated with gender differences in precollege math performance as measured by SAT scores.

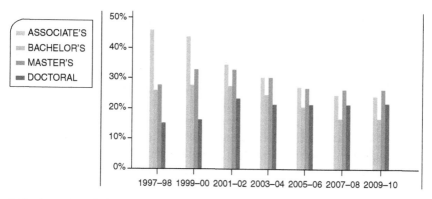

FIGURE 4.4   Female Percentage of Computing Postsecondary Degrees, 1998–2010

They found that differences in high school SAT scores—which are also contested measures of ability—accounted for less than half of the total gender gap in major choice, and they maintained that differences in academic preparation constituted only a small portion of the explanation for the persistence of gender segregation in majors. They concluded that "[D]ifferences in preferences, labor market expectations, gender-specific effects of college experience, and unmeasured aspects of academic preparation account for the main part of today's gender gaps in choice of academic major."[34]

Dickson's study of race, gender, and ethnicity and their impact on choice of academic major corroborated Turner and Bowen's results, but also found that women of all races and ethnicities were significantly more likely to change their major to a non-STEM field, even after initially declaring a STEM major. These results held constant even when the female participants had the same preparation and qualifications as the male participants.[35] These results further suggested that the effects of race and ethnicity on college major choice are small when compared to the differences by gender.

Mullen's study of gender and college major subsequently corroborated these studies, finding evidence of traditional gender divisions in students' choice of major, as well as ways in which major choices were further complicated by social class. At the state school studied, Mullen's subjects drew on gender stereotypes of what women "should be" and memories of childhood socialization to explain their choice of traditionally female majors, such as education and social work.[36] These majors also offered women in the study future jobs that they perceived were less demanding, allowing them to spend time with their planned-for children as well. At the elite private university just two miles away, female students' choices were also shaped by gender and class assumptions; many chose to study fields like anthropology and art history, understanding that these majors would not easily lead to high-paying jobs or even careers at all. Many of the elite school women Mullen studied assumed that their future (male) mates would have occupations that were economically rewarding, so that they would not have to rely on having their own jobs for income, though these subjects did not indicate that this choice was due to future offspring.

College men at both universities, according to Mullen's analysis, followed gender and social class patterns as well. Mullen found that a majority of the men indicated that they felt pressure to choose a major based, in part, on their acceptance of expectations of men as breadwinners.[37] State school men spoke about choosing majors based on their connection to potential income, differing from their higher status colleagues largely in their level of economic aspiration. In other words, men knew the economic rate of return that their majors were likely to offer, and selected their majors to fit the professions they felt they were likely to obtain. Elite school men focused on majors that were likely to lead not only to high levels of income, but also to status and prestige. Tellingly, not one woman in Mullen's study—at either the elite school or the state school—stated that the prestige of their major mattered with regard to their future plans.[38]

A school's curriculum and culture—the ethos associated with the school, whether cultivated, ascribed, or both—are essential elements for understanding how gender differences in men's and women's expectations of their futures influence their academic and social behaviors during college.[39] Mullen's findings, together with Lips's concept of "future selves" and Kerr's "future day" scenarios, comprise a strong body of research that implicates gender norms, social class expectations, and institutional contexts as profound influences on students' college behaviors and their plans for the future. Rather than acting as disrupters of gendered expectations, college experiences often reinforce and/or exacerbate them. These findings appear to hold true across most permutations of race, ethnicity, and first-generation college status; when a young adult represents the first in a family to attend college, she or he is not only expected to succeed, but to do so in a way that will result in raising the socioeconomic status of the entire family.[40] Reproduction of cultural patterns of behavior, according to these researchers' findings, overpower the potential career opportunities and income that the degree represents. If the two conflict, particularly for women, traditional expectations influence their decisions even more strongly.

Explanations for Differential Enrollment and Engagement

What might be said about men, women, and U.S. college attendance since the 1950s, then, can be encapsulated by the following:

- More people of all genders, races, ethnicities, and social classes have enrolled in and completed college, but since the 1980s, more women have enrolled in and completed college than men.

- There are approximately 1.35 females for every male who graduated from a four-year college and 1.3 females for every currently enrolled male undergraduate.
- Black and Hispanic students have only somewhat lower rates of postsecondary school enrollment than whites and Asians, but have much lower levels of educational completion by their mid-20s.
- Women of color have not begun a new trend—they continue to attend and complete college at greater rates than men of color.
- The more prestigious the school, the greater the gender parity.
- Choice of college major is strongly influenced by gender, mediated by social class, race, ethnicity, and institutional context.

The advantage/crisis argument is largely based on the first point only; together, these trends do not foretell a significantly new problem. What academic and public perseveration about white males and higher education reflects, however, is shifting American economic and labor market perceptions and realities, cultural expectations and norms of masculinity and femininity, and changing structural conditions of education, producing an environment where schooling is cast as the enemy. Exploring the intersections of these themes relative to higher education can explain how positive gains in overall postsecondary school attendance are recast as unfair advantages for women and negative gains for men.

Economic Lure and Labor Market Issues

The most widely discussed and researched explanation for men's relatively lower enrollment in and completion of higher education is the college degree and its return on investment: Does the labor market reward men's scholastic efforts? Men may be receiving what is often referred to as a "garbled" market signal. That is, high school males—particularly those on the fence about college attendance—may be getting unclear messages about the economic importance of obtaining a college degree, even though it has been clear for three decades that overall earnings for college graduates are significantly greater than those without them. "Among 25 to 34-year-olds," write Schmitt and Boushey, "a college graduate earned 25 percent more than a high school graduate at the end of the 1970s, and by the late 2000s, the pay premium for college graduates in the same age range climbed to 60 percent."[41] Standard economic theory, they point out, would predict that knowing this information would lead more young people, men and women alike, to pursue college degrees.

But for many adolescents on the cusp of adulthood, the economic case for attending college may not be as clear-cut as it seems. Men, more than women, make decisions about college attendance based on their perceptions of the worthiness of schooling in relation to the strength of the labor market.[42] The male opportunity cost of getting a college degree—even an associate's degree—is perceived by many men as too burdensome when the possibility of getting a "good job" directly out of high school is still a reality, particularly in parts of the labor market that have been traditionally male.[43]

Indeed, Schmitt and Boushey's 2010 analysis of low, average, and high-earning male and female college graduates from 1979 to 2009 shows that while many college graduates make more money than the average high school graduate, "an important portion of college graduates earn *less* than the average high school graduate in the same age range" (italics original).[44] For men in their study, low-earning college graduates consistently earned less than their high-school-only contemporaries did. Researchers at the Martin Prosperity Institute argue the same: even later in life when men are more likely to have families, men *without* postsecondary degrees often earn more money than women *with* degrees.[45] Still other analyses show that women with some college or higher make more money than men with only high school degrees, but this gap narrows with degree attainment, so that women with bachelor's degrees earn, on average, what men with associate's degrees earn.[46] The future male college wage premium thus becomes a male opportunity cost, particularly in the short term, providing fewer incentives for men to attend college post-high school, as well as to return to college later in life.

Apart from the lure of immediate earnings, another reason men are not pursuing higher education at the same rate as women appears to be due to a greater aversion to debt. Given the increasingly high cost of higher education relative to individual earnings, men seem to be less willing to borrow money to fund their educations.[47] Dwyer, Hodson, and McCloud's study of the relationship between college attendance, debt, and degree completion found that anticipation of higher levels of debt is more associated with dropping out of college for men than it is for women.[48] They argue:

> In the short run, men who drop out of college do not experience a wage penalty in comparison to their peers who go on to graduate. It may be harder for men than for women to see the advantage of staying in college because in the early years after college, men who complete college make no higher pay than men who drop out.[49]

Men's unwillingness to take on as much debt as women may partly explain women's lesser earnings later in their careers, even when achieving higher levels of education. With more debt, in combination with the disparity in men's and women's pay and women's general employment in lower paying fields, a college degree may be more of an economic burden than boon for many women.

Further, since men can earn a living wage in traditionally male fields that may require some post-high school training but no college degree—for example, police officers, construction workers, and insurance salespeople—they often do not see a need for more schooling; indeed, young males are more likely to say that they will not need more education for their jobs as a reason for not attending college.[50] Men's post-high school decisions to enter the workforce immediately upon graduation may also be influenced by their perception (if not also the reality) of increasingly available high-paying jobs in computing and other high-tech firms, as well as what they believe to be greater opportunities for independent business ownership (see Chapter 5).

Bureau of Labor Statistics (BLS) data confirm that two-thirds of the available jobs nationwide in May 2013 were in occupations that required a high school diploma or less education.[51] The next 10 years look similar: Between 2014 and 2024, the BLS predicts that of the 15 occupations with the most job growth, 11 of them will be in sectors that typically can be entered with a high school diploma or less (see table 4.2).

And, of the next decade's 15 fastest growing occupations, the Bureau of Labor Statistics predicts that just over half of them will require an associate's degree at most, with one-third of them needing only a high school diploma or less.[52] With college debt a reality, and the promise of an immediate return on a college investment unsure, it is not surprising that young men, in particular, would be drawn to the workforce, especially when jobs are available. Autor's analysis of job opportunities in the U.S. labor market further helps explain this trend: Between 1999 and 2007, he found that only occupations in the bottom fourth of the skills distribution were increasingly available, whereas those in the higher three-quarters of the skills distribution remained flat or declined.[53] Skilled jobs, to many young people, may simply not be worth the financial or intellectual investment if their availability is not readily apparent.

Debates about economic gains for college graduates also too often mask the unequal wages that black and Hispanic degree holders can expect from the labor market. Even with college degrees in hand, the return on investment is much lower for black and Hispanic graduates than it is for white graduates. Researchers at Demos, a public policy organization, find that a black family at the median income level has a $4,846 return from completing a four-year degree, a Latina/o family has a $4,191 return, and a white family—a return of $55,869 (see figure 4.5).[54]

Dwyer, Hodson, and McCloud's research corroborates these figures, finding further that black and Hispanic or Latina/o students drop out of college at lower levels of debt than white students.[55] Often having fewer family resources to help pay off this debt, black and Hispanic students with some college education may turn out to be in more financial peril than students who never attempt college. These findings are rarely articulated in the crisis/advantage arguments, making debates about postsecondary education, employment, and gender dangerously color-blind, and definitely oversimplified.

Thus, while many college graduates' earnings are rising, all college costs have risen significantly, and young men in particular do not have evidence that

TABLE 4.2 Occupations With the Most Job Growth, 2014–2024 (Numbers in Thousands)

Occupation	Employment		Change, 2014–24		Median annual wage, 2014	Typical education needed for entry
	2014	2024	Number	Percent		
Total all occupations	**150,539.9**	**160,328.8**	**9,788.9**	**6.5**	**$35,540**	—
Wind turbine service technicians	4.4	9.2	4.8	108.0	48,800	Some college, no degree
Occupational therapy assistants	33.0	47.1	14.1	42.7	56,950	Associate's degree
Physical therapist assistants	78.7	110.7	31.9	40.6	54,410	Associate's degree
Physical therapist aides	50.0	69.5	19.5	39.0	24,650	High school diploma or equivalent
Home health aides	913.5	1261.9	348.4	38.1	21,380	No formal educational credential
Commercial drivers	4.4	6.0	1.6	36.9	45,890	Postsecondary nondegree award
Nurse practitioners	126.9	171.7	44.7	35.2	95,350	Master's degree
Physical therapists	210.9	282.7	71.8	34.0	82,390	Doctoral or professional degree
Statisticians	30.0	40.1	10.1	33.8	79,990	Master's degree
Ambulance drivers and attendants, except emergency medical technicians	19.6	26.1	6.5	33.0	24,080	High school diploma or equivalent
Occupational therapy aides	8.8	11.6	2.7	30.6	26,550	High school diploma or equivalent
Physician assistants	94.4	123.2	28.7	30.4	95,820	Master's degree
Operations research analysts	91.3	118.9	27.6	30.2	76,660	Bachelor's degree
Personal financial advisors	249.4	323.2	73.9	29.6	81,060	Bachelor's degree
Cartographers and photogrammetrists	12.3	15.9	3.6	29.3	60,930	Bachelor's degree

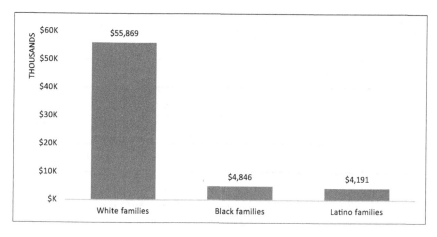

FIGURE 4.5 Median Wealth Return to College Graduation

attending higher education is a wise or necessary investment. Combined with still-strong working class cultural norms about masculinity and schooling, it is highly plausible that an increasing number of men of all races and ethnicities would make a rational choice not to go to college, while more women would attend, with equal rationality. And with women earning degrees at higher rates than men, the perceived value of these credentials may be called into question: If college is perceived to be something that women do, men may be more likely to eschew attending.

Real Men Don't Study: Cultural Expectations and Norms of Masculinity and Femininity

Cultural expectations of gender and definitions of masculinity and femininity create powerful messages about the importance of schooling in one's life, even beyond its financial impact, in ways that differ significantly for men and women. Messages about gender identity are perhaps the strongest noneconomic influencers on men's college participation, in ways that are markedly different from the influence of gender identity on women's college engagement, with both mediated by social class, race, and ethnicity.

Masculinity is a key analytic and political concept in Western culture, and over the last several decades cultural expectations of masculinity in America have not changed radically.[56] Western masculinity has never been broadly defined by its affinity for study and deep thought, and "boys being boys" continues to carry a biology-is-destiny model wherein "real men" restrict their energies to actions that involve muscles and stoicism.[57] Even in a time when gay marriage is legal and metrosexuality is a recognizable state of being, to be a *man*, one still needs to be tough. "Real men" are expected to be independent, and to display heterosexuality by playing and/or watching sports. And, they *definitely* do not study hard. Leonard Sax writes without irony:

> There's a long tradition of iconic American boys who disdain school, from Tom Sawyer to Ferris Bueller. But while those boys weren't heavily invested in school, they were still highly motivated to succeed—on their own terms, pursuing their own schemes. Tom Sawyer is determined to outwit Injun Joe, to go exploring with Huck Finn, and to win the affection of Becky Thatcher. Ferris Bueller disdains school because he has other more important and engaging missions to accomplish in the real world— which for him is any world outside of school.
> "Girls care about getting good grades. Geeks care about grades. Normal guys," he concludes, echoing one of his 14-year-old informants, "do not care about grades."[58]

While public figures like Sax loudly advocate for "saving" boys and men from the perceived femininity of formal schooling, researchers note that these discussions lean on very old, highly entrenched ideologies of traditional masculinity that harbor a "pervasive culture of anti-intellectualism."[59] The continued existence of the "aura of machismo"[60] has been thoroughly documented throughout virtually all U.S. subcultures, with academic and public sources alike noting (and often graphically displaying) the continuous development and entrenchment of stereotypical masculinities and their effects on men's and boys' lives.[61]

Current definitions of femininity chafe at intellectualism in their own way. Although females have a wider range of culturally acceptable emotional states, "real women" are frequently not defined with much more subtlety than men: Women are still judged, first and most strongly, by how well they adhere to Western beauty standards.[62] In fact, the definition of femininity has not really changed at all; rather, it is the meaning of femininity in relation to masculinity that has changed. "As the oppositional logic of the failing boy has taken hold," writes Ringrose, "the successful girl, attains ever greater status as 'common-sense' truth."[63] With femininity now being defined as intellectual—at least as the female advantage argument has it—women's educational success becomes threatening, not just to men overall, but to men's conceptions of what women should be.[64]

Current research bears this out. For example, in 2014, Rahbari reported the results of her investigation of college professors' ideas of educated women's beauty. Of the 20 male lecturers interviewed, two-thirds agreed with the idea that "women who enter higher education are uglier than the less educated."[65] Rahbari's analysis indicated that men in her study correlated beauty with femininity—since women pursuing higher education were not acting in ways the men thought were feminine, they therefore were less beautiful than women outside academia. In a patriarchal system, male prioritization of women's physical attractiveness does not diminish, and in fact traditional standards of beauty may be more strictly reinforced when men perceive that women are acting in ways that breach gender norms. As Walkerdine famously noted, when women dare to transgress the idea that femininity is defined by lack, and instead—as in the case of higher education achievement—constitute the feminine as equal or better, they become constituted as a threat to men.[66]

Cultural definitions of masculinity and femininity in higher education continue to hinge on essentialist definitions about what it means to be male or female, then, usually without complication of social class, race, or sexual orientation.[67] The ways in which the intersections of gender, race, and ethnicity manifest themselves in relation to men's and women's college attendance are still too-frequently overlooked as well. The intersections of black masculine identity and underachievement have gained currency in some empirical literature and popular press[68] but studies of black, Hispanic, and Latina/o men and women in relation to higher education performance are still too few, substituting white men's and women's experiences for all college students.

Searching for Explanations

Indeed, the 21st century has produced a large body of work endeavoring to explore, explain, and ultimately correct the perceived and real imbalances of how formal educational enterprises differentially impact males and females. Throughout many of these studies and commentaries regarding men and education, the structure of school itself—teachers, curriculum, and school rules and practices—is offered as explanation for differences in school success. Much of this work has been conducted in or centers on K–12 schools and is used as the basis for understanding why boys and men do not attend college. Why, the authors ask, would men volunteer to attend higher education, when their experiences with K–12 schooling have been so untenable?

Among the most prevalent of these explanations, surprisingly used even in some empirical work, is the biologically rooted one: The practices and structures of schooling do not "fit" boys' and men's natures. Gurian and Stevens declare: "Boys and girls learn differently!" arguing that because of neuro-physical differences in boys and girls, they have distinct educational needs.[69] They claim that if boys are not taught "correctly," they will not want to attend school of any kind. Sax, likewise, asserts that gender is so a primary human difference that teaching boys and girls using the same techniques could actually cause harm, echoing the 20th-century assertions that women who studied too much risked future uterine damage. Among Sax's claims are that boys hear less well than girls, and that boys' brains are better at seeing action, while girls' brains are better at seeing the nuance of color and texture. Although major researchers counter claims like these, many people read and remember Gurian and Stevens's, and Sax's well-publicized arguments, accepting the explanation that males are naturally inclined to drop out of the educational process, including college attendance, because it somehow no longer fits them.

Some popular writers argue that boys simply find school boring and reading even more boring; others argue that what one learns in school is irrelevant to (boys') work.[70] Many of these commentators add that males need things like movement and freedom in order to learn optimally, claiming that school rules like sitting in rows and hand-raising are counterproductive to male learning, even though studies of educational development conclude that active learning is more productive for *all* learners. Still other writers contend that the school curriculum simply *repels* men, while the less strident among them make the argument that males do not want to be in school because their interests and learning styles are not accommodated. In the end, most popular writers stick to what they claim is "basic" schooling, arguing that males want a path that is "literal, linear, and pragmatic."[71] The educational system, now including higher education, is apparently unfit for males.

Circumventing Female Schooling Through Digital Technology?

Digital pathways to post-high school learning have been presented as an avenue by which men (and women) can circumvent the purportedly feminized structures of the modern American university. Both empirical and journalistic authors have argued that the *digital turn* in schooling, with its individualized, computer technology-driven focus, provides possibilities for male and female students to get what they need from school without having to engage in outmoded and many times unfair, educational practices. This would be a potentially positive turn of events if there were evidence that digital technologies offered a viable alternative pathway to good-quality higher education credentials for all students. But this is not the case. As a solution to the advantage/crisis dilemma, the digital turn in the structure of higher education seems to be an incendiary device for educational equity: Student enrollment in and completion of partial and fully online (digital) degree programs is even more female-heavy than its brick-and-mortar sibling. The "turn" does not seem to have changed male college enrollment or completion patterns, nor has digital education proved advantageous for those who could benefit from it most: black and Hispanic women, and women *and* men in lower socioeconomic levels.

The digital turn in higher education is both technical and theoretical: It is defined by a major organizational focus on online courses and degree programs, and it is the wholesale embrace of the idea that credentials can be delivered in bulk to a much wider swath of the population than traditional higher education can achieve. Both not-for-profit and for-profit schools have embraced this development, but since 2005, for-profit universities have been associated largely with almost fully online coursework, degrees, and pathways to professional credentialing.[72] According to the National Center for Education Statistics (NCES), between 1990 and 2012, undergraduate enrollment at private, for-profit institutions increased by 634 percent, from 0.2 million students in 1990 to 1.5 million in 2012. Most of this growth occurred between 2000 and 2010 when undergraduate enrollment at private for-profit institutions quadrupled (from 0.4 million to 1.7 million students). In 2011, women made up the majority—57 percent—of students at these schools.[73]

However, as the analog world goes, so goes its digital shadow: For-profit institutions offer no different picture of female advantage than brick-and-mortar schools. Women attend and graduate from for-profits at rates significantly higher than men, and black and Hispanic women, in particular, graduate at higher rates than black and Hispanic men.[74] Yet, as Chapter 6 will show, male for-profit degree holders reap more financial rewards from these credentials than women do, a finding that mirrors the gender pay equity gap in the population at large.[75]

Amidst the worry about the lack of males' college attendance overall, there is strangely little worry about their for-profit attendance. This may be because women who enroll in for-profit degree programs are more often from lower socioeconomic levels;[76] while they outnumber men just like women at brick-and-mortar schools do, women at for-profit schools may not be perceived as threatening—they do not have enough power to upset the status quo and so their increased digital degree pursuit ironically contributes to the maintenance of patriarchal equilibrium. It is not low-status women who threaten to upend patriarchal order, but high-status women, for it is the latter who can gain access to power by attending college and taking up (presumably male) space in and after college. Women of lower socioeconomic status may gain higher education that offers them skills, but little access to power, and credentials that offer scant career advancement and a huge amount of student debt.

With more financially marginalized people taking part in higher education, believing that their degrees will offer them power to better their life circumstances, for-profit and not-for-profit digital higher education programs siphon money from those who can least afford them. If such students finish the degree or program, they possess credentials that, on balance, do not provide the same kind of cultural capital as traditional programs do. Nonetheless, belief in the American Dream is fed anew, particularly to women, with potentially empty credentials.

College for All

President Obama introduced his administration's *2020 plan* in 2009, the fulfillment of which, according to the President, would allow America to "once again have the highest proportion of college graduates in the world."[77] Other current and aspirational U.S. leaders have also outlined their plans for broader access to affordable college programs, as well as for college student debt relief.[78] Americans he message: Everyone should go to college. A greater percentage of _..cans than ever before now attend college of some kind, at some point ιn their lives, largely with the hope and expectation that doing so will gain them credentials that will in turn offer more economically profitable careers.

Until recently, this expectation has been a reasonable one. "During much of the 20th century," Folbre notes, "most people with access to higher education could expect a reliable rate of return on investments in their own skills. In the golden age of human capital, the labor market richly rewarded educational credentials."[79] In the last 40 years, women followed this advice most sincerely, believing that such credentials would help ensure their financial security and independence, as well as narrow, if not altogether eliminate, the long-standing pay disparity between men and women. College was the new arbiter of gender equity and when women finally breeched its ivy-covered banks, they believed the credentials would speak for themselves. They—we—believed that old gender stereotypes would diminish if not disappear altogether. This is the promise whispered on the backs of sheepskin.

Yet this whisper is tangled in ivy, turned cultural kudzu—a web of realities that render the promises of higher education more than troublesome: (1) higher education credentials are no longer dependable guarantors of excellent jobs and steady career paths; (2) achieving a college degree does not alone overcome social class or racial or ethnic disparities, and (3) cultural expectations for women, in particular, have not been altered by college as profoundly as 21st-century American culture would suggest. As the cultural importance of college changes and is increasingly questioned, men may be starting to reposition themselves through alternative acquisitions of skills, knowledge, credentials, and contacts. By strategically *not* investing in the institution that women, underrepresented minorities, and the working class have committed to, a greater proportion of men with privilege may believe that economic power, as well as dominant masculinity, is no longer found in higher education. Chapter 5 shows what might be happening instead.

Notes

1. Gilder, G. (2005). The idea of the (feminized) university. *National Review, 57*(24), p. 26.
2. Ibid.
3. Pratto, F., & Stewart, A. L. (2012). Group dominance and the half-blindness of privilege. *Journal of Social Issues, 68*(1), p. 28.
4. National Center for Education Statistics (NCES). (2014). *The condition of education.* Retrieved from https://nces.ed.gov/
5. According to Frank T. Rhodes, President Emeritus of Cornell University (*Chronicle of Higher Education*, 8.24.2006).
6. Lee, S. (2012, August 9). The for-profit higher education industry, by the numbers. *Pro Publica.* Retrieved from www.propublica.org/
7. National Center for Education Statistics (NCES). (2015). *The condition of education.* Retrieved from https://nces.ed.gov/

8. United States Senate. (2012). *For-profit higher education: The failure to safeguard the federal investment and ensure student success.* Retrieved from www.help.senate.gov/imo/media/for_profit_report/Contents.pdf
9. Kinser, K. (2005). A profile of regionally accredited for-profit institutions of higher education. *New Directions for Higher Education, 2005*(129), 69–83.
10. National Center for Education Statistics (NCES). (2013). *The condition of education.* Retrieved from https://nces.ed.gov/
11. National Center for Education Statistics (NCES). (2016). *The condition of education.* Retrieved from https://nces.ed.gov/
12. Buchmann, C., & DiPrete, T. A. (2006). The growing female advantage in college completion: The role of family background and academic achievement. *American Sociological Review, 71*(4), p. 516.
13. National Center for Education Statistics (NCES). (2012). *The condition of education.* Retrieved from https://nces.ed.gov/
14. Pew Research Center. (2014). Retrieved from www.pewresearch.org/fact-tank/2014/03/06/womens-college-enrollment-gains-leave-men-behind/
15. Williams, A. (2010, February 7). The new math on campus: When women outnumber men at a college, dating culture is skewed. *The New York Times*, pp. ST1, 8.
16. Jacobs, J. A. (1996). Gender inequality and higher education. *Annual Review of Sociology, 22*(1), 153–185.
17. Bielby, R., Posselt, J. R., Jaquette, O., & Bastedo, M. N. (2014). Why are women underrepresented in elite colleges and universities? A non-linear decomposition analysis. *Research in Higher Education, 55*(8), 735–760.
18. Similar to Bowman, N. A., & Bastedo, M. N. (2009). Getting on the front page: Organizational reputation, status signals, and the impact of "U.S. News and World Report" on student decisions. *Research in Higher Education, 50*(5), 415–436.
19. Espenshade, T. J., Hale, L. E., & Chung, C. Y. (2005). The frog pond revisited: High school academic context, class rank, and elite college admission. *Sociology of Education, 78*(4), 269–293.
20. Persell, C. H., Catsambis, S., & Cookson, P. W. (1992). Differential asset conversion: Class and gendered pathways to selective colleges. *Sociology of Education, 65*(3), 208–225.
21. Ibid., p. 221.
22. Armstrong, J. E. (1910). The advantages of limited sex segregation in the high school. *School Review, 18*, p. 337.
23. Jacobs, J. A. (1996). Gender inequality and higher education. *Annual Review of Sociology, 22*(1), 153–185.
24. Goldin, C., Katz, L. F., & Kuziemko, I. (2006). The homecoming of American college women: The reversal of the college gender gap. *The Journal of Economic Perspectives, 20*(4), p. 135.
25. Goldin, C. D. (2004). The long road to the fast track: Career and family. *The Annals of the American Academy of Political and Social Science, 596*(1), 20–35.
26. Wirt, J. et al. (2004). *The condition of education 2004. U.S. Department of Education.* National Center for Education Statistics. Washington, DC: U.S. Government Printing Office.
27. Snyder, T. D., & Dillow, S. A. (2011). *Digest of education statistics 2010 (NCES 2011–015).* National Center for Education Statistics. Washington, DC: U.S. Department of Education, Institute of Education Sciences.
28. National Science Foundation. (2003, 2004, 2006). *New formulas for America's workforce: Girls in science and engineering* (Document No. NSF 03207). Retrieved from www.nsf.gov
29. National Science Foundation, 2004.
30. Mullen, A. L. (2010). *Degrees of inequality: Culture, class, and gender in American higher education.* Baltimore, MD: Johns Hopkins University Press, p. 171.

31. Beede, D. et al. (2011, August). *Women in STEM: A gender gap to innovation.* ESA Issue Brief #04–11. Office of the Chief Economist, U.S. Department of Commerce, p. 6.
32. Johnson, J. P. (1982). Can computers close the educational equity gap? *Civil Rights Quarterly Perspectives, 14*(3), 20–25.
33. Ashcraft, C., Eger, E., & Friend, M. (2012). *Girls in IT: The facts.* Boulder, CO: National Center for Women in Information Technology, p. 18.
34. Turner, S. E., & Bowen, W. G. (1999). Choice of major: The changing (unchanging) gender gap. *Industrial & Labor Relations Review, 52*(2), p. 309.
35. Dickson, L. (2010). Race and gender differences in college major choice. *The Annals of the American Academy of Political and Social Science, 627*(1), 108–124.
36. Mullen, A. L. (2010). *Degrees of inequality: Culture, class, and gender in American higher education.* Baltimore, MD: Johns Hopkins University Press, p. 171.
37. Ibid., pp. 180–182.
38. Mullen, A. L. (2014). Gender, social background, and the choice of college major in a liberal arts context. *Gender & Society, 28*(2), p. 306.
39. Ibid., 294.
40. Brown, S. W. (2008). The gender differences: Hispanic females and males majoring in science or engineering. *Journal of Women and Minorities in Science and Engineering, 14*(2), 205–223.
41. Schmitt, J., & Boushey, H. (2010). The college conundrum: Why the benefits of a college education may not be so clear, especially to men. *Center for American Progress.* Retrieved from www.americanprogress.org/wp-content/uploads/issues/2010/12/pdf/college_conundrum.pdf
42. See, for example, England, P., & Farkas, G. (1986). *Households, employment, and gender: A social, economic, and demographic view.* Hawthorne, NY: Aldine Publishing; Jacob, B. A. (2002). Where the boys aren't: Non-cognitive skills, returns to school and the gender gap in higher education. *Economics of Education Review, 21*(6), 589–598; Chiappori, P. A., Iyigun, M., & Weiss, Y. (2009). Investment in schooling and the marriage market. *The American Economic Review, 99*(5), 1689–1713.
43. Bailey, M. J., & Dynarski, S. M. (2011). *Gains and gaps: Changing inequality in US college entry and completion* (No. w17633). Cambridge, MA: National Bureau of Economic Research.
44. Schmitt & Boushey, 2010, p. 8.
45. Martin Prosperity Institute. http://martinprosperity.org
46. Institute for Women's Policy Research (IWPR). (2015). *The status of women in the United States. 2015: Employment and earnings.* Washington, DC. Retrieved from http://statusofwomendata.org/app/uploads/2015/02/EE-CHAPTER-FINAL.pdf
47. NCES, 2012.
48. Dwyer, R. E., Hodson, R., & McCloud, L. (2013). Gender, debt, and dropping out of college. *Gender & Society, 27*(1), 30–55.
49. Ibid., pp. 45–47.
50. Jacob, B. A. (2002). Where the boys aren't: Non-cognitive skills, returns to school and the gender gap in higher education. *Economics of Education Review, 21*(6), 589–598.
51. Bureau of Labor Statistics, U.S. Department of Labor. (2014). *Career outlook.* Education level and jobs: Opportunities by state. Retrieved from www.bls.gov/careeroutlook/2014/article/education-level-and-jobs.htm
52. Bureau of Labor Statistics, U.S. Department of Labor. (2015). *Employment projections, 2014–2024.* Report USDL-15-2327. Retrieved from www.bls.gov/news.release/pdf/ecopro.pdf
53. Autor, D. (2010). *The polarization of job opportunities in the U.S. labor market: Implications for employment and earnings.* Washington, DC: Center for American Progress and the Hamilton Project.

54. Sullivan, L., Meschede, T., Dietrich, L., Shapiro, T., Traub, A., Ruetschlin C., & Draut, T. (2016). *The racial wealth gap: Why policy matters*. Institute for Assets and Social Policy, Brandeis University (Boston) and Demos, New York, NY. Retrieved from www. demos.org/sites/default/files/publications/RacialWealthGap_1.pdf

55. Dwyer et al., 2013, p. 47.

56. Haywood, C., & Mac an Ghaill, M. (2012). What next for masculinity? Reflexive directions for theory and research on masculinity and education. *Gender and Education*, *24*(6), 577–592.

57. Kimmel, M. (2008). *Guyland: The perilous world where boys become men*. New York, NY: Harper Collins.

58. Sax, L. (2007). *Boys adrift: The five factors driving the growing epidemic of unmotivated boys and underachieving young men*. New York, NY: Basic Books.

59. Weaver-Hightower, M. B. (2010). Where the guys are: Males in higher education. *Change: The Magazine of Higher Learning*, *42*(3), 29–35.

60. Tsolidis, G. (2006). Strategic encounters: Choosing school subcultures that facilitate imagined futures. *British Journal of Sociology of Education*, *27*(5), 603–616.

61. For example, Connell, R. W. (1995, 2005). *Masculinities*. Berkeley, CA: University of California Press; Kimmel, 2008; and Martino, W., & Pallotta-Chiarolli, M. (2003). *So what's a boy? Addressing issues of masculinity and schooling*. Philadelphia: Open University Press.

62. Aronson, P. (2008). The markers and meanings of growing up: Contemporary young women's transition from adolescence to adulthood. *Gender and Society*, *22*(1), 56–82; Ringrose, J. (2013). *Postfeminist education? Girls and the sexual politics of schooling*. London, UK: Routledge.

63. Ringrose, J. (2007). Successful girls? Complicating post-feminist, neoliberal discourses of educational achievement and gender equality. *Gender and Education*, *19*(4), 471–489.

64. Foster, V. (2000). Is female educational "success" destabilizing the male learner citizen? In M. Arnot & J. A. Dillaough (Eds.), *Challenging democracy, international perspectives on gender, education and citizenship*. London, UK: Routledge-Falmer, pp. 203–215.

65. Proceeding of the Global Summit on Education GSE 2014 (E- ISBN 978-967-11768-5-6) 4–5 March 2014, Kuala Lumpur, Malaysia. Organized by WorldConferences. net, p. 360.

66. Walkerdine, V. (1990). *Schoolgirl fictions*. London, UK: Verso Books.

67. See Armstrong, E. A., & Hamilton, L. T. (2013). *Paying for the party: How college maintains inequality*. Cambridge, MA: Harvard University Press; and Williams, A. (2010) for important exceptions to this.

68. Boyd-Franklin, N. B., & Franklin, A. J. (2000). *Boys into men: Raising our African American teenage sons*. New York, NY: E. P. Dutton; Cuyjet, M. J., & Associates (Eds.). (2006). *African American men in college*. San Francisco, CA: Jossey-Bass; Davis, J. E. (2003). Early schooling and academic achievement of African American males. *Urban Education*, *38*(5), 515–537.

69. Gurian, M., & Stevens, K. (2005, May 2). What is happening with boys in school? *Teachers College Record*. Retrieved from www.tcrecord.org ID Number: 11854

70. For example, Pollack, W. (1999). *Real boys: Rescuing our sons from the myths of boyhood*. New York: Random House; Tyre, P. (2009). *The trouble with boys: A surprising report card on our sons, their problems at school, and what parents and educators must do*. New York: Three Rivers Press; Whitmire, R. (2010). *Why boys fail: Saving our sons from an educational system that's leaving them behind*. New York: American Management Association.

71. Houston, M. (2006, November 27). *The truth about boys*. The Age. Retrieved from www.theage.com.au

72. Ruch, R. (2001). *Higher ed. Inc.: The rise of the for-profit university*. Baltimore, MD: The Johns Hopkins University Press.

73. *Participation in education: Postsecondary enrollment.* 2014–15. National Center for Education Statistics. Washington, DC. Retrieved from https://nces.ed.gov/programs/coe/pdf/Indicator_CHA/coe_cha_2014_05.pdf
74. Ibid.
75. Chugh, D., & Brief, A. P. (2008). 1964 was not that long ago: A story of gateways and pathways. In A. P. Brief (Ed.), *Diversity at work* (pp. 318–340). Cambridge, UK: Cambridge University Press.
76. Ibid.
77. Retrieved from www.whitehouse.gov, 2.24.09.
78. See, for example, Hilary Clinton's College Compact, www.hillaryclinton.com/briefing/factsheets/2015/08/10/college-compact-costs/; and Tennessee's Drive to 55 program, http://driveto55.org/. See also www.insidehighered.com/news/2015/07/09/oregon-passes-free-community-college-bill-congressional-democrats-introduce-federal for details about other free and almost-free college programs.
79. Folbre, N. (2014, October 15). Should you go to college? In K. Geier, N. Folbre, A. Clark, & S. Feiner (Eds.), *The Nation.* Retrieved from www.thenation.com/article/should-you-go-college/

5

AMERICAN MEN

Other Places to Be

Helen Smith, a forensic psychologist who takes issue with what she sees as the feminist direction of American culture, writes:

> If women were fleeing the nation's universities and colleges, we would have a national uproar, but men are now fleeing in large numbers and society barely notices. . . . Universities are increasingly becoming feminized . . . [and men] feel emasculated in [them]. . . . Manliness wants to compete, to win, to boast, to glory, even to fail honorably against the best. This is disallowed to men on campus. Men have decided that they don't belong in college and, consciously or unconsciously, they are going on strike.[1]

Smith's criticisms of American higher education read like a foot-stomping rant against all-those-girls who have apparently upended the natural order. According to her analysis, men are leaving college because the institution no longer allows for the bygone era of unexamined curriculum, didactic teaching methods, and extra-collegiate cultural behaviors that allowed "boys to be boys." Men have no choice, she claims, but to go elsewhere.

Despite Smith's hyperbolic view of manliness, her point that there is something different about men's college-going behaviors rings true. As the evidence indicates, men, taken as a whole, *are* entering college less than women and when enrolled, completing college with less frequency than women, even though there are slightly more men of traditional college-age than women.[2] But where Smith's arguments miss the mark is their lack of accounting for persistent male dominance in virtually all other parts of American life. Men get credit—and power—just for being men. Since graduating from college is not as exclusive to males as it once was, "[w]e need to consider the possibility," as Bennett stated, "that patriarchal institutions can shift and change without much altering the force of patriarchal power."[3] In other words, it is possible that in accommodating large numbers of women, higher education has changed its population and perhaps a fair amount of its structure, while simultaneously diminishing in stature as men create channels of power elsewhere.

Put another way, the cultural worry surrounding gender differences in college enrollment and success may be a bellwether for a bleaker trend: that men are leaving college precisely *because* women are succeeding in it. Through this view, as men reposition themselves by not investing in the institution in which women have invested, the cultural importance of formal postsecondary schooling may be on the path to decreasing significance. Wood claims that while the price of college has skyrocketed, its rewards have slumped.[4] But for whom? According to Autor and Wasserman, real earnings growth for males has been "remarkably weak" and even among men with four years of college, growth in real hourly wage levels is half of what it is for women with four years of college.[5] In other words, women have benefitted significantly from higher education, with highly educated women, according the authors, making "especially sharp gains."[6]

These figures seem to support the female advantage argument: In the last several decades, women have attended college at increasingly higher rates, and during the same time period, their real hourly wages have risen. But such analyses are a diversion: it is not women's increased wages that indicate the presence of advantage so much as it is men's decreased wages compared to women. Given the general returns on college degrees, in combination with the gender pay gap, men should be seeing *more* benefit from college credentials than women, not less. That college attendance and degree attainment result in higher real wages for

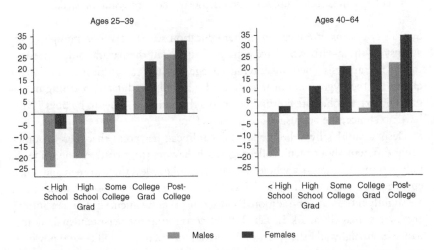

FIGURE 5.1   Percent Changes in Real Hourly Wage Levels, 1979–2010, by Education and Sex

women overall tells us that a strange interaction between gender, college credentials, and paid labor is at work.

What if the cultural forces that shape American attitudes regarding gender function more like rubber bands, as Bennett suggests, snapping men's dominant status back into place, in reaction to a perceived threat by highly educated women? Numerous studies across world populations demonstrate that when a country's women are more highly educated, there are enormous opportunities for social transformation, growth, and greater social equity for everyone.[7] Western women of the last two centuries have experienced extraordinary life changes—reflected in part by their college enrollment and completion—but this has not reflected wholesale change in their overall status, and particularly not in their levels of power to control the structures that maintain male dominance. The cries of "where have all the boys and men gone?" may be the echo of a threatened cultural norm, shifting attention away from newly developing locations of male economic and political power, while simultaneously placating worry over the presence of large numbers of women in college. By emphasizing a discourse of individualism—that is, by highlighting the ways in which individual women have gained increased wages and status, the cultural narrative of female advantage in college distracts from the story of shifting male power. This kind of cultural conversation preserves an attitude of American autonomy, while hiding static or even retrograde ideological beliefs about gender.

Gender researchers have noted this possibility over the past 20 years. "When there begins to be a predominance of female members in any area," states Sturnick, "the value of that area goes down."[8] Levanon, England, and Allison (see Chapter 1) note the same phenomenon in their census data analysis, showing that whenever women moved into occupations in large numbers, those jobs begin paying less, even after controlling for work experience, education, race, geography, and skills.[9] Current U.S. employment data reveal, for example, that in human biology, veterinary medicine, and pediatrics, as women have dominated each profession in numbers, the value, reflected by pay within the profession, has diminished.[10] These professions require years of higher education, and yet each has seen its status decline.

There may be "a time not too distant when degrees are not so prized and skipping college might be a wiser career choice," notes Koerner. Sturnick puts it more bluntly. Through corporate-sponsored schools and alternative means to careers, she asks,

> Will we set up a separate track for education which will primarily benefit men, which will allow them to enter the job market with higher pay . . . while women continue up the baccalaureate track, end up debt-laden, and then wind up three or four years behind in a profession?[11]

A 2013 poll conducted by the College Board and National Journal underscores the more general worry that many Americans may no longer see obtaining a college degree as a necessity: 46 percent of the respondents, including over 50 percent of those ages 18–29, agreed that a college degree was not necessary to be successful.[12] As indicated in Chapter 1, the Public Agenda's *Public Opinion on Higher Education 2016* survey results corroborate this belief, finding that 57 percent of their respondents believed that college was not necessary for work success, a 14 percent increase since their 2009 survey.[13]

Kimmel also sees worrisome trends in Americans' changing beliefs in the value of college, adding that while changes in male college enrollment and achievement undergird the current boy crisis, its political origins are older and more familiar. "Peeking underneath the empirical façade," he writes, helps explain much of what is occurring. "Fears of 'momism'—that peculiar cultural malady that periodically rears its head—have returned. . . . Now the problem with mothers is that they read *The Feminine Mystique* and ran out to pursue careers."[14] Fears of dominant women, coupled with a recurrent ideological focus on manliness, fuel the "advantage/crisis" debate. Like water that is blocked from one pathway, diverting to other channels to find a new path, men may be following such routes.

Men's waning interest in formal higher education, coupled with their subsequent movement to careers that are independent, masculine, and not traditionally intellectual, can be seen through four broad avenues: (1) the changing nature of formal college credentials, in conjunction with the ascendance of digital educational technologies and rewards; (2) the rise of the do-it-yourself vanguard; (3) resurgence of occupations that underscore stereotypical masculinity; and (4) the creation of industries and occupations that prize independence and keep distance from much or any formal schooling. These trends are built on a rhetoric of crisis that feeds an increasingly large slice of American political mentality, as dependent on calamity as it is contemptuous of formal education. They have been increasingly apparent, but they are not a spontaneous phenomenon. A thousand small betrayals of the American belief in formal education, combined with what to many people feel like attacks on Americans' presumptive world superiority, have led to this point. To recognize these current developments as a set of comprehensive counterforces is to acknowledge that an increasingly female-dominated higher education domain may have diminishing returns not just for individual women of all races and social classes, but also threaten its bright promise as a lever for gender equity.

The Changing Nature and Perception of Formal Higher Education Credentials

In the swirling dust of massive, open, online courses (MOOCs), for-profit schools, and fully online and hybrid degrees, many have begun to question universities' privileged positions as expensive gatekeepers of credentials that lead to career and life success. In combination with a college-for-all leitmotif in which higher ed credentials are expected to lead directly to a better life, the resulting precipice on which higher education sits makes it ripe for extraordinary change, and a soapbox for many who claim their roles as sages and saviors of the enterprise. On the one hand, higher education is all but reified as one of the best, if not one of the only ways in which young adults, career changers, and just about everyone finds jobs that lead to more satisfaction, money, and power; on the other hand, higher education's prominent place in the development of human skills, knowledge, and future social connections is being questioned, not only because of its cost, but also because of its physical inaccessibility, and in many cases, its decreasing worth as a transmitter of canonical knowledge.

"Advantage/crisis" conversations are occurring in the midst of these college value debates, and their temporal proximity raises the question: Is the emphasis on college-for-all a distraction, obscuring debates about broader knowledge dissemination and better jobs? None of the new educational developments are male by definition; in fact, their general creed of "open-to-all" runs counter to that exclusivity. However, it is evident that though new kinds of credentials may be increasingly available to all, their power feeds highly male domains, while women's success in obtaining "old higher ed" credentials may offer fewer possibilities for economic and sociopolitical gain.

Alternative college credentials, as a whole, are part of a massive reassignment of access to higher education and its knowledge bases. Populations that formerly had little connection with or ability to participate in college are now enrolling at historically high rates.[15] Only 40 years ago still an important site for maintaining American male privilege, college has since developed into a more welcoming experience for many, with the expectation of better career development and higher economic returns. Carnevale sees this as a development that allows expanding college opportunity without surrendering responsibility; students still have to do their homework and earn a high enough GPA in order to succeed.[16] Women, as discussed in Chapter 3, have been responsible in this manner, and even more recently, the working class and poor have been encouraged to attend college in order to increase their chances at procuring better jobs, particularly in light of fluctuating economic conditions. Rather suddenly, higher education is no longer a place for and by men.

By pursuing a college degree, people "become somebody" and through the process of interacting with others, they reflect on who they believe themselves to be.[17] If higher education has become a place where white males, in particular, perceive their identities to be overshadowed by female identities, then it seems reasonable to expect that fewer males would choose to attend. Chapter 4 examined how the prevailing definition of American masculinity rests increasingly on less formal intellectual development, and it may be that this development is comprehensible—even reasonable—if we see it as the work of a masculine cu~ turning weak academic performance in college into gendered advantages other cultural sectors. In other words, by turning the *lack* of a college creden~

into the more valuable commodity, through emphasis on the money and power to be gained in alternative sectors, an adult version of "if the girls have it, we don't want it" comes into play. This, in conjunction with currently changing dynamics of middle and working class men's labor force participation, may partly explain why post-high school options other than higher education are appealing to males, particularly for those that have traditionally had or have potential for high levels of power. If the lessons of men's resistance to high school a century ago are indicative of current thinking, we can wonder if the same pattern now applies to college degrees: Why get them and compete with women if power can be conferred via different credentials?

Career and Technical Education: Apprenticeships and Postsecondary Certificates

Career and Technical Education (CTE) is a long-standing American tradition, focused on applied learning methods and on teaching field- and occupation-specific skills.[18] Synonymous with apprenticeships and vocational education, CTE occupies a lower status than most other postsecondary educational paths due to its association with working class jobs and careers such as truck driving and hairstyling. Americans have a complicated relationship with CTE; given the deeply held belief that higher educational attainment via a very proscribed kind of schooling—namely, a four-year degree—is the best route to the middle class, attaining a post-high school certificate feels to many people as an abdication of that dream, even if the reality does not offer evidence that such paths cut off that possibility. As the authors of the 2012 CTE Report, *Five Ways That Pay*, put it,

> A majority of Americans do not think everyone should go to college, but the vast majority of parents think their sons and daughters should go, and the students themselves feel the same way. In other words, Americans tend to support alternatives to college for other people's children, but not their own.[19]

Nonetheless, postsecondary education via traditional four-year degree programs represents only 35 percent of the entire postsecondary education and training system. Employer-provided education programs, on-the-job training, apprenticeships, and many other programs constitute much of the rest of the system in which adults of all ages gain skills and training outside of traditional higher education institutions.

Postsecondary certificates that attest to one's mastery of such abilities constitute an increasingly viable alternative to a college degree: One has a definable skill set that directly translates to the job market. Such certificates have been expanding rapidly—roughly 300,000 certificates were awarded in 1994, roughly 1 million were in 2010, and in 2012, certificates overtook both associate's and master's degrees as the second most popular postsecondary award after bachelor's degrees.[20] Certificates are also extremely sex segregated; women tend to cluster in health care, administrative office work, and cosmetology, while men work in auto mechanics, construction, electronics, transportation, HVAC, and refrigeration.[21] Men get more value from earning a training certificate than do women; the labor market tends to reward men and women who enter blue-collar professions differently, and, in fact, men's jobs in these areas tend to be seen as careers, whereas women's are perceived as low-level jobs. Simply put, states Fain, "men get much more value than women do from a certificate."[22] Female certificate holders receive only 16 percent more in pay than workers with only a high school degree. Male certificate holders, on the other hand, make on average more than 27 percent more than males with only a high school degree.[23] Frankly, states Carnevale, "women are really better off going higher [on the educational ladder]," in order to get the same pay that men get from only a certificate.[24]

A similar pattern holds for apprenticeships that, in 2008, were 90 percent male.[25] With over 50 percent of all apprenticeships in the construction fields, and with even more in technical and digital industries, women do not gravitate to formal apprenticeships, even though, like postsecondary certificates, they offer viable, often highly profitable routes to careers. Many more traditionally male jobs become available to men than women this way—not by law or design, but by culturally accepted norms. Aside from persistent beliefs that men and women should be in one kind of occupation or another, if it is the case that women are better off "going higher" in education in order to earn the same amount of money as a man with lower or more streamlined education credentials, it is understandable that they would enroll in some form of degree-granting education more often than men. This gendered analysis, however, is not usually mentioned in the current national push for alternative credentials or in the discussion of why women might actually need to obtain college credentials in ways that men might not.

Learning via Digital Means

The development of digital technologies and their use within education has been named by many as a revolution: People around the world, according to Collins and Halverson, are taking their education out of school and into places where they can decide what, when, and how they want to learn. The use of digital technologies in higher education has also been seen as a paradox: Students' access to knowledge and ways of being can be greatly expanded via digital means, even as such avenues simultaneously offer tempting possibilities for uncritical pursuit of credentials that leave students neither educated nor skilled enough to gain better job and life opportunities. Over the last two decades, higher education's "digital turn" has put pressure on students and teachers to learn via technologically mediated ways that, frequently in the hands of for-profit colleges and degree programs, have created new, often unstable or degraded credentials. Traditional institutions of higher education have also developed online and hybrid credentialing programs, with tuition-driven colleges using them to compete for a declining population of high school graduates.

The proliferation of digital education, whether online, on-ground, or hybrid, has made such delivery into a kind of credentialist savior: If students can gain the skills they need via screens, games, and commodities that sell products, but without the exposure to knowledge they see no hope of using, why would such an avenue not be the logical and desired place to go? Digital learning is offered as an alternative to traditional education, available to all, purportedly free from the bias of the physical world, as well as from geographic and monetary constraints. Anant Agarwal, president of the open source, online higher education platform edX, claims as much, stating in his introduction to the company that "online learning is the ultimate democratizer."[26]

Much has been written about the universality of digital education and its potential to beget the end of higher-education-as-we-know-it; the intent here is not to argue to veracity of those arguments but, rather, to highlight the ways in which digital access and acquisition of knowledge is stratified by gender and social power. That is, the knowledge resources available by digital means may be technically available to all via an open Internet, but the ways in which individuals have time, support, money, permission, and power to take advantage of such resources are dependent on structural inequities that remain intact. "To hear some ed tech enthusiasts tell it, online learning is sweeping aside the barriers that have in the past prevented access to education," notes Annie Murphy Paul, "but such pronouncements are premature. As it turns out, students often carry these barriers right along with them, from the real world into the virtual one."[27] When college goes digital, the parameters by which people undertake study remain virtually the same, making online credentials earned by women subject to the same questions of power as those they earn via traditional means.

Like traditional degree programs, more women than men participate in online degree programs, and since 1995, single-parent, minority, and low-income women have become the largest group among online adult learners.[28] This is not particularly surprising since, unlike the brick-and-mortar world, women have been not only allowed but in some cases also encouraged to engage in off-campus learning for at least a century.[29] Distance learning, usually through correspondence courses, allowed women who had other responsibilities like children and home care to participate on the margins of postsecondary education. They were, however, as online degree pursuers of both sexes still are, considered to be "individuals working on the sidelines of higher education to fulfill individual goals, rather than as thousands of women responding to social constraints, taking a common action to change their social and educational situation."[30] Considering those who pursue online degrees as *individuals* silences the structural issues with which these individuals struggle as a group, and negates the inequalities that still exist on people's paths to education.

Sugata Mitra's *School in the Cloud* project is a clear example of this. The project offers "free learning" to everyone, through the company's computer kiosks placed in some of India's poorest communities. Ritu Dangwal, educational consultant for the Hole-in-the-Wall project, which is part of the *School in the Cloud* initiative, states "we do not find any discrimination [in this project] . . . except gender."[31] Indeed, a five-country comparison of digital inequality, reported in 2007, found that in three of the five countries studied, having a computer in one's home did not guarantee women's use of that computer; access does not always translate into use.[32]

MOOCs are perhaps the prime example of digital education sources that are technically available to all but that benefit more men than women. At one level, they are exactly as described: "courses" of knowledge focused on a particular topic, available to anyone who has Internet access. They are usually offered for no fee and no credit, though MOOCs that are offered by companies related to elite institutions of higher education (e.g., edX—MIT, Harvard, Berkeley, UT; Coursera—Stanford, Yale, and 32 university partners) have opportunities for students to pay for proctored final exams. The pedagogical medium is lecturing, with occasional pauses in the lecture for students to respond to short quizzes or other formative assessments. These are usually not graded by anyone other than the user, and there are virtually no mechanisms by which the instructor can help individual students, or assess whether they are understanding the material. The lack of support for one's learning is one of the major reasons why many women and first-generation, part-time, and lower-income individuals of both sexes struggle, and ultimately do not complete, online courses of any kind, including MOOCs.[33]

According to researchers at the University of Pennsylvania, significantly more males worldwide than females take MOOC courses.[34] These data show that in the United States, women and men *enroll* in MOOCs at roughly the same rates, but this and other studies indicate that in the United States, as in the rest of the world, those who *complete* them are largely men. The world of "masculine open online courses,"[35] as Straumheim puts it, is further bolstered by the predominance of men who lecture in them. A 2013 analysis of the MOOCs listed on three major university-associated online learning sites revealed the tiny proportion of women who taught on such sites: 12 percent of edX's courses, 16 percent of Coursera's, and 6 percent of Udacity's courses offered that year were taught exclusively by women.[36] EdX makes a particular point of using its brand association with Harvard and MIT to sell access to prestigious professors, particularly in the STEM fields, which make up, according to the same analysis, over 50 percent of edX's offerings, and whose professors are almost exclusively men.

Enrolling in a MOOC is not the same as enrolling in an online degree program, of course; one could argue that the predominance of women in online degree programs, and the equal enrollment by women in MOOCs in the United States, is evidence that the educational equity promised by digital means is occurring. However, this bifurcation of women in online degree programs and men in MOOCs only furthers the point that while formal higher education degree programs, online and on-ground, may be skewing female, alternative, informal means of gaining postsecondary skills, knowledge, and connections is gaining legitimacy—and becoming identified with males. New technologies built on old biases seem to reproduce the same gender inequalities.

The Rise of the Do-It-Yourself, No-College Movement

Strongly connected with the credentialist perspective and the belief that the digital education world offers the possibility of access without gender bias is the idea that no college degree is necessary for success, and that even taking the time and money to pursue a traditional college degree could be harmful to one's future. The *un-college* or the *do-it-yourself (DIY) college* movements embody "technoventurists'" advocacy of higher education, freely available to all, without the necessity of actually taking a formal class or program of study. Bolstered by examples like Bill Gates, Mark Zuckerberg, and Steve Jobs, the DIY group promotes "hacking" one's education, learning focused on specific job skills, and making money fast. With arguments ranging from the opportunity costs of higher education to the denigration of the entire collegiate enterprise, a number of people now make the claim that college is a waste of time, and that one is better off getting an education by pursing it individually. In fact many proponents of these initiatives argue that such initiatives avoid prejudice altogether, though none of them acknowledge the social, cultural, and financial capital needed in order to benefit from their proposals, regardless of gender, race, or social class. In this atmosphere, writes Kamenetz,

> Everyone explores . . . virtually and actually. Everyone contributes something unique. Everyone learns. This is the essence of the DIY U idea. It takes us back to the basics. . . . People everywhere will have a greater ability to create their own learning communities and experiences.[37]

Proponents of "no college equals success" have the racial and financial privilege to gain access to people, places, and knowledge that universities usually offer. Women and people of color are rarely mentioned (though often pictured) in no-college success stories; there is no discussion of any kind of privilege required to be able to achieve success without formal schooling. Further, do-it-yourself education perpetuates and expands the already-intense culture of anti-intellectualism, particularly for males. Western masculinity is again defined as independent, non-book-learning, and entrepreneurial, with the primary goal of being rich and therefore powerful.

The un-college or no-college movement emphasizes arguments regarding skyrocketing costs of higher education. Granieri writes:

> The idea that the educational experience is so valuable that no price is too high rests on assumptions about the intrinsic value of knowledge that cannot stand up to economic scrutiny.
>
> When colleges push that myth too far and the price of attendance becomes too high, the willing suspension of disbelief consequently erodes.[38]

Others, like James Altucher, take the no-college argument much further, denouncing higher education as a scam and financial Ponzi scheme, while he wonders aloud if parents should simply forget encouraging children to attend higher education, and suggest that they find their own path instead.[39] Indeed, as more adolescents and adults are encouraged to attend college, more face the reality of its costs, making the enterprise ripe for questions regarding its worth. It has become fashionable to make collegiate voodoo dolls, with authors sticking pins in college mascots and sounding strikingly familiar in tone to those who bemoan traditional education's abandonment of boys.

Stories of those-who-made-it-big without college offer apocryphal examples of getting rich. Fertig categorizes these tropes as: the techie (Bill Gates), the jock (Kobe Bryant), the scribe (Ray Bradbury), and the loudmouth (Glenn Beck).[40] Fertig rightly identifies the figures who occupy each of these categories as outliers, noting that they usually make poor examples of what one can do without a college degree because they are exceptions to the rule. Young adults, he maintains, are tempted to follow these examples, without clear ideas of how to do so. From here, however, he explains that every successful alternative to college is a positive step toward dismantling the foundation of all contemporary higher education, and that, given higher education's "dismal" ROI, alternative postsecondary options for young adults are essential.

What Fertig does not highlight is that no matter what the alternative to college, and no matter how rare or common the pathway, such possibilities are only real choices for those who have the power to take advantage of them. In his listing of non-college attending outliers, for example, he does not acknowledge that all of his examples are men. A few women make the list of "others" he says he could have named, but they, without his saying so, are the exceptions even within the exceptions.

Nonetheless, in an atmosphere where entrepreneurship is seen as the new common sense, and success in it the invitation to comment upon and guide broader social policy, entire companies are being built on selling un-college to disaffected late adolescent men. Not going to college is simply good business, according to this narrative. Dale Stephens even developed a product that names this un-action: The *UnCollege* urges young adults to "hack their education by finding their own pathways to success. . . . If you want to learn," he says, "college is the last place to go."[41] *UnCollege* takes credentialism at its most blunt definition; Stephens argues that if a young adult can get into an elite school, she or he should, using it only to take advantage of its status, but not its learning. "A semester or two may be all you need . . . to gain the advantages associated with the school's name brand."[42] Stephens is adamant that *not* going to college makes one a better learner because individuals have to figure things out for themselves, without the coddling of a college experience. Get the elite institutional status, but make it on your own, he offers paradoxically.

Further, not going to college, according to Stephens, is just smart business. "Self-directed learners, or hackademics, as I like to call them," he says, "aren't just learning for a fraction of the costs [of college attendance]. In many cases, they're doing it for absolutely free."[43] He joins Kamenetz in naming resources from Udacity to the Khan Academy, all of which claim to offer to the fundamentals of regular college courses, without accumulating a crushing debt. Stephens and others like him view access to the knowledge resources brought by the Internet as free-floating, open channels of information, with which individuals can interact as they choose, without the burden of debt or worry about grades . . . and also without intellectual guidance, feedback, support, business connections, ideological challenges, or the institutional stamp of approval, for better and worse, that comes with collegiate association.

Perhaps the prime example of the no-college trend is the Thiel Fellowship. Peter Thiel, himself a two-time Stanford graduate and creator of PayPal, created the fellowship in 2010, offering grants to people under the age of 20 who show evidence of being able to produce a "grand idea"—with the stipulation that they do not go to college. Recipients are awarded $100,000 for two years of work toward building a company or some other kind of product. There are no demographic requirements, and the finalists are judged through interviews with Thiel and his associates. The results? As of 2016, 127 Thiel Fellowships had been awarded, all but 23 of them to men. In other words, only 18 percent of the Fellows are not "fellows."

Stephens, Thiel, and other men like them point to the "hundreds and hundreds" of entrepreneurs who did not graduate from or attend college. Taking a handful of men out of the college pool for each of four years, as Thiel does, is certainly alone not evidence of a seismic gender shift, but the larger idea behind the Thiel Fellowship and similar ideas is that a shift from formal education to alternative credentialing pathways, where few women are willing or able to go, is underway. In fact, as Thiel's fellowship program matures, writes Tom Clynes, "each class begins to look more like the creator himself."[44] Women, by and large, do not have the power to just do-it-yourself; Western gender norms see women without degrees as merely uneducated, while seeing men—at least privileged white ones—as mavericks, entrepreneurs, and visionaries. Most women and underrepresented minorities cannot afford to ask the question: "Is college worth it?" In order to make a living, they need a credential to be considered competent to get a job. So while these tech eduventures are, well, *technically* offered to everyone, it is with men for whom the offers resonate, and it is to these offers that predominantly adolescent men increasingly gravitate. The unspoken call of the un-college boys' club, visible but not articulated, is powerful motivation for its participants.

Resurgence of Occupations That Underscore Stereotypical Masculinity

In addition to the attention focused on the potential benefits of postsecondary certificates, digital knowledge resources, alternative college credentials, and no college at all, jobs that underscore stereotypical masculinity have concurrently taken on increased importance. After years of steady, incremental gains by women in traditionally masculine fields such as policing, firefighting, and emergency work, there is evidence that this trend may be reversing itself. A longtime female police officer asks,

> I've been working with police officers for nearly 30 years. The spirits of the female officers I know are every bit as expansive as their male counterparts. They burn equally with heroic desire, and they're willing to put themselves on the line. So why aren't there more of them? With all the gains women have made in the past 30 years, why have they stalled in policing?[45]

In fact, men are increasingly overrepresented in higher risk industries such as construction, mining, firefighting, military, farming, fishing, and protective services,[46] and it is possible that the stalled integration of women into traditional male occupations is another piece of evidence of cultural retrenchment; if masculinity is threatened, increases in occupational segregation and the resurgence of jobs with traditions of masculine orientations may be causally related to what is perceived as irreversible female educational dominance.

A resurgence in attention to and respect for masculinized occupations, coming in tandem with a decline in men's (and white men's in particular) interest and enrollment in formal higher education is not proof of a relationship, however. Nonetheless, the trifecta of a decline in men's interest in formal higher education, an increase in attention to and respect for hyper-masculine occupations both old and new, and the stagnation of women's participation in occupations that are perceived as male suggest a relationship among these trends. Masculine jobs—high-risk jobs, dirty jobs, and dangerous jobs—may in fact be in the process of a kind of cultural overhaul, taking on a renewed importance in places where masculinity has traditionally dominated, as ideas of where women and men belong are again renegotiated. Given that one of the primary ways in which people define their identities is through their occupations,[47] jobs that are highly stressful, disturbing, and dangerous, make questions of identity construction even more distinctive.[48] People want to work in places where their senses of self align with the work they perform, and desiring a heightened sense of masculinity would enhance the importance and attractiveness of jobs that are seen as adding to such an identity.

Police Officers and Firefighters

One does not need a college degree for community service jobs such as police officers, firefighters, and emergency service (EMS) personnel. Respected professionally in most communities (though recent waves of protest against racial profiling and racist police behavior temper this), but still needed in all of them, these occupations are avenues for young men to have respectability and legitimacy without needing to gain formal higher education credentials. College degrees can enhance one's position in each, but entry-level positions in these jobs are immediately available through specialized training directly from the organization.

Most research in the culture of policing demonstrates that there has been remarkably little change in its "cult of masculinity," which valorizes danger, excitement, and physical strength.[49] The highly masculine institutional cultures of police and fire organizations have traditionally served as gendered barriers in several ways: Higher numbers of men discourage women from breaching clearly male bastions, and they serve to protect the organizations' tendencies toward sexist behaviors, which then perpetuates the cycle of fewer women applying for these positions. Researchers have observed the production and maintenance of this dominance via their study of law enforcement academy training, noting that workplaces are "key sites where . . . a seemingly gender-neutral organizational logic embeds gendered assumptions and practices deeply into the fabric of modern work."[50] Other researchers found that police instructors' and male students' language, curriculum materials, and behaviors defined policing as a particular kind of masculinity, one in which physical violence, discussion of personal sexual behaviors, and "natural" dominance over women was the norm. Further, studies of the discourse of police academies in the United States and Britain within the last 20 years revealed training that encouraged police officers to see women as objects to be denigrated and ridiculed, and treated purely as objects for sexual gratification.[51]

Despite the maintenance and promotion of masculinity in police academy training, women had been making slow, steady gains into the policing profession, increasing their presence at about one half of 1 percent per year since 1971.[52] By 2000, women comprised approximately 14 percent of all police officers in the United States.[53] Beginning in 2001, this trend began to stagnate, and then to decline.

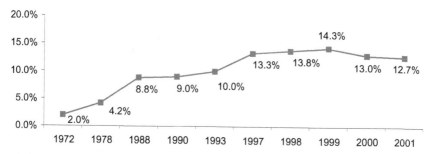

FIGURE 5.2 Percentage of Sworn Women in Law Enforcement Agencies With 100+ Sworn Personnel, 1972–2001

Sklansky argues that the modern police department is "not your father's police department," that changes in police demographics over the past four decades have been profound and largely ignored, and that shifts in gender and racial law enforcement demographics have been transformational, particularly with regard to community policing.[54] His demographic data mirror views offered by other researchers: Women, at the turn of the new century, occupied from single digits to up to 25 percent of police departments in urban areas (though in these departments they made up much more of the civilian workforce, not officers). But even with his optimism regarding a new, more gender-equitable police force, Sklansky admits that the gender integration of the late 1990s has stalled, and agrees with the National Center for Women and Policing that the United States is now seeing a reversal, with numbers of sworn female police officers declining.[55]

The number of women in the firefighting profession is even fewer than that of police ranks—3.4 percent of all U.S. firefighters were women in 2012, a slight decline from 3.8 percent in 2008.[56] The authors of the 2008 *National Report Card on Women in Firefighting* (NRCWFS) questioned those who made attributions about women and men, and their representation in the firefighting workforce:

> When fire department leaders are challenged about these numbers, they traditionally respond that women do not want and cannot handle the job, so that low numbers are to be expected. Are they right? . . . To their male peers, women firefighters represent more than competitors for positions they want and constraints on the free-wheeling aspects of firehouse life. They also silently challenge the self-esteem male fire-fighters derive from perceiving themselves as doing a job for which only a select few have the "right stuff."[57]

According to the same report, women in the firefighting profession encounter issues similar to those of female police officers in their training and job execution.

The job of firefighting is suffused with images of maleness, steeped in highly masculine codes and values that prize risk and danger, heroism, fearlessness/courage, physicality, and body strength, or what some refer to as "body capital,"[58] and recent research findings suggest that firefighters' occupational identities continue to be based in such masculine codes, along with a high degree of group solidarity.[59]

The 2008 NRCWFS speaks about necessary changes in this organizational culture, including the necessity of making firefighting an occupation where sexual harassment and daily gender discrimination are no longer the norm. Pacholok's 2013 investigation of the ways in which gender relations play out in times of disaster reveals gendered micro-interactions between firefighters and the structural masculinity that defines the profession. If females receive the messages that this and other like professions are not for them, and men inherently understand that such professions are for the most part theirs alone by virtue of their sex, it makes sense that the profession would remain heavily male-dominated—even though NRCWFS authors maintain that roughly 17 percent of women who responded to their survey report an interest in the profession.[60]

Even without the statistical reports, women know from general exposure to media and cultural norms that professions like policing and firefighting are men's to be had, and that to enter them is almost an invitation to accept the harassment that comes as a result of infringing on male territories.[61] What makes firefighting and police work relevant to the decline in men's overall participation in higher education is the idea that if higher education is perceived as increasingly female-dominated, the attractiveness of highly male-dominated professions increases. As such, women continue to disregard these professions as places to attend after high school, even as they remain viable and increasingly attractive places for men.

Military Service

The military's institutional framework is built on a foundation of masculinity. Closed to women for most of its history, enlistment in all branches has been an option that many young men have taken in lieu of or as a precursor to formal higher education; 84.2 percent of all 18–24 year olds who choose enlistment are men—about 145,000 men per year.[62] This mirrors the overall gender demographics in all branches of the military, in which 85–86 percent of active personnel (enlisted and officers) are male.[63] The army alone recruits approximately 64,000 more college-age, high school graduate men than women per year into active duty.[64] While the number of female enlisted military personnel *relative* to the number of men has increased since 1973, their numbers have steadily declined since 1998, not long after the time at which women's enrollment in higher education began exceeding men's.[65]

The military continues to be a place where men with fewer socioeconomic resources, independent of race and ethnicity, can see a more direct path to achieving educational and other life goals than gaining a college degree offers.[66] For black men, as their treatment by the armed forces has gotten significantly better overall, enlistment has been even more appealing in the last 30 years, which may account for much of the increase in male military enrollment.[67] It has also been the case that for black men, enlisting in the military has been a direct way to make up for educational and socioeconomic disparities of their childhoods, including their unequal treatment in school; indeed, a number of analysts have proposed that the reasons why black men over-enlist in the military (approximately 16.8 percent of the total) is because they perceive it to be a more meritocratic and racially tolerant place than the civilian world.[68]

Different reasons are offered for the rate of black women's military enlistment, which offers an exception to the bifurcation of women and men and their choices of formal education post-high school. Black women comprise nearly one-third of all women in the military, with a higher enlistment rate than men or women of any other racial or ethnic background.[69] With black women's enlistment rate accelerating in the early 1980s, Melin makes the argument that welfare reform, in conjunction with a rise in female-headed households and the 2008 financial crisis, precipitated such high enlistment. She contends that such enlistments are born of "desperate choices" and that it is unclear whether such enlistment helps disadvantaged black women achieve more social and economic mobility than would be available without having enlisted.[70]

For men of all races, reasons for their enlistment in the military remain less murky: Whether they want more education, or because of a host of other reasons such as travel, a steady income, and needing some definable path after high school, they find a highly masculine home in the armed services. Since 2008, all branches of the military showed increased enlistment, which analysts credit, in part, to economic pressures and to the reintroduction of a GI Bill, in which service members who spend at least three years on active duty can attend any public college at government expense or apply the payment toward tuition at a private university. Given that the number of new active-duty recruits with high school diplomas dropped 12 percent from 2003 to 2008, the promise of an education could indeed be more powerful now. The 2012 DOD Report indicates that 78.6 percent of all active-duty enlisted personnel have a high school degree, a GED, or some college (but less than a bachelor's degree).[71]

The highly masculine nature of the military makes it possible for men of all races and socioeconomic classes to embrace a stereotypical code of masculinity, gaining an education and a place of belonging without what enlisted men may perceive as an unwanted feminine influence.[72] Certainly the possibility of improved socioeconomic status for men, decreased racial and ethnic discrimination, and more money and opportunities for travel are interwoven in men's reasons for enlisting in the military. Combined with a corresponding lack of women, even with their representation at higher levels than in previous generations, these factors continue to make the post-high school military option a powerful one for men. The stagnation of white women's enlistment, in combination with rising black women's enlistment, however, adds troubling considerations to women's post-high school educational choices. Military enlistment may be a desperate choice that solves financial problems in the short term, but doing so does not appear to offer female veterans ways to counteract continued male dominance in socioeconomic realms outside of military life.

Sports

Sports have always been a greater employment avenue for men than for women. The culture of sports in the United States is pervasive, defined by a masculinity that is "strong, dominant, independent, and unemotional."[73] Given the cultural context in which many young men are expected to discuss, play, and watch sporting events from golf to fantasy football, they frequently develop a much greater working knowledge of U.S. sports culture, and have, over the past century, developed many avenues for employment with professional or semiprofessional sports. Yet even this long-standing, gender-weighted reality did not predict the explosive growth in sports-related occupations, and men's employment in them, in the last decade.

Nationally, much of the growth in sports-related jobs has been in the organizations' business offices, with the occupational category of *Promoters of Performing Arts, Sports, and Similar Events* growing by 30 percent between 2010 and 2014, followed by *Agents and Managers for Artists, Athletes, Entertainers, and Other Public Figures*, which grew by 17 percent, according to Careerbuilders.com and Economic Modeling Specialists.[74] The pervasive culture of sports and its tie to stereotypical masculinity in the United States makes a visible place for many American men to look for jobs. Although women are employed in some aspects of sports— broadcast journalism, cheerleading, and some athleticism (and ironically, they are overrepresented in sports management degree programs)[75]—the pay and opportunities for women in any aspect of sport is a fraction of what is available for men.

The Bureau of Labor Statistics categorizes sports jobs along with entertainment; among the categories of employment are "athletes and sports competitors," "coaches and scouts," and "umpires, referees, and other sports officials." Only coaches and scouts require any college credential, according to the BLS, and sports officials and athletes need only a high school degree or equivalent.[76] Added to these job opportunities are also international sports leagues, Hispanic leagues, semiprofessional sports leagues, and more recently, sports management positions. Though these requirements vary greatly by state, region, specific sport, and locality, these positions are nonetheless considered viable and available job opportunities that high school educated men are increasingly taking at much higher rates than women.[77]

New Opportunities in Old Professions: Organized Crime and Gangs

Most researchers agree that crime is a virtually all-male activity.[78] What is not often acknowledged, however, is that crime, particularly *organized crime*, constitutes a legitimate career aspiration for men in communities where the cultural context accepts organized crime as a viable part of life.[79] Drug trafficking and gang activity define significant growth in this area, in which 46 percent of the new participants in the trade are aged 12–29 years old,[80] making lucrative, albeit illegal and dangerous, new paths for young men in the last few decades.

Gang activities have increased by over 30 percent since 2002,[81] with membership bringing not only money but also strong social relationships, not unlike those formed in residential colleges. Immediate access to money, as well as a profound sense of belonging have always attracted potential members. Counterintuitively, perhaps, it is not just young men with little or no access to money who join organized crime, nor is it those who simply could not succeed in educational endeavors.[82] Increasingly, argue crime experts, it is the "pulling power of the social environment" that attracts many kinds of young men to become involved, as well the myriad business opportunities that offer lucrative opportunities without investment of time.

Hispanic and Latino males, in particular, are susceptible to gang membership in lieu of high school completion and therefore college attendance; only half of U.S. Hispanic and Latino males complete high school, and of those students, only 34 percent enroll in college, as opposed to 44 percent of Hispanic and Latina females.[83] High school educators too often assume that males of color are already criminalized, contributing to the dominant cultural portrayal of Hispanic and Latino men as street-focused as opposed to academically focused. In some cases, the disinvestment of Hispanic and Latino males from schooling occurs in order to prevent bullying by gang-affiliated peers; gangs provide group belonging in the face of disenfranchisement, as well as a place to develop an identity.[84] With Hispanic and Latino youth representing 46 percent of the three-quarters of a million gang members in the United States, gang availability offers quick access to cash and a chance to become "somebody" in ways that, at least for a while, align with predominant characteristics of stereotypical Hispanic and Latino masculinity.[85]

Rios[86] argues that for youth of color, an additional consequence of proximity to criminal activity such as gangs and subsequently the criminal justice system is the development of a kind of hyper-masculinity, which scholars define as the "exaggerated exhibition of physical strength and personal aggression" that is often a response to a gender threat "expressed through physical and sexual domination of others."[87] This definition of masculinity is typically oppositional to schooling, leading young men who rely on gang identity away from any kind of high school or post-high school opportunities.

Further, just like any other business, organized crime offers opportunities for social mobility, particularly in communities where other kinds of mobility are hard to achieve.[88] With the advent of more women of all social classes graduating from college and gaining what many claim is their subsequent advantage in the workforce, it may be that organized crime offers an increasingly attractive place for men who are part of a hyper-masculinized culture to gravitate—one that they are all but certain women will not follow. Women participate in activities of organized crime as well, usually in relationship to men who are directly involved, and almost always as part of traditionally female roles rather than as "active offenders."[89] But being part of organized crime, for women, is simply not a viable career path. For an increasing number of men of color, however, the chance to be a key and respected community member, along with earning immediate money, organized crime is a career option many see as too great to pass up.

New Industries and Occupations That Prize Independence and Keep Distance From Much or Any Formal Schooling

At the turn of the 21st century, Koerner and others in the business world warned *U.S. News & World Report* readers that the increasing number of tech jobs was allowing male high school graduates to immediately enter the job market ahead of women, warning that such a trend could prove to be problematic.[90] He likely had no idea how prophetic his comments were. In addition to the traditional settings that welcome many more post-high school men than women, the development of tech versions of professional boys' clubs may be the places where a female *dis*advantage is most evident. New industries in which the independent worker dominates—the loner techie or the geek, for example—have been portrayed as the standard against which emerging professions are measured.[91] It may seem a positive development that there is already a healthy conversation about such nascent professions' collective dearth of women. But the "woman problem" in these industries and organizations seems likely a new code built on an old male framework—that is, women may have been busy earning college degrees only to find that their credentials do not unlock these new office doors.

Silicon Valley and the I.T. Profession

The most notorious female-limited opportunities lie in the relatively new field of information technology development (I.T.). Nicknamed "The Valley of the Boys"[92] in which "a young guy's dreams come true,"[93] the I.T. market offers the epitome of a get-rich-quick boys' club that often requires no conventional schooling. Men who have dominated I.T. fields offer examples of success, and *Business Insider* and *Forbes* regularly run articles like "Top 100 Entrepreneurs Who Made Millions Without a College Degree"[94] and "High Paying Jobs that Don't Require a Bachelor's Degree."[95] The vast majority of these entrepreneurs are male and from the tech industry. "[I]n recent decades," writes Caldwell in *The New York Times*, "the biggest rewards have gone to those whose intelligence is in new directions on short notice."[96] Laszlo Bock, senior vice president of People Operations at Google said recently: "For every job, the number one thing we look for is general cognitive ability and it's not IQ. It's learning ability. It's the ability to process on the fly [and] pull together disparate bits of information."[97] Google's hiring process involves leadership, coding, and teamwork, but, according to their *How We Hire* site, "We're less concerned about grades and transcripts and more interested in how you think."[98]

It does not matter in Silicon Valley that women are gaining more college degrees, for its doors most frequently open to men. According to *Catalyst*, only 5.7 percent of employed women in the United States work in the computer industry.[99] The National Center for Women and Information Technology (NCWIT) offers a different view of the same picture, citing that 26 percent of the computing workforce occupations in the United States in 2013 were held by women—3 percent of the workforce was black women, and 2 percent was Hispanic women.[100] While this pattern is partially due to the small number of women majoring in computer science (the major experienced a *64 percent decline* in women's enrollment between 2000 and 2012), much more of it is the gendered culture of I.T. and computing, and the influence of stereotypes on women's perceptions of being a computer scientist. Indeed, the percentage of computing occupations held by women in the United States has been declining steadily since 1991, when it reached a high of 36 percent.

Silicon Valley of the 1990s trumpeted its meritocracy as a "secret weapon," where only IQ counted, and everything else was ignored.[101] Companies wanted the "best, youngest Technorati," but then promoted employees that looked like Michael Dell, Steve Jobs, and Bill Gates. As context shapes identity, Silicon Valley's context demanded technical knowledge and expertise that they deemed masculine,[102] with engineering and computer cultures defining success and professional competence as aggressive, technical self-confidence, while simultaneously devaluing characteristics such as cooperation and communication—those

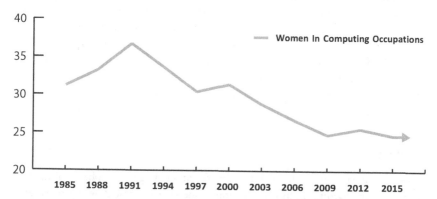

FIGURE 5.3 Percentage of Computing Occupations Held by Women Since 1985

more associated with women. This "nerd masculinity" became common in the high-tech world and was glorified in descriptions of Silicon Valley. Those with the kind of masculinity that in earlier eras would have invited bullying and belittling got revenge in one of the oldest ways possible: Beat up on someone else.

Even more progressive companies are still heavily male: Google's workforce is 70 percent male, and 83 percent of its technical employees are men.[103] Misa notes that even the discourse of I.T. reflects its male-favored culture:

> You start a computer by booting it, if it unexpectedly crashes or bombs an expert might do a code dump, you execute instructions or programs, or if something goes wrong you kill or abort them, a code warrior dreams of creating a killer app.[104]

Focusing on how stereotypes of a field drive gender differences in interest by those not already in it, Cheryan and colleagues showed how the stereotype of someone who works in I.T.—"a genius male computer hacker who spends a great deal of time alone on the computer, has an inadequate social life, and enjoys hobbies involving science fiction"[105]—affects girls as early as elementary school. Tobias calls this depiction the "boy wonder icon"—the association of male traits with an obsessive focus on and success in science at an early age—and attributes this depiction as one of the earliest ways in which men are funneled to, and women away from, technological pursuits.[106] Margolis and Fisher zero in on the bottom line, arguing in *Unlocking the Clubhouse* that "the study of computer science education can be seen as a microcosm of how a realm of power can be claimed by one group of people, relegating others to outsiders"; the need to feel as though one belongs to the profession, to a group of people who accept the passion and interests of one's own, is a weighty influence on women's participation in a male-dominated occupation.[107] Though the authors are discussing computer science, they could be describing organized crime or construction work as well.

Concludes Misa, "It appears that the fall in enrollments, number of graduates, and computing workforce numbers are closely related. Indeed, we suspect that the educational and workforce tail-offs together actually reflect some broader, as-yet-unrecognized social or cultural shift."[108] Between these powerful stereotypes, the current employment statistics in the fields of information technology, and the cultural beliefs that support I.T. skills as something innate, it is easy to see how men regard I.T. as a highly attractive place to go directly from high school. It is also easy to see why women would not regard I.T. as a place where they are welcome, with higher education credentials or not.

Gaming

Closely associated with the new female-free and college-free spheres of the tech world lies the gaming industry. Gaming is one of the fastest growing worldwide industries; revenue in 2009 was estimated at $10.5 billion;[109] by the end of 2016, the total market forecast is over $86 billion.[110] In Massachusetts alone, video game employment has jumped nearly 80 percent since 2009, with the vast majority of those jobs going to men who do not need a college degree. According to A.J. Grand-Strutton, CEO of *Dlala Studios*:

> The reality is, a degree is effectively gravy compared to an actual portfolio. If I'm hiring you for a job I'm not interested in whether you did three years at University and were judged good enough to get a certificate by someone else, I'm interested in you being able to show me practical application of your skill.[111]

Anthony Castaro of *Howcast* hedges, but ultimately says the same:

> Do you have to go to college to get into the game industry? The answer to that question is no. When you send in your resume . . . if you have that degree, it might set you apart. It's not necessarily going to give you a leg up when you start your job.[112]

Higher education has followed the gaming money, developing gaming and engineering degrees at a dizzying rate[113] to capitalize on the feeding frenzy of the gaming business, even though the majority of those who work in the industry do not have or need college degrees: They need to be able to program, and they apparently need to be male. In 2014, women still held only 11–22 percent of the jobs in the industry, according to the International Game Developers Association (IGDA), even though the Association estimates they make up over 43 percent of the gaming population.[114]

According to the IGDA, women occupy 10–12 percent of the artist and designer roles, and are fewer than 5 percent of industry's programmers. Women's roles in gaming tend to be weighted heavily toward operations and human resources, public relations, and marketing/production.[115] Most attribute women's lack of participation in the gaming industry to its "frat boy" culture and the hypersexualization of female game characters,[116] as well as the gender pay gap; in 2014, female programmers made, on average, $15,000/year less than male programmers, and female animators made $21,000/year less than their male counterparts.[117]

The frat boy mentality permeates the gaming culture, drawing late adolescent boys to the highly lucrative business, which requires little or no college expense before beginning and offers a steadily growing number of jobs and a work culture that celebrates *guyness*. The promise of an extended adolescence that such a culture often provides may be as much a draw for post-high school men as the work of gaming itself. The billion-dollar video game industry is growing, but women remain outsiders. "If you are a woman in the industry," states Marleigh Norton, cofounder of and game developer at Green Door Labs, "there are all these little signals that you are not part of the club, that this is not your tribe."[118] Young women might be tempted to dismiss the game industry entirely, likening it to a playground that, though they are excluded from it, they did not wish to enter anyway. Yet as gaming becomes bigger business, related to the growth in the sports and entertainment industries, not only does females' exclusion severely hamper the jobs they can get in a lucrative industry, but it also works to relegate women (and to allow them to relegate themselves) to more obligatory tasks that reinforce the gender stereotype of women as too serious and too dedicated to their studies and to children and families to pay attention to gaming.

Researchers Winn and Heeter found evidence of such a phenomenon in their recent study of gaming, gender, and time in college. Their results confirmed the gender gap in gaming; 70 percent of male undergraduates in their study played a digital game the week of the survey, compared to only 25 percent of the female undergraduates.[119] Further, their study found that one reason women played fewer games was because they had less free time; they studied more, and had more duties to fulfill. This distinction in male and female behaviors becomes a vicious cycle: Women are busier than men in studious and extracurricular tasks of college, believing that hard work in college will equate to better lives and jobs outside it; men spend more time in college developing skills that come through gaming, whether or not they represent part of their official college curriculum, believing that they will succeed once outside college, not necessarily connecting their behavior with post-college outcomes. Upon graduation, men subsequently have more gaming skills, which are increasingly prized by I.T. companies, with or without the college credential.

The Gig Economy

Finally, an important college-not-required space where men may be disproportionally gravitating is the gig economy: work that boasts small-scale entrepreneurship, freelance tasks with little connection to an employer, and, above all, independence. The *Wall Street Journal* defines the term "gig" as "an alternative work arrangement job."[120] Contingent workers are not new to the American or world economic picture, of course; agricultural workers, child care workers, tutors, and textile mill workers have been paid as independent contractors for centuries. But with digital tech companies and the arrival of other peer-sharing, crowd-sourcing, or on-demand companies, combined with the valorization of working for yourself and not getting into college debt, the decades-long shift to flexible work arrangements[121] has transformed the contingent economy into the gig economy—one that boasts new opportunities, lots of independence, and lots of men.

Analysis of just what constitutes a gig job drives the way gender is counted in these occupations, and it is difficult to get an accurate measure of the current number of them; according to most labor market analysts, the gig economy grew

18 percent of all jobs between 2001 and 2014, rising from 20 million to over 32 million workers in those years.[122] The Bureau of Labor Statistics notes:

> More and more, we have what many people have called a "gig economy"— with the looseness of a musician's one-night engagement at a club now defining in many cases everything from construction and retail work to adjunct professorships at prestigious universities.[123]

In addition to chauffeuring services like Uber and Lyft, gigs include butlering with The Alfred Club, cleaning with Handy cleaners and TaskRabbit, and arranging others' accommodations through Airbnb. Economists debate the scope of the gig economy; depending on how one analyzes part-time workers, it is possible that the size of the independent workforce has stayed constant or risen slightly to 35 percent, as a share of overall employment, in the last 20 years.[124] The Freelancers Union claims roughly the same percentage, but argues that the impact of freelance workers is grossly underestimated.[125] Depending on how one defines contingent, independent, freelance, or part time, one can get widely varying statistics on who is employed doing what in the U.S. economy.

Even with the malleability in the definition, it seems clear that in the United States, gig workers are increasingly men.[126] Many analysts find that occupational segregation by gender and race is particularly important in this economy; when workers are defined as "solopreneurs," they are much more likely to be men; when they are defined as "sidegiggers," they are more likely to be women.[127] The allure of the independent life and the possibility of high wages—in other words, the identity of being an independent entrepreneur—increasingly drives larger numbers of young, white men to pursue gigging as an entrepreneurial strategy, whereas for women and for underrepresented minorities of both sexes, gigging is likely to be a new term for people who try to earn a living through multiple part-time jobs.[128] For example, a Boston-based company called HourlyNerd connects alumni of top business schools and other specialized programs to companies with projects in need of completing, like market analysis or examinations of pricing strategy. There are a number of experts in the company, they report, who earn well over six figures, and young men gravitate to statistics such as this. Most in this economy earn significantly less, however, with many people working in what some call the "gray market"—the place occupied by "discouraged workers" who take gig jobs because there are many fewer full-time jobs to be found.[129] Many in this category do not even make minimum wage.[130]

Tellingly, the gig economy is also referred to as "Uberization," due to the technology company's domination of the independent chauffeuring market. Uber serves as a striking picture of how male this way of working can be. The "It" company of the 21st century, Uber has become a preeminent symbol of on-demand services, with an employment model that claims to allow its drivers and riders ultimate freedom. Uber's chief advisor, David Plouffe, cites an internal

Uber study finding that "87 percent of drivers say a major reason they chose Uber was that they wanted to be their own boss and set their own schedule."[131]

Uber's driver statistics offer a window into the business and its underlying model. "[People] are joining," says Badger of *The Washington Post*, "at a breakneck pace."[132] The people joining, however, are primarily men: 86 percent of Uber's drivers are male, with close to 50 percent of its drivers (male or female) having no college degree.[133] Lyft, a rival chauffeuring service, has a better gender balance at the executive level—14 of its 30 executives are women—but its drivers are also overwhelmingly male—70 percent of them.[134] Although these numbers generally mirror the U.S. taxi drivers and chauffeuring industry demographics—approximately 13 percent of the industry was female in 2015[135]—the gender imbalance in companies like Uber and Lyft is striking because men are choosing to join the services in record numbers, whereas men—white men in particular—are increasingly leaving the taxi industry.[136]

The gender imbalance in this new version of ride-hailing services may feed on itself, creating a company that feeds on a "nerd masculinity" and occupational racial segregation. According to journalist Steven Greenhouse, Uber's white, male, ULCA-dropout founder, Travis Kalanick, "once joked to GQ magazine that his company should be called 'Boober' because it made it such a cinch for him to attract women."[137] If the CEO sees his company this way, and most of its employees are men, it seems unsurprising that new chauffeuring companies are deemed male work territory, just as the older taxi services have been. But where taxi driving is increasingly non-white and perceived as the ghost of Business Past, Ubering seems the white male way of Business Future.

Even with a highly malleable definition of what the gig economy is, who works in it, and why they do, what seems to be clear is that a young, white male who is comfortable with digital technologies and who wants to make money without first engaging in formal education will be able to look for work in this sector. Millennials—those aged 18–34 in 2015—are now the largest share of the U.S. labor force, and the largest share of the gig economy.[138] With the draw of independence and money without formal higher education, young men continue to be attracted to its promises.

With the opportunities, real and perceived, for young adult American men, it may not be surprising that their interest in formal higher education is waning. But what about the supposed female advantage in college completion and success? Given the numbers, should there not be evidence of more equity in women's post-collegiate lives over the past 40 years? A proportion of the U.S. population seems to think so. In *The End of Men*, Hannah Rosin writes,

> What if the modern, postindustrial economy is simply more congenial to women than to men? For a long time, evolutionary psychologists have claimed that we are all imprinted with adaptive imperatives from a distant past: men are faster and stronger and hardwired to fight for scarce resources . . . ; women

are programmed to find good providers and to care for their offspring. . . . But what if men and women were fulfilling not biological imperatives but social roles, based on what was more efficient throughout a long era of human history? What if that era has now come to an end?[139]

Chapter 6 explores this assumption.

Notes

1. Smith, H. (2013). *Why men are avoiding college.* Minding the Campus: Reforming our Universities. Retrieved from www.mindingthecampus.org/2013/05/why_men_are_avoiding_college/ From *Men on Strike: Why men and boycotting marriage, fatherhood, and the American Dream and why it matters.*
2. National Center for Education Statistics (NCES). (2014). *The condition of education.* Retrieved from https://nces.ed.gov/
3. Bennett, J. M. (1997). Confronting continuity. *Journal of Women's History, 9*(3), p. 82.
4. Wood, P. (2011). Higher education's precarious hold on consumer confidence. *Academic Questions, 24*(3), p. 1.
5. Autor, D., & Wasserman, M. (2013). *Wayward sons: The emerging gender gap in labor markets and education.* Washington, DC: Third Way, p. 12.
6. Ibid.
7. See, for example, The Clinton Foundation and The Bill and Melinda Gates Foundation. (2015, March). *No Ceilings: The Full Participation Report.* Retrieved from www.noceilings.org.
8. Koerner, B. I. et al. (1999). Where the boys aren't. (Cover story). *U.S. News & World Report, 126*(5), p. 46.
9. Levanon, A., England, P., & Allison, P. (2009). Occupational feminization and pay: Assessing causal dynamics using 1950–2000 US census data. *Social Forces, 88*(2), 865–891.
10. Irvine, L., & Vermilya, J. R. (2010). Gender work in a feminized profession: The case of veterinary medicine. *Gender & Society, 24*(1), 56–82; Lincoln, A. E. (2010). The shifting supply of men and women to occupations: Feminization in veterinary education. *Social Forces, 88*(5), 1969–1998; Williams, A. P., Domnick-Pierre, K., Vayda, E., Stevenson, H. M., & Burke, M. (1990). Women in medicine: Practice patterns and attitudes. *Canadian Medical Association Journal, 143*(3), 194–121; Williams, A. P., Pierre, K. D., & Vayda, E. (1992). Women in medicine: Toward a conceptual understanding of the potential for change. *Journal of the American Medical Women's Association, 48*(4), 115–121.
11. Koerner et al., 1999, p. 54.
12. Porter, E. (2013, November 13). Rethinking the rise of inequality. *The New York Times.* Retrieved from www.nytimes.com/2013/11/13/business/rethinking-the-income-gap-and-a-college-education.html, p. 1.
13. Public Opinion on Higher Education. (2016, September 12). Retrieved from www.publicagenda.org/pages/public-opinion-higher-education-2016
14. Kimmel, M. (2006). A war against boys? *Dissent, 53*(4), 65–70.
15. Smith, W., & Bender, T. (2008). Introduction. In W. Smith & T. Bender (Eds.), *American higher education transformed: 1940–2005* (pp. 1–11). Baltimore, MD: Johns Hopkins University Press.
16. Carnevale, A. P. (2008, January/February). College for all? *Change,* 23–29.
17. Wexler, P., Crichlow, W., Kern, J., & Matusewicz, R. (1992). *Becoming somebody: Toward a social psychology of school.* London, UK: Falmer Press.

18. Carnevale, A. P., Jayasundera, T., & Hanson, A. R. (2012). *Career and technical education: Five ways that pay along the way to a B.A.* Washington, DC: Georgetown Public Policy Institute, Center for Education and the Workforce.
19. Ibid., p. 13.
20. Carnevale, A. P., Rose, S. J., & Hanson, A. R. (2012). *Certificates: Gateway to gainful employment and college degrees.* Washington, DC: Georgetown University Center on Education and the Workforce. Retrieved from http://cew.georgetown.edu/certificates/
21. Ibid.
22. Fain, P. (2012, June 6). Certificates are misunderstood credentials that pay off mostly for men. *Inside Higher Ed.* Retrieved from www.insidehighered.com/
23. Ibid.
24. Ibid.
25. U.S. Department of Labor, Office of Apprenticeship.
26. Agarwal. A. edX: *How it works.* Video. Retrieved from www.edx.org/how-it-works
27. Paul, A. M. (2014). *The MOOC Gender Gap.* The Hechinger Report. www.slate.com Retrieved from www.slate.com/articles/technology/future_tense/2014/09/mooc_gender_gap_how_to_get_more_women_into_online_stem_classes.html
28. Peter, K., & Horn, L. (2005). *Gender differences in participation and completion of undergraduate education and how they have changed over time.* Postsecondary education descriptive analysis reports (NCES 2005–169). Washington, DC: U.S. Department of Education.
29. Kramarae, C. (2003). Gender equity online, when there is no door to knock on. In M. Moore & W. Anderson (Eds.), *Handbook of distance education* (pp. 261–272). Mahwah, NJ: Erlbaum.
30. Ibid., p. 262.
31. Watters, A. *Hacking at education: TED, technology entrepreneurship, uncollege, and the hole in the wall.* Retrieved from http://hackeducation.com/2013/03/03/hacking-your-education-stephens-hole-in-the-wall-mitra
32. Ono, H., & Zavodny, M. (2003). Gender and the internet. *Social Science Quarterly,* 84(1), 111–121.
33. Kramarae, 2003.
34. Christensen, G. et al. (2013). *The MOOC phenomenon: Who takes massive open online courses and why?* Working Paper (November 6). Philadelphia, PA: University of Pennsylvania.
35. Straumheim, C. (2013, September 3). Masculine open online courses. *Inside Higher Ed.* Retrieved from www.insidehighered.com/news/2013/09/03/more-female-professors-experiment-moocs-men-still-dominate
36. Ibid.
37. Kamenetz, A. (2010). *DIY U: Edupunks, edupreneurs, and the coming transformation of higher education.* White River Junction, VT: Green River Publishing.
38. Granieri, R. J. (2010). The worst of both worlds: The crisis in American higher education. *Quarterly Review,* 4(3), p. 34.
39. Altucher, James. (2010, August). *Seven reasons not to send your kids to college.* Retrieved from https://collegerealitychat.wordpress.com/dont-go-to-college/saying-no/james-altucher/
40. Fertig, J. (2011, August). Success without college. *Academic Questions,* 24, 291–299.
41. Oljavo, H. E. (2012, February 2). Why go to college at all? *The New York Times,* https://thechoice.blogs.nytimes.com/2012/02/02/why-go-to-college-at-all/?_r=0
42. Ibid.
43. Ibid.
44. Clynes, T. (2016, June 5). Peter Thiel's Dropout Army. *The New York Times,* p. A5.
45 VanBrocklin, V. *Why aren't there more women in police work?* Retrieved from www.policeone.com/women-officers/articles/6539439-Why-arent-there-more-women-in-policework/

46. See Messing, K. et al. (2003). Be the fairest of them all: Challenges and recommendations for the treatment of gender in occupational health research. *American Journal of Industrial Medicine, 43*(6), 618–629; Gerarda Power, N., & Baqee, S. (2010). Constructing a "culture of safety": An examination of the assumptions embedded in occupational safety and health curricula delivered to high school students and fish harvesters in Newfoundland and Labrador, Canada. *Policy and Practice in Health and Safety, 8*(1), 5–23, for more evidence.

47. Collinson, D. L. (2003). Identities and insecurities: Selves at work. *Organization, 10*(3), 527–547; Tracy, S. J., & Trethewey, A. (2005). Fracturing the real-self ↔ fake-self dichotomy: Moving toward "crystallized" organizational discourses and identities. *Communication Theory, 15*(2), 168–195.

48. Tracy, S. J., Myers, K. K., & Scott, C. W. (2006). Cracking jokes and crafting selves: Sensemaking and identity management among human service workers. *Communication Monographs, 73*(3), 283–308.

49. Brown, J. (2007). From cult of masculinity to smart macho: Gender perspectives on police occupational culture. *Sociology of Crime, Law and Deviance, 8*, 205–226.

50. Prokos, A., & Padavic, I. (2002). "There oughta be a law against bitches": Masculinity lessons in police academy training. *Gender, Work & Organization, 9*(4), p. 440.

51. Brown, J. (2007); Prokos & Padavic, 2002.

52. VanBrocklin, V. *Why aren't there more women in police work?* Retrieved from www.policeone.com/women-officers/articles/6539439-Why-arent-there-more-women-in-policework/

53. Ibid.

54. Sklansky, D. A. (2006). Not your father's police department: Making sense of the new demographics of law enforcement. *The Journal of Criminal Law and Criminology (1973–), 96*(3), 1209–1243.

55. Ibid., 1239.

56. Bureau of Labor Statistics, U.S. Department of Labor. (2012). *Education and training outlook for occupations 2012–2022*. Retrieved from www.bls.gov

57. Hulett, D. A., Bendick, M., Thomas, S. Y., & Moccio, F. (2008). *National report card on women in firefighting*. Institute for Women and Work, School of Industrial and Labor Relations (ILR). Ithaca, New York: Cornell University.

58. Monaghan, L. (2002). Hard men, shop boys and others: Embodying competence in a masculinist occupation. *Sociological Review, 50*(3), 334–355.

59. Thurnell-Read, T., & Parker, A. (2008). Men, masculinities and firefighting: Occupational identity, shop-floor culture and organisational change. *Emotion, Space and Society, 1*(2), 127–134.

60. NRCWFS Report, 2008.

61. Ibid.

62. Post-secondary Pathways, 2012.

63. U.S. Department of Defense. (2014). 2014 demographics: Profile of the military community. *Office of the Deputy Assistant Secretary of Defense* (Military Community and Family Policy). Retrieved from http://militaryonesource.mil

64. Weaver-Hightower, M. B. (2010). Where the guys are: Males in higher education. *Change: The Magazine of Higher Learning, 42*(3), 29–35.

65. Patten, E., & Parker, K. (2011). Women in the military: Growing share, distinctive profile. *Pew Social & Demographic Trends*. Retrieved from http://pewsocialtrends.org

66. Kleykamp, M. A. (2006). College, jobs, or the military? Enlistment during a time of war. *Social Science Quarterly, 87*(2), 272–290; NRC, 2003.

67. Cox, T. (2007, December 14). Blacks using military to get ahead. *National Public Radio* Audio Broadcast]. Retrieved from www.npr.org/templates/story/story.php?storyId=17259797

68. Angrist, J., Lang, D., & Oreopoulos, P. (2006). *Lead them to water and pay them to drink: An experiment with services and incentives for college achievement* (No. w12790), pp. 1–61.

Cambridge, MA: National Bureau of Economic Research. Retrieved from www.nber.org/papers/w12790; Latty, Y. (2004). *We were there: Voices of African American veterans, from World War II to the war in Iraq.* New York, NY: Harper Collins/Amistad; Moskos, C., & Butler, J. S. (1996). *All that we can be: Black leadership and racial integration the army way.* New York, NY: Basic Books.

69. Patten, Eileen, & Parker, Kim. (2011). Women in the U.S. military: Growing share, distinctive profile. *Pew Research Center.* Retrieved from www.pewsocialtrends.org/2011/12/22/women-in-the-u-s-military-growingshare-distinctive-profile/; Office of the Assistant Secretary of Defense for Personnel and Readiness, Department of Defense, Population Representation in the Military Services Annual Report, 2013.

70. Melin, J. (2016). Desperate choices: Why Black women join the US military at higher rates than men and all other racial and ethnic groups. *New England Journal of Public Policy, 28*(2), p. 8.

71. Office of the Deputy Assistant Secretary of Defense (Military Community and Family Policy), 2012 Demographics. Profile of the Military Community. pp. 1–221, p. 40.

72. Brennan, T. J. *Women in combat? Sometimes marines react.* Retrieved from http://atwar.blogs.nytimes.com/2013/01/29/women-in-combat-some-marines-react/?_r=0

73. Kimmel, M. (2008). *Guyland: The perilous world where boys become men.* New York, NY: Harper Collins.

74. *Sports-related employment is on the rise and creating jobs in other industries, according to new research from CareerBuilder and economic modeling specialists.* Retrieved from www.prnewswire.com/news-releases/sports-related-employment-is-on-the-rise-and-cre ating-jobs-in-other-industries-according-to-new-research-from-careerbuilder-and-economic-modeling-specialists-272991311.html

75. See *Paying for the Party* for an excellent analysis of sports management and gender.

76. www.onetonline.org/link/summary/27–2023.00

77. BLS 2014, http://data.bls.gov/projections/occupationProj

78. Chesney-Lind, M., & Pasko, L. J. (2003). *The female offender: Girls, women and crime.* Thousand Oaks, CA: Sage.

79. Abidansky, H. (2009). *Organized crime.* Belmont, CA: Cengage Learning.

80. Kleemans, E. R., & de Poot, C. J. (2008). Criminal careers in organized crime and social opportunity structure. *European Journal of Criminology, 5*(1), 69–98.

81. *Teen violence statistics.* Retrieved from Teenviolencestatistics.com

82. Kleemans & de Poot, 2008.

83. Contreras, F. (2011). *Achieving equity for Latino students: Expanding the pathway to higher education through public policy.* New York, NY: Teachers College Press; Pew Research Center, 2013.

84. Huerta, A. H. (2015). "I didn't want my life to be like that": Gangs, college, or the military for Latino male high school students. *Journal of Latino/Latin American Studies, 7*(2), 119–132.

85. Ibid., p. 3.

86. Rios, V. M. (2009). The consequences of the criminal justice pipeline on black and Latino masculinity. *The Annals of the American Academy of Political and Social Science, 623*(1), 150–162.

87. Harris, A. P. (2000). *Gender, violence, race, and criminal justice.* Retrieved from www.nccd-crc.org/nccd/pubs/2007jan_justice_for_some.pdf (accessed April 10, 2008).

88. Lyman, M. D., & Potter, G. W. (2000). *Organized crime.* Upper Saddle River, NJ: Prentice Hall.

89. McCarthy, B., & Gartner, R. (2014, August). *Five facts about women's involvement in organized crime.* OUP Blog. Retrieved from www.blog.oup.com

90. Koerner et al., 1999, p. 7.

91. Szeman, I. (2015). Entrepreneurship as the new common sense. *South Atlantic Quarterly, 114*(3), 471–490.

92. Winn, J. (2004). Entrepreneurship: Not an easy path to top management for women. *Women in Management Review, 19*(3), 143–153.
93. Bushweller, K. (2001). The new networkers: The path to hot IT jobs begins in high school. *American School Board Journal, 188*(1), 16–19.
94. *Business Insider,* January 19, 2011.
95. *Forbes,* December 19, 2013.
96. Caldwell, C. (2007, February 25). The way we live now: What a college education buys. *The New York Times Magazine,* pp. 15–16.
97. Friedman, T. (2014, February 16). Start-up America: Our best hope. *The New York Times,* p. SR1.
98. How we hire. Retrieved from www.google.com/about/careers/lifeatgoogle/hiringprocess/
99. International New York Times, October 5, 2013.
100. By the numbers. (2014). *National Center for Women & Information Technology (NCWIT).* Retrieved from www.ncwit.org/bythenumbers.
101. Shih, J. (2006). Circumventing discrimination gender and ethnic strategies in Silicon Valley. *Gender & Society, 20*(2), 177–206.
102. Turkle, S. (1988). Computational reticence: Why women fear the intimate machine. In C. Kramerae (Ed.), *Technology and women's voices: Keeping in touch* (pp. 41–61). New York, NY and London, UK: Routledge and Kegan Paul; Cockburn, C. (1988). *Machinery of dominance: Women, men, and technical know-how.* Boston, MA: Northeastern University Press.
103. International New York Times, May 28, 2014.
104. Misa, T. J. (Ed.). (2011). *Gender codes: Why women are leaving computing.* San Francisco, CA: John Wiley & Sons, pp. 11–12.
105. Cheryan, S., Plaut, V., Handron, C., & Hudson, L. (2013). The stereotypical computer scientist: Gendered media representations as a barrier to inclusion for women. *Sex Roles, 69*(1–2), 3, 58–71.
106. Alper, J. (1993). The pipeline is leaking women all the way. *Science, 260,* 409–411.
107. Margolis, J., & Fisher, A. (2002). *Unlocking the clubhouse: Women in computing.* Cambridge, MA: MIT Press.
108. Misa, 2011, p. 6.
109. *Trends in the gaming industry.* Retrieved from www.esrb.org/about/video-game-industry-statistics.aspx
110. *Top five gaming industry trends for 2015.* Retrieved from www.internap.com/2014/12/01/top-five-online-gaming-industry-trends-2015/
111. Stuart, K. *How to get into the games industry: An insider's guide.* Retrieved from www.theguardian.com/technology/2014/mar/20/how-to-get-into-the-games-industry-an-insiders-guide
112. *Is a degree necessary in the video game industry?* Retrieved from www.howcast.com/videos/500611-is-a-degree-necessary-video-game-careers/
113. Gandel, C. *Discover 11 hot college majors that lead to jobs.* Retrieved from www.usnews.com/education/best-colleges/articles/2013/09/10/discover-11-hot-college-majors-that-lead-to-jobs
114. Reported in *The Orlando Sentinel,* August 23, 2014.
115. Haines, L. (2004). *Why are there so few women in games?* Manchester, UK: Media Training Northwest.
116. Burrows, L. *Women remain outsiders in the video game industry.* Retrieved from www.bostonglobe.com/business/2013/01/27/women-remain-outsiders-video-game-industry/275JKqy3rFylT7TxgPmO3K/story.html
117. Gamasutra Salary Survey 2014. Retrieved from www.gamesetwatch.com/2014/09/05/GAMA14_ACG_SalarySurvey_F.pdf
118. Burrows, L. *Women remain outsiders in the video game industry.* Retrieved from www.bostonglobe.com/business/2013/01/27/women-remain-outsiders-video-game-industry/275JKqy3rFylT7TxgPmO3K/story.html

119. Winn, J., & Heeter, C. (2009). Gaming, gender, and time: Who makes time to play? *Sex Roles, 61*(1), 1–13. DOI:10.1007/s11199-009-9595-7

120. Crook, D. and McGill, B. (2016. November 30). Who's working in the 'gig economy'? The Wall Street Journal Online. Retrieved from https://www.wsj.com/articles/whos-working-in-the-gig-economy-1479920400

121. Hanauer, N., & Rolf, D. (2015). Shared security, shared growth. *Democracy Journal, 37*, p. 6.

122. Economic Modeling Specialists, International. As noted in Scheiber, N. (2015, July 12). Growth in the 'gig economy' fuels workforce anxieties. The New York Times. Retrieved from https://www.nytimes.com/2015/07/13/business/rising-economic-insecurity-tied-to-decades-long-trend-in-employment-practices.html?_r=0

123. Perez, T. E. *Rising to the challenge of a 21st century workforce*. Retrieved from www.bls.gov/opub/mlr/2015/article/rising-to-the-challenge-of-a-21st-century-workforce.htm

124. Fox, J. *Keep digging to find the gig economy*. Retrieved from www.bloombergview.com/articles/2015–09–25/keep-digging-to-find-the-size-of-the-gig-economy

125. Horowitz, S. *The Gig Economy Goes Mainstream*. Retrieved from FreelancersUnion.org

126. Torpey E., & Hogan, A. *Working in a gig economy*. Retrieved from www.bls.gov/career-outlook/2016/article/what-is-the-gig-economy.htm

127. Taylor, K. *The difference between a solopreneur and a side-gigger*. Retrieved from Entrepreneur.com www.entrepreneur.com/article/239522

128. Hightower, J. *Need proof that the "gig economy" is painful? Just ask people who work for Uber or Lyft*. Retrieved from www.salon.com/2016/05/12/need_proof_that_the_gig_economy_is_painful_just_ask_people_who_work_for_uber_or_lyft/

129. Hill, S. *How big is the gig economy?* Retrieved from https://medium.com/the-wtf-economy/how-big-is-the-gig-economy-e674c7986a28#.pbuytk83h

130. Schieber, N. *Growth in the 'gig economy' fuels work force anxieties*. Retrieved from www.nytimes.com/2015/07/13/business/rising-economic-insecurity-tied-to-decades-long-trend-in-employment-practices.html?ref=business

131. Greenhouse, S. (2015, December 7). Uber: On the road to nowhere. Uber drivers are getting creative in their fight for workplace rights. *The American Prospect*. Retrieved from http://prospect.org/article/road-nowhere-3

132. www.washingtonpost.com/news/wonkblog/wp/2015/01/22/now-we-know-many-drivers-uber-has-and-how-much-money-theyre-making%E2%80%8B/

133. *Uber's ever-renewing workforce: One-fourth of its current U.S. drivers joined last month*. Retrieved from www.forbes.com/sites/ellenhuet/2015/01/22/uber-study-workforce/#37c12d2d1244

134. Nagy, E. (2015, January 22). The women leaders driving Lyft's impressive growth. Fast Company Inc. Retrieved from https://www.fastcompany.com/3041106/most-creative-people/the-women-leaders-driving-lyfts-impressive-growth

135. *Women in the labor force: a databook*. Retrieved from www.bls.gov/cps/cpsaat11.pdf

136. *Uber's ever-renewing workforce: One-fourth of its current U.S. drivers joined last month*. Retrieved from www.forbes.com/sites/ellenhuet/2015/01/22/uber-study-workforce/#37c12d2d1244; *Taxi and limo drivers in the US*. Retrieved from www.schallerconsult.com/taxi/taxidriversummary.htm

137. *Freelancing in America*. Retrieved from http://prospect.org/article/road-nowhere-3

138. www.upwork.com/press/2015/10/01/freelancers-union-and-upwork-release-new-study-revealing-insights-into-the-almost-54-million-people-freelancing-in-america/

139. Rosin, H. (2010, June 8). The end of men. *The Atlantic*. Retrieved from www.theatlantic.com/magazine, p. 4.

6

HIGHER EDUCATION, LESS POWER
Gender Equity Post-College

The promises of a college education are alluring and the payoffs for many are real: So strong is Americans' belief in the power of education to fix gender inequities that scholars and journalists in large numbers have declared that the shift in the rate at which women are graduating with college degrees fundamentally changes everything. The war against boys was fought and the end of men may be the result. Ringrose puts their argument this way:

> The educational failing boys' discourse of male disadvantage, inculcates what Foster (2001) calls a "presumptive equality"—the widespread belief that women have achieved equality with men in society. These sets of presumptions orienting educational debates bolster the quintessential . . . post-feminism argument "that girls and women are doing fine, feminism is unnecessary . . . the movement is over . . . girls have attained all the power they could ever want" and may actually "have too much power in the world."[1]

"Education is always the answer," agrees Covert, "for the person who would rather put the onus of eliminating sexism, racism, and class on individuals, not on the collective."[2] Americans have seen that on the whole, women are earning myriad college degrees at faster rates than men. Increases in white and Hispanic women's higher education participation, along with black women's continued historically higher rates of participation, indicate that at the very least, many women are invested in college enough to believe that its credentials and knowledge will gain them many things: better careers, stronger earning power, more knowledge, perhaps security.

But likening these developments to the wholesale upending of cultural norms that have favored men for centuries is, at the very least, dismissive of many realities; the claim of women's social domination via higher education indicates a blindness to the multiple ways in which the power of being male in the United States—particularly a white male—remains unshaken. Conflating college success with women's economic and sociopolitical dominance is damaging hyperbole; wholesale gender equity, particularly across racial, ethnic, and social class lines in the United States, remains a fiction. Not only is an increase in college numbers not evidence of a decrease in gender bias, the rise in women's successful college participation may signal a further *decrease* in women's social power and in the credentials they have so ambitiously earned.

Kathleen Gerson claims that we are "poised at a moment when changing lives are colliding with resistant institutions."[3] Tremendous shifts in the patterns and expectations of how people across their life courses engage in work, create families and friend networks, and pursue education have been evident in American life over the last 50 years. But cultural expectations are tenacious—men and women have internalized norms of masculinity and femininity, reminding them of what they are supposed to do and to be; race, ethnicity, and social class intersect and complicate these expectations. Combined with institutions whose organizational practices remain rooted in outdated and white-privileged ideas of gender, women's educational advances have not altered the ways in which they are allowed—and allow themselves—to live their lives.

The tensions between women's individual advances in educational achievement and Americans' conflicted beliefs about gender, race, and social class result in complicated and at times paradoxical outcomes, particularly for women who have operated with the sincere belief that gaining more formal education would advance not only their individual life trajectories but also contribute to overall greater gender equity. Underlying the female advantage in higher education arguments are unspoken questions: An advantage over whom? For what? Although women's increased educational attainment may offer greater job access and better pay to women than those without college credentials, it is not the case that they stand *pari passu* with men—not with those whose credentials match their own, and by many measures, not even with those men who have markedly fewer credentials and training.

Indeed, accumulating evidence indicates that women's successes in higher education may be reproducing if not also exacerbating the gender inequities that female advantage proponents claim have been eradicated. Men's navigation around traditional degree paths now shared or dominated by women, combined with cultural norms regarding women's romantic and familial roles and entrenched racial and economic barriers, offers an uncomfortable vision: American women may be better educated than men, but they are *not* better situated.

Powerful Sex and Romance Norms Influence Women's and Men's Behaviors in College . . . and Out of It

The attainment of an "M.R.S." degree was a serious joke that resonated for middle and upper class white women and men in the mid-20th century: Many Americans thought (and some still do, as we saw in Chapter 1) it perfectly logical that women would enroll in college primarily as a way to find a husband. For many, earning a college degree was about being exposed to an eligible pool of men, as well as preparation for a career and greater knowledge accumulation. Reframing college as a marriage market may, in fact, have been a way to mitigate some of the discomfort of the influx of women in academia. As women on college campuses became the norm, however, such societal assumptions about women's reasons for attending higher education faded, as women's seriousness about studying, their independence, and their plans for future employment became evident.

Astin's seminal analysis, *The Changing American College Student*, chronicled the shifting trends in the attitudes of college freshmen between 1966 to 1996 highlighting, among other surprising data, that the proportion of female college freshmen who agreed with the statement "the activities of married women are best confined to the home and family" dropped from 44 percent to 19 percent during that period.[4] Four years later, the situation on college campuses seemed to be similar: Stone and McKee's study of almost 1,200 college undergraduates found that over 60 percent of both men and women, consistently across race, ethnicity, and social class, felt that a career was "most important" in their lives.[5]

Yet the career aspirations of college women, then and now, sit nestled within a "culture of romance"[6] that cross-cuts against women's career goals. This normative culture of heterosexual romance, sex, and dating has had a continued effect on college men's and women's behaviors, which in turn affects their actions post-college. Studies of dating behavior in colleges have elicited the same gendered patterns of interaction over the last 40 years.[7]

In the early 1980s, anthropologists Holland and Eisenhart conducted one of the first studies of how the archetypal dating system works in conjunction with higher education.[8] As mentioned in Chapter 1, the researchers surveyed over 300 women at one predominantly white and one predominantly black university over four years, finding that as the participants progressed throughout their schooling, the culture of romance on campus encouraged many women to compromise their own career goals in order to support their male partners' goals. White women were particularly susceptible to changing their career plans in order to fit future plans of men they hoped to remain with, a surprising finding even in the late 1980s.

Black women in the study also indicated interest in marriage, but stated that it conflicted with their plans for financial independence, and as such, indicated their intent to work after college before pursuing long-term relationships.[9]

These findings anticipated trends in black women's future college attendance and marriage rates; in 2007, close to 60 percent of all black women in America had attended some college or earned a bachelor's degree, but they are currently among the group of women least likely to be married.[10] Black women are also the least likely among all racial groups to marry outside their race; only 12 percent of the black women who married in 2013, for example, married men who were not black.[11] Taking these trends into account, claims about women's college degree attainment in relationship to their proclivity for marriage need to be examined differently for white and black women in particular.

Even accounting for racial differences, Holland and Eisenhart maintained that from an anthropological perspective, the behavior of the women in their study made sense: American culture prizes male achievement in status and financial reward, whereas women are still judged on an underlying assessment of their relationships with men. This reality seems to lead to more marriage among white college-educated women, whereas with black women it leads to less, thereby decreasing black women's opportunities to gain financially from long-term partnerships.[12] In a similar later study, Eisenhart[13] described college participants' gradual acceptance of this system of romance, along with their acceptance of diminishing academic agency, as a kind of cultural acquisition: That is, the participants develop gradual expertise in the system (in this case, romance) to the point at which they become agents in their own reproduction of the pattern and deny any frustration they might have with it. They come to accept and even welcome that following their boyfriends' career trajectories and dreams is not only romantic, but *right*.

This alteration of their career goals by women themselves—the reproduction of their own inequality—calls into question the assumption that college credentials are a chief architect of social equity post-college. Eisenhart's, as well as Kerr's "perfect future day fantasy" findings (Chapter 1) mirror those in Astin's study, even at the end of his 30-year investigation: While only 19 percent of all his female college respondents agreed that women's rightful place was at home, 33 percent of all college men in his study believed that women's lives should revolve around home and children. Given Holland and Eisenhart's window into the ways that college women bent their career plans for men, Astin's findings resonate. These researchers' results challenge the female advantage notion and its assumptions that women's overall success in college means that men's beliefs about their future families and children no longer apply.

Park and colleagues, in their recent investigation of women in science, technology, engineering, and math (STEM) majors,[14] hypothesized that college women distanced themselves from STEM majors whenever they were specifically prompted to think about the cultural message that men do not like smart women.[15] As Holland and Eisenhart found 30 years earlier, Park and company discovered that when their participants' romantic goals were activated by environment or personal choice, women were less interested and invested in STEM activities, pursuits, and careers. Even *viewing* romantic images or overhearing about a romantic date—everyday occurrences—led study participants to report less positive attitudes toward STEM, and to show less preference for majoring in math/science relative to other fields. Interestingly, women in this study reported *greater* interest in majoring in what are typically defined as feminine domains (e.g., arts, English/foreign languages) when primed with romantic goals, but for men, there were no such changes in major preferences when primed with romantic goals.[16]

Park and colleagues observed that women are socialized to prioritize romance and downplay power and autonomy, but what makes their study especially compelling is that they identified specific mechanisms that triggered women's lower interest in what are considered the masculine domains of math and science.[17] Romantic cues such as hearing or being part of discussions about dating, as well as more direct activities like pursuing romantic goals (e.g., going on dates, flirting) were significantly related to women's lesser pursuits of their intellectual goals. As the researchers put it, "Whereas men are encouraged to excel in masculine domains, women are socialized to downplay intelligence goals in masculine domains in romantic contexts, consistent with traditional romantic scripts and gender norms that exist in Western cultures."[18] Small and frequent reminders that romance and "male" intellectual pursuits are not compatible with women's ambition, particularly in male-dominated domains, create the fabric of many women's college experiences—a stereotype-threat "costume" that becomes daily clothing—and a message that translates to incompatibility of romance and career aspirations for women in general. These incompatible messages, then, help explain how women could have a college credential and a set of potentially emancipatory experiences, but not a mindset that allows them to use these things to bring about sociocultural and economic equity.

More recently, Armstrong and Hamilton demonstrated how gendered cultural patterns interact with social class norms in college, revealing how college women are still subject to powerful romantic norms. In their study of women in what they classify as a "party dorm," the researchers showcased mechanisms of gender norm replication within social events on college campuses.[19] Their findings—that in matters of [heterosexual] dating, beauty matters more than brains, and "pretty girls" get attention and date higher social class men—are not surprising; where their data are revelatory is their explication of the ways in which higher education constructs students' experiences, playing directly off of the gendered norms it purports to equalize. Armstrong and Hamilton's analysis pointed to, among many structural facets, the recent university trend of creating undemanding majors that require little skill acquisition, but which focus instead on stereotypically feminine traits and country club-like socialization processes. Such majors, and the gendered expectations that accompany them, encourage too many women to take "easy majors" because they anticipate marrying wealthy men.[20]

"Easy majors," according to Armstrong and Hamilton, are "characterized by ease of obtaining a high GPA, little evidence of general skills improvement during college, and a heavy focus on appearance, personality, and charm."[21] Many of the women they studied were what the researchers termed "business lite" majors, those that existed outside the circle of the highly competitive business school at their university. Such majors included arts management, sport and recreational sport management, outdoor recreation and resource management, communications broadcasting, sports communication, and apparel merchandising. These majors allowed the women in them to be exempt from more rigorous college requirements (like the foreign language competency), to obtain higher GPAs by taking less demanding coursework, and to have time to participate in the college social and romantic networks to which they aspired. Many of the participants in Armstrong and Hamilton's study anticipated marrying financially well-off men, even as they experienced tension between fulfilling their own career aspirations and traditional gendered expectations of many of the men with whom they attended college.[22]

The easy-major route may be the "M.R.S. degree" in new packaging with an added considerations for social class. Directly admitting that one is attending college, even in part, for the purpose of finding a mate is no longer socially acceptable; focusing on less intense courses of study with the mindset that one will not be financially self-sufficient or professionally self-directed may be a new way to acquiesce to an old set of still-powerful gender norms. As the evidence from these researchers demonstrates, gendered expectations of women and men do not disappear at the college door. The tension between being a career-oriented college student and a woman may be strong, particularly for women who are first-generation college students. Less academically well-prepared than women from higher social class backgrounds, "first-gen" students have to negotiate new student identities that may conflict with family-of-origin gender norms.[23]

Further, the pressure to succeed in college at any cost, given the pressures that come with being the first in a family to attend college, may lead women to gravitate toward majors that seem, or are, in fact, easier than others. These majors, according to Armstrong and Hamilton, are often cast as "feminine" majors.[24] Between increased familial pressures to succeed in college overall, and internalized cultural messages to sublimate future career goals to those of men, college women without adequate messages to the contrary may choose to alter their academic trajectories because the culture of romance, and perhaps their cultures of origin, quietly reminds them that their career and intellectual needs are not as important as men's needs are.

Marriage market analyses lend complexity to this belief. In 2014, the Pew Research Center reported that for the first time ever, American women are "marrying down" educationally; that is, wives are now more likely to have greater educational attainment than their husbands.

In 1960, 13.5 percent of newlywed husbands had more education than their wives, whereas only 6.9 percent of wives had more education than their

More Women Marrying "Down"
% of currently married couples

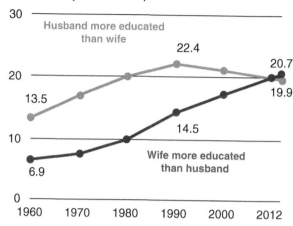

FIGURE 6.1 Husbands' and Wives' Educational Achievement, 1960–2012

Source: Pew Research Center analysis of the Decennial Census and American Community Survey, IPUMS files.

husbands—in other words, more women than men married educationally "up." In 2012, that pattern was reversed for the first time—20.7 percent of wives had more education attainment than husbands, whereas only 19.9 percent of men had more education attainment than their wives. The researchers report that this pattern is likely because more men and women attend college overall—the number of couples in which *both* spouses have a college degree has risen sevenfold between 1960 and 2012.

As indicated earlier in this chapter, "marrying up" and "marrying down" are not racially monolithic trends. In addition to black women's low rates of marriage overall, in combination with their comparatively low rates of marriage outside their race, their marriages are disproportionally likely to be to someone with a lower education level than they have; black men's college degree attainment rates have dropped considerably in the last 30 years. By 2007, 57 percent of U.S.-born black women aged 30–44 had attended (36 percent) or graduated from (21 percent) college, compared to the 48 percent of black men who had attended (31 percent) or graduated (17 percent).[25] The sharp decline in marriage rates for black women and black men overall, in spite of black women's striking rise in educational attainment, may be key to explaining some of the disparate effects that college completion has on women of different races.

Further complicating the effects of marriage and education is the fact that marrying down educationally does not mean marrying down economically. The 2014 Pew Report also indicated that the majority of newlywed women who married someone with less education actually "married up" economically. According to these data, in 2012, only 39 percent of newlywed women who married a spouse with less education earned more than their husband; a majority of them (58 percent) made less than their husband.[26] The 2011 National Research Center for Career and Technical Education report corroborates these conclusions. The Center identified 16 career clusters that represented the full array of related occupational opportunities and education requirements. The report's authors found that well-paying, high school level jobs were available in male-dominated career clusters: manufacturing and construction. (The transportation business had not been affected by Uber and Lyft at the time of this study.) See table 6.1. Further,

> The study confirm[ed] that women need postsecondary education to earn the same wages as men with only a high school diploma. For instance, whereas a man can earn $35,000 with a high school diploma in the manufacturing career cluster, a woman must obtain a postsecondary credential and work in healthcare to earn as much.[27]

In other words, many women will have to choose to "marry up" or "credential up" just to achieve economic parity with men. The first scenario asks that a woman partner with someone in order to achieve economic stability, and the second asks that she spend more money and time to achieve credentials that allow for her to achieve *less* stability than men with the same level of education.

Gender role attitudes held by young adults offer important clues about how they plan to balance their work and romantic lives.[28] If women and men are still strongly primed by traditional gendered cultural expectations about romance, marriage, and their future family lives, their pursuit of college degrees will be shaped by these expectations. Coupled with economic realities that virtually all adult men and women face, earning a college degree may be the equivalent of an "unfunded mandate" for women—necessary credentials they are responsible for earning and for which they must pay, but for which they receive no advantage over the men they work with, or the men they love.

Parenthood Norms

Deeply connected with the culture of romance, American cultural norms around gender and parenthood—specifically motherhood—affect college women's and men's behaviors, even though only 26 percent of all undergraduate college students are parents, according to a 2014 study from the Institute for Women's Policy Research.[29] Long before they consider whether to have children, young men's and women's beliefs about what is best for their *future* children shape their college behavior. The reams of research and numerous popular articles devoted to the "work–family debate" attest to its continuing presence in Americans' lives. Their overwhelming conclusion: Just like romance, cultural expectations about parenthood are formidable determinants of both sexes' behaviors.

TABLE 6.1 Best-Paying Opportunities for Women in Middle Skill Jobs and Best-Paying Opportunities for Men With High School Diploma or Less

The best opportunities to earn a living wage with less than high school or high school diplomas are concentrated in career clusters where men dominate.

Career cluster	New and replacement job vacancies 2008–2018 (thousands)		High school diploma or less (%)	Males per cluster (%)	Rate of growth (% change in employment)	Fastest rate of growth (rank)
	Less than high school	High school diploma				
Manufacturing	420	1,250	9	71	−1	16
Architecture and Construction	760	1,200	11	98	7	11
Transportation, Distribution, and Logistics	560	1,800	13	85	4	14
Hospitality and Tourism	1,670	3,190	27	50	12	6
All other clusters	1,230	5,670	40			

60%

Source: The Georgetown University Center on Education and the Workforce forecast of educational demand through 2018.

Under the female advantage argument, college gives women credentials that make them equally as powerful as, or more powerful than, men but the logic assumes that becoming a parent is a gender-neutral event. College credentials are women's, but so is the responsibility to negotiate using them alongside motherhood. The "cult of true womanhood" may be gone, but according to Poelmans, "normative beliefs about working parents and careers are imbedded in the multiple layers of context created by the spousal relationship, the occupation, the organization, and the national or ethnic culture."[30] Studies of college, women, men, and careers often sidestep the existence of masculine "breadwinner" ideologies that, together with long-standing debates of what it means to be a "good mother" in America, are still very powerful influences on women's and men's behaviors in college, regardless of whether or not they have children of their own.

Studies of recent college students illustrate this point. Goldberg and colleagues surveyed 955 culturally and ethnically diverse college undergraduates, asking them about their attitudes toward maternal employment and their own employment, as well as their work–care domains. They found that the majority of the students had mothers who had returned to paid work when they were very young, and consistent with the power of modeling behavior, these students generally believed that there were few costs [to children] of maternal employment. Yet these same students also indicated that they saw few benefits to maternal employment; that is, beyond the income gained by working, students in this study did not see that their future children gained enough materially, or they themselves gained enough interaction, perspective, or career advancement, to justify their continued working. Men's continued working after parenthood was never questioned, and male college students in this study saw maternal employment as more problematic than women did.[31]

In a later study, Goldberg and Lucas-Thompson investigated the impact of young women's beliefs about the effects of maternal employment on their career decisions. They hypothesized that if college women overestimated the negative and underestimated the positive effects of full-time maternal employment for children, they would make educational and career decisions while in school that would render them as the primary child care provider. Their results revealed that overall, college women consistently overestimated the negative effects of full-time maternal employment on children; women who held to traditional gender norms unsurprisingly had the most negative stereotypes about mothers' full-time employment.[32] Hispanic women in this study had the most positive views of mothers' full-time employment. (Black women were not part of the sample.)

Goldberg and colleagues' results illustrated that stereotypes remain powerful influences on women, with white women in particular strongly affected by larger cultural expectations that often communicate traditional gender ideologies.[33] Left to negotiate their own choices about college majors, activities, and career goals, many 21st-century women continue to reproduce a stereotype that is built on gendered tradition more than fact. In 2004, Goldin examined how these beliefs could still remain—how female college students managed to hold onto ideas about motherhood and work that many people would dismiss as outmoded. Using labor force data and demographic histories of women, she identified five distinct cohorts of women who had negotiated both motherhood and the workforce (see figure 6.2).

Goldin notes it is only recently that women have been able to think realistically about having career and family simultaneously; roughly one quarter of women in the fifth cohort (approximate birth interval 1958–68) reported attaining both. This "long road to the fast track," as Goldin states, is indicative of "loosening constraints and shifting barriers" over time,[34] and it would be reasonable, given these data, to assume that the number of women having-it-all would continue to increase over time. Yet at the end of the fifth cohort boundary, Goldin observed a leveling off in female labor force participation rates; by 1990, women were no longer showing steep gains—or even rises—in full-time work. The workforce participation rate of women in their 30s has stayed at about 76 percent for the last 15 years, though Goldin found that during this time, women also had children later in life, thus increasing the child care burden even as they continued working.

The norms of modern work, as Goldin and others continue to find, are still set on male-as-breadwinner ideologies in which women are expected to be primary child care givers and men are expected to be full-time pursuers of careers. "The social conditions that make . . . shared parenting and housework possible," Arlie Hochschild famously said, "remain out of reach."[35] Goldin notes that early in the feminist movement, women pushed for flexibility of workplace and work hours so that men could also participate in home and work, but the cultural understanding required to go from an attitude that men and women "could share" both, to one in which men and women "will share" both did not—and has not—occurred.

Thébaud and Pedulla recently offered mixed evidence, with muted optimism, that young men and women might someday negotiate different work–family responsibility arrangements. The researchers noted the cultural clash between employers' continued desire for "ideal workers" who are singularly devoted to the workplace at the expense of almost everything (and everyone) else, and

TABLE 6.2   Five Cohorts of College Graduate Women

Cohort	Interval when graduated	Approximate birth interval	Characterization of desired (or achieved) family and career from four-year college path
1	1900–19	1878–97	Family or career
2	1920–45	1898–1923	Job then family
3	1946–65	1924–43	Family then job
4	1966–79	1944–57	Career then family (13–18 percent)
5	1980–90	1958–68	Career and family (21–27 percent)

Source: Georgetown University Center on Education and the Workforce.

(white) culture's increased expectation that parents (particularly mothers) be "ideal." Yet even if young men had access to supportive work–family policies, the researchers found, the men in their study would be no more or less likely to prefer an egalitarian relationship with their partner, whereas women were significantly more likely to prefer such a relationship.[36] Citing men's privileged structural position in labor markets and families, Thébaud and Pedulla argue that men would have more to lose in income, social status, and masculinity if they were to take advantage of such policies. In a subsequent study, the researchers examined whether the effect of young men's work–life attitudes are dependent on their perceptions of masculinity norms about these issues. "Men's responses to supportive work-family policies," Thébaud and Pedulla state, "depend largely on their perceptions of what they believe their male peers want, and by extension, what kind of behavior they would hold them accountable to."[37] In short, they found that influencing men's attitudes about gender equity, at least as measured by willingness to adopt a work–life equity with their partners, might depend on men seeing that "other guys are doing it too."

Studies of current workplace culture reflect the attitudinal and practical ambivalence found by Goldberg and others: Fathers who embody the "breadwinner" status are still rewarded by the marketplace. Williams found that male breadwinners married to traditional homemakers earned 30 percent more than workers in two-job families, and were regarded with more favor at work.[38] Current college students—women and men alike—indicate that they understand they will likely be held to these same working norms as well; young adults are primed to reproduce the cultural ideology of which they are a part. Fuegen and colleagues offered an illustration of this dynamic: Their study of 200 undergraduates revealed that the students already expected that males would be held to less strict workplace performance and commitment standards when they became fathers because employers understood that men were "the providers" and needed to maintain their jobs even if they were not performing up to standards.[39] Likewise, both male and female students anticipated that motherhood would have a detrimental effect on women's career opportunities because of the stereotype that mothers are less professionally committed.

Williams offers that while men may well be policed into this breadwinner role,[40] the surrounding ideology hurts men as well as women, shaming men who do not live up to the provider status, and making conditions in which they can comfortably change their working definitions of masculinity daunting. Jacobs and Gerson echo this idea; their analysis of the 1997 *Changing Workforce Survey* data indicated that many men with young children wanted to spend more time at home with them, but that workforce pressure to be the financial provider did not allow them to do so.[41] Gerson's 2009 study of 18–32 year olds about their experiences growing up, their work and family strategies, and their future outlooks elaborated extensively on these earlier findings; interviews revealed young women and men who professed wanting similar, egalitarian ways of working and living, but who were also preparing for a very inegalitarian reality. Gerson writes,

> Despite the large overlap in women's and men's aspirations, their second-best strategies point to a new gender divide that differs starkly with the one touted by media analysts and social critics. In contrast to the popular argument that young women are "opting out" of the workplace, almost three-quarters of the women . . . see work as essential to their survival and marriage as an appropriate option only if and when they can find the right partner. Men, however, worry that equal parenting will cost them at work, which they believe must remain their first priority. Seventy percent of men are planning to fall back on a neo-traditional arrangement that leaves room for their partner to work but reserves the status of primary breadwinner for themselves.[42]

Men-as-breadwinner, of course, also reinforces the companion ideology of women-as-good-mother. The belief that women who work full time and who do not subscribe to a certain kind of motherhood are not "good mothers" is even more powerful than the expectation of motherhood itself. For women in college, many of whom already try to answer the cultural expectations of perfection in everything from grades to weight to participation in activities, this powerful cultural construct further influences women's decisions about their college majors, careers, and their everyday student behaviors. Understanding how this gendered expectation shapes women's college participation is critical to seeing how higher education credentials do not buy women the power they seek, or offer them the equity that college completion promises.

Ideal Mother, White Mother

The centrality of motherhood in cultural constructions of women's identities is what some now refer to as the "ascendant ideology of intensive mothering"—that is, being a good mother is not enough. Now, one needs to be an *ideal mother*.[43] Susan J. Douglas defines it this way:

> The insistence that no woman is complete or fulfilled unless she has kids, that women remain the best primary caretakers of children, and that to be a remotely decent mother, a woman has to devote her entire physical, psychological, emotional, and intellectual well-being, 24/7, to her children.[44]

In the academic and popular press, it is impossible for women *and men* to escape others' beliefs and idealized norms of what "good mothers" should be and do. From women's magazine articles to all-out online rants, the society in which some claim gender equity has been realized nonetheless reveals strong opinions about mothers who go to work:

> Mothers who choose to work full-time jobs and routinely leave their young children with others for much of the day are not normal. . . . Maybe a little stigma is exactly what [working mothers] deserve for abandoning their children. [As a society] we are committed to "leaving no child behind" unless it is by his mother hustling off to make her career.[45]

Given that by 2000, 60 percent of all married couples in the United States had two earners, and single-parent families, overwhelmingly headed by women, claimed a growing proportion of U.S. households,[46] such a statement sounds ridiculous to many younger college students, more than half of whom grew up with mothers who were part of the labor force for some if not all of their childhoods.[47] Born in a cultural moment in which they and their partners assumed that women worked for pay at the same time they mothered, most young women in college no longer think that there will be a question that they can have a career and children, if they "want" them.[48] But no matter what they say they believe, they still have heard the message that women are supposed to be at home with children. This explains how traditional college-aged women—and most of their male friends—can espouse support for women having careers and children simultaneously, while also believing that *ideal* mothers do not work full time or at all.[49]

Recent studies explain how some of the ideology of the "ideal mother" works to disable the messages of career pursuit and pay equity that college educations promise. Higher education was designed around men's lives[50] (both faculty members and students) and men and women see, firsthand, that men are still the star professors, lead administrators, and board members. The new, "hot" majors—STEM, engineering, neuroscience, digital technologies of many kinds—are built around measures of accomplishment defined and evaluated by male standards of practice that assume future workers in these fields will have wives, ex-wives, or partners who take on most of the child-rearing responsibilities and housework so that they can pursue their own academic careers.[51] Coupled with gendered romantic norms, the tension between ideal mother norms and ideal worker norms—defined by majors that lead to professions that demand one's "all"—pushes college students in many cases to create what Gerson names a "neo-traditional" view of parenthood. "[T]his outlook," Gerson writes, "makes room for an employed spouse without undermining men's position as specialists in breadwinning. Because this strategy frames women's—but not men's—work as 'optional,' it converts belief in a child's need for intensive parenting into an injunction for 'intensive mothering.'"[52]

College women, as a whole, understand that working and leaving one's children in anyone's care other than their own is still devalued; the message is even clearer in policy than it is in expectations for maternal practice. The United States is one of the only countries in the world that lacks universal paid maternity leave—who will take care of the children if women do not intend to leave paid work?[53] Further, there is no national cultural or business support for high quality, part-time work and multiple surveys indicate that many mothers do not seek employment when they lack adequate child care.[54] "Good" jobs in the United States are usually regarded as an all-or-nothing proposition, as jobs like those of Silicon Valley reiterate. As Williams states: "Women will continue to be disadvantaged if employers insist in designing the most desirable jobs around someone available 24/7—in other words, a man with a stay-at-home wife."[55] The unspoken career rules of undergraduate education perpetuate this design, and let women know that they are expected to make an either-or decision.

Even more subterranean than discussions of the ideal mother is that the ideology of intensive mothering is largely based on constructions of a *white* mother. Because social and historical constructs of racial and income inequality influence the definition of ideal motherhood, they are based on white norms.[56] Women of color have historically needed to work—or been forced to do so. The first non-native, black women in this country worked as slaves, taking care of their own as well as other people's children as they did so; no debate about whether or not maternal employment was good for children entered their lives.[57] Except in rare cases, low-income women, working class women, black women, and other women of color have always been worker and mother simultaneously; they often hold "integrative views" of motherhood, and as such often see paid work as an important dimension of motherhood.[58]

Philyaw notes the relative absence of black women's voices in mainstream U.S. discourse about motherhood. In naming the dearth of "mommy memoirs" by writers of color, she underscores how the whiteness of the ideal mother construct contributes to the opaqueness of the argument that pits paid work against motherhood. "Black women have always worked," writes R. J. Barnes, who notes that in spite of this reality, white and privileged assumptions of intensive mothering begin to influence women of color as well once they pursue a college degree.[59] As more black women complete higher education, the conflicted identities of race, gender, and mother are likely to align more closely with white women's mothering ideologies.

A whitening-of-mothering ideology does not bode well for college-educated women of color, any more than it has enhanced equity in white men and women's gender relationships. Gerson's "Changing Lives, Resistant Institutions" study also found that the overwhelming majority of men and women she interviewed—across race, ethnicity, and social class lines—were committed to share paid work and family caretaking.[60] If motherhood becomes "whiter" as women become more credentialed, the patterns already evident seem to indicate less equality than these men and women anticipate.

Motherhood Penalties, Fatherhood Bonuses

Once in the paid workforce, economic penalties for mothers continue to influence women's decisions about pursuing their degrees. Women know that not only will female college graduates likely make less than their male classmates in their first job no matter what school they attended, major they chose, grades they got, or job they accepted—they also are fairly certain that they will be penalized for becoming mothers (see figure 6.3).[61] The Pew Research Center found in their 2013 *Social & Demographic Trends* project that 63 percent of the Millennial women (aged 18–32 years) in their survey believe that they will be paid less than men for doing the same job, and assume that if and when they have children, it will be harder for them to advance in their careers.[62]

In fact, these beliefs reflect reality. In the same study, researchers found that "among working parents of all ages with children younger than 18, mothers are three times as likely as fathers to say that being a working parent has made it harder for them to advance in their job or career."[63] Corbett and Hill of the American Association of University Women confirm that women just one year out of college who were working full time earned, on average, 80 percent of what their male peers earned, even after controlling for hours worked, college major, occupation, and employment sector.[64] According to Pew Research Center data, this disparity worsens quickly, though it differs according to racial and ethnic categories.

If the gender pay gap exists just 12 months out of college, and most women expect that their earnings and opportunities will diminish upon getting married and having children, then it is not surprising that women, while in college, make decisions that anticipate—and perhaps try to compensate for—further gender biases.

Still more confusing, if not also galling, is the fatherhood *bonus* that seems to be applied to many men after having children, even as women experience a motherhood penalty. Michele Budig, researcher for the *Third Way*, reports that becoming a father often leads to "significant wage bonuses for men that cannot be explained by differential selection into fatherhood on factors that lead to higher wages."[65] Fathers' (or their partners') changed work hours following the birth of a child do not explain this bonus. Budig concludes that fatherhood may be acting as a signaling device, indicating characteristics valued by employers such as greater work commitment, stability, and deservingness. In other words, employers may interpret men's willingness to become fathers as indicators that they are people who will remain loyal, not only to their families, but to their work organizations as well.

By comparison, women across the racial and social class spectrum are negatively impacted by motherhood when it comes to their employment. The "motherhood penalty" is well-documented, though it is most severe for those who are least educated and earn the least to begin with.[66] The average penalty for women is a 4 percent decrease in salary for each child she bears, though the figure can be as high as 6 percent for low-wage earners, and almost nonexistent for high-wage

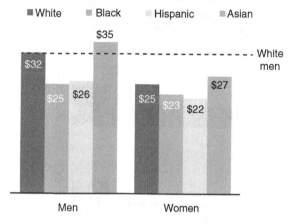

Controlling for education, white men still out-earned most groups in 2015

■ White   ■ Black   Hispanic   ■ Asian

FIGURE 6.2   Median Hourly Earnings Among Those Aged 25 and Older With Bachelor's Degree or More

Note: Based on civilian, non-institutionalized, full- or part-time workers with positive earnings. Self-employed workers are excluded. Hispanics are of any race. Whites, blacks and Asians include only non-Hispanics. Asians include Native Hawaiian and Pacific Islanders.

Source: Pew Research Center tabulations of 2015 Current Population Survey data.

earners.[67] Nonetheless, having a college degree (or several degrees) does not exempt women from this penalty.

Finally, among those with the highest levels of college education, even policies intended to mitigate against motherhood penalties may be doing exactly the opposite. Tenure clock-stopping policies in higher education have been initiated in many universities in order to acknowledge and ameliorate the impact that childbirth and infancy have on faculty in their pursuit of tenure.[68] These policies theoretically allow women and men who are new parents to use some of the time in which they would be researching and writing to care for very young children, with the assumption that their academic work would be resumed at a regular speed in the future, thus leveling the field with non-childbearing colleagues (namely men). In a recent study, however, researchers found that after the implementation of a gender-neutral clock-stopping policy, the probability of females getting tenure at their university *decreased* by 22 percent, while male tenure rates at the same university *rose* by 19 percent.[69]

The researchers conclude that clock-stopping policies like the one they studied do not adequately reflect the productivity losses that come in the wake of having children.[70] With similar results in other high-skill, high-education occupations likely, the study points to the difficulty of ameliorating deep, long-standing gendered practices and time divisions between men and women who are raising

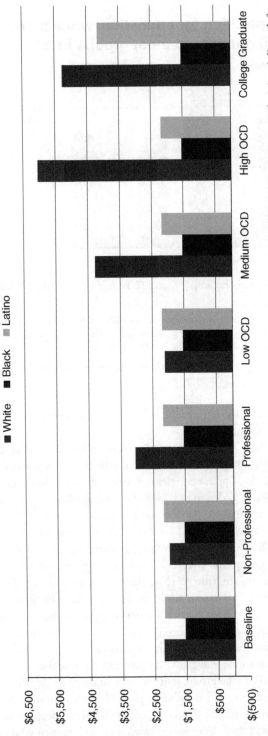

FIGURE 6.3 Fatherhood Bonus in Dollars, by Professional Status, Occupational Cognitive Demands (OCD), and Race/Ethnicity, Adjusted for Human Capital

Source: The Third Way, 2014

children, even when a structural change—like the change in an institutional promotion policy—is attempted.

The Myth of "Opting Out"

An influential cultural meme illustrates the continued and neo-Victorian tensions surrounding college-educated mothers' workforce participation, and the influences that (mis)shape college women's understandings of their purportedly advantageous credentials. In a 2003 *New York Times Magazine* article, Lisa Belkin famously attempted to explain why some women with powerful professional careers leave the very positions for which college prepared them, offering the idea that one way to understand this phenomenon is to think of women choosing to leave the workforce as an "opt-out revolution":

> Why don't women run the world?
> Maybe it's because they don't want to.
> Attitudes cluster in place and time. This is particularly true of a college campus, where one-quarter of the student population turns over every year. Undergraduates tend to think that the school they find is the one that always was, with no knowledge of the worldview of those even a few short years before.[71]

This extraordinary turn in the way that the discussion of women and their increasing participation in higher education and the workforce was framed has shaped a large swath of public conversation over highly educated, white women's labor force participation throughout the last decade. "The opt-out narrative in American newspapers," writes Williams, "predominates over alternative narratives that give weight to social or family pressures pushing women out of the workforce."[72] Together with her colleagues at the *Center for Work Life Law*, Williams analyzed newspaper storylines from 1980–2006 to find that opt-out stories reified "traditional," white values of stay-at-home moms and breadwinner dads, thereby delivering a generation's worth of messages proclaiming that motherhood, fatherhood, and work at the turn of the American 21st century did not need to change, even though the women who fit this category accounted for only 5 percent of all married, stay-at-home mothers with working husbands.[73]

But much has changed: Most mothers now participate in the paid workforce. According to the Bureau of Labor Statistics, the labor force participation rate in 2013 of mothers with children under 18 years of age was 69.9 percent—74.7 percent for mothers with children 6–17 years of age, 63.9 percent for mothers with children under 6 years of age, 61.1 percent for mothers with children under 3 years of age, and 57.3 percent for mothers of infants. College women, of course, live in the cultural milieu that generates these data, and with the unspoken expectations of society and the partners with whom they are looking to live. Presumed to want powerful careers or at least highly paying and/or highly rewarding jobs after graduation, they also are presumed to be thinking about potential husbands or partners, children, and adult lives. They hear, see, and feel the narratives around them, undifferentiated by social class and race, communicating that they have "all" the advantages; they also hear, most perniciously, that many men will not choose them as partners and wives if they focus on their careers instead of being ideal romantic partners, wives, and mothers. Increased college attendance might not feel like an advantage over these realities.

Perhaps worse, even if a young woman does not want to be married or a mother, the potential for her to *be* one affects others' perception of her job performance and the realities of her job preparation, no matter how many college degrees she has.[74] This perception holds true across race and class lines. Burgess's review of the motherhood penalty literature[75] cites multiple studies showing that women's competence and organizational commitment are called into question if employers also see them as potential mothers.

Professions and Their Relationship to College Credentials

Not surprisingly, college students' internalized norms of masculinity and femininity, as well as their conflicting ideas about romance and parenthood, do not change once they graduate and find work. Thus, even though in 2012 women made up 63 percent of all accountants/auditors, 33 percent of all physicians, and 30 percent of all lawyers in America,[76] studies of these and other professions suggest that the rebalancing processes of patriarchal equilibrium work to diminish the prestige and pay of fields in which women now dominate: structural, cultural, and interactional mechanisms continue to shift, re-creating new albeit subtle, forms of gender discrimination.[77]

Uhlmann and Cohen observed this trend in their 2005 study of job discrimination, in which they found evidence that hiring committees redefined the criteria for job success according to the specific credentials that a candidate of the desired gender happened to have.[78] In other words, committee members' evaluation of a potential co-worker's success changed in order to have their gender and job perception align. Levanon, England, and Allison's investigation (see also Chapter 1) into what they termed "occupational feminism" explored this dynamic in depth. Questioning the relationship between occupational pay and the predominance of women in a specific profession, they analyzed 50 years of census data to determine if a profession that is already paid poorly attracts women, or if the number of women in a profession leads to lower pay. They found substantial evidence of a "devaluation view"—the effect that female dominance in a profession leads to subsequent later wage reductions.[79] In other words, as women begin to occupy a profession, its value, at least as measured by its average wage, begins to decrease.

Importantly, these researchers found no evidence that the relationship between women's dominance in a profession and its value worked in the opposite direction. That is, they did *not* find that as wages in a profession fell, employers tended to hire more women. According to this study, the effect women have on the economic value of a profession is unidirectional: It is women's increased presence in an occupation that causes its devaluation, not a devalued wage that leads women into the profession.

Exploring the relationship between gender, occupation, and value in different ways, numerous professions' employment data offer evidence that increased representation of women has not offered proportional decreases in bias against women in those professions, or in the structural inequities that maintain such bias. The academic community has studied this phenomenon, turning its investigatory lenses on itself: The 1999 MIT report on women and science was a famous and early case demonstrating that the increased presence of educated women did not change the underlying gender inequities of the institution. Rutgers University's analysis of Integrated Postsecondary Education Data System (IPEDS) data followed in 2003, finding that women made up 40 percent of all faculty members in the United States, but with each corresponding rise in rank, their numbers decreased; at the highest faculty level (professor), only 24 percent were women.[80]

Even as the numbers of highly ranked professors come closer to gender parity, the reward system in academia continues to shift, accommodating the work of men in new ways. The numbers of full-time, tenure-track positions in higher education are decreasing, being replaced with clinical and adjunct positions that offer little security or room for advancement—these ranks are filling with women.[81] Grant activity, an increasingly important and valued part of academic work as the funding structures of research change, is disproportionally and increasingly the work of men in research universities.[82] Further, the structure of academic decision-making, funding, and advancement is still rooted in individualistic mythology—that the "lone researcher" toils away with his data until he "discovers" something and is thereby rightly rewarded for his individual work.[83] This distance from everyday practices allows the structure to maintain, virtually invisibly, the myth of the male as the producer of new disciplinary truths, while women in the academy do the great majority of the "academic housekeeping" necessary to keep students happy, educated, and properly advised.[84]

Nowhere in the U.S. research hierarchy is the mythology of the lone researcher more rooted than in the STEM disciplines. Both in academe and other "bench" careers available upon graduation, the gender and race disparities in the natural sciences, digital and computer technologies, engineering, and mathematics continue to offer the most compelling evidence that women's numbers in any discipline are flags for changing stature and practice: Whether proportionally underrepresented (physics, chemistry, digital and computer technologies, engineering, mathematics) or overrepresented (biology, veterinary science, parts of earth science, family medicine, nursing), the proportion of women to men in these fields offers a continuing view of how power, importance, and advantage flow to where men are.

Numerous studies, articles, and calls for change have documented what is commonly referred to as the "leaky pipeline" in STEM fields, chronicling the loss of women from high school science classes through higher education and on to work in STEM professions.[85] At each stage of this path from early adolescence through one's establishment in a career, researchers have noted the loss of girls and women. Blickenstaff names nine different themes that cut across the "leaky pipeline" literature—from biological differences in men's and women's STEM abilities to a chilly climate for girls and women in science class to an inherent masculine worldview of the knowledge and study of science—concluding that science educators in higher education are responsible for amending the issues under their control.[86]

But the enormity of the gender cultural change process is such that even if scientists and science educators are successful in bringing more women into the field, this will not be sufficient in bringing more women into STEM careers. In fact, the mounting evidence regarding women's experiences in STEM professions is perhaps the most important indicator that the "female advantage" argument is a warning sign for the decreasing value of higher education, and the shifting cultural mechanisms that uphold gender inequity.

Veterinary medicine offers an illustrative case. Between 1980 and 1990, the number of practicing female veterinarians increased 288 percent, with an additional 78 percent increase between 1990 and 1998. By 2008, women made up nearly 50 percent of practicing veterinarians, making veterinary medicine the most feminized of the comparable health professions.[87] Yet, among private practice veterinarians, women's incomes are only 75 percent of men's earnings.[88] Even in occupations in which women maintain occupational dominance, the advent of men in the profession can create a stratified gendered professional status, with men's status rising while women remain or become decreasingly devalued in the profession overall. Naming this mechanism the "glass escalator"—the mechanism that offers men a ride to higher wages and faster promotions—Williams and other researchers found its presence in a multitude of professions.[89] Nursing, still very much the province of women, offers such evidence. Even though men in the nursing profession make up only 9 percent of the field, they out-earned females by nearly $7,700 per year in outpatient settings and nearly $3,900 in hospitals.[90]

Wingfield's research into the ways in which race and gender intersect with glass escalator effects adds an important nuance to such findings. He found that black male nurses experienced "starkly different" and much less positive receptions from female colleagues than white men. Black male nurses, for example, were mistaken for custodians, as opposed to their white male counterparts who were mistaken for doctors. Therefore, white men were able to capitalize on racialized structural assumptions whereas black men were disadvantaged by them.

Studies of business, law, and publishing professions offer further examples of greater male success in spite of women's greater participation in corresponding higher education. Women, for example, make up half the country's new law school graduates and 45 percent of law firm associates,[91] but only 22 percent of the federal judiciary and 26 percent of state judges.[92] Women also stay in the profession less than men, and even when they do stay, according to the *American Bar Association's Commission on Women in the Profession Goal III Report* 2015, they face bias in the major factors that shape a legal career—evaluations, assignments, and compensation.

Finance careers offer a similar picture: Women often have more education but less pay and prestige, even in a profession where the pay is extraordinary. Roth, for example, demonstrated how men and women in Wall Street financial firms were "sifted into different and differentially remunerated positions [even though they enter the profession with the] same amount of motivation, ambition, and human capital [schooling]."[93] Interviewing men and women who graduated from the same five elite graduate MBA programs in finance, Roth found that in their first year, women's earnings were 60.5 percent of men's and that sex segregation within equity firms occurred at the beginning of the respondents' careers by funneling women into the functions that paid less (like support functions, equity research, and public finance), while men were more likely to begin in asset management or corporate finance. Moreover, lack of considerations for family issues, blocked mobility, and outright discrimination prevented many females from advancing or even staying in finance careers.

The high-tech industry, or Silicon Valley, also offers occupational places where women, no matter what their college degrees and training, are not welcome, at least in any significant number. According to most experts, *almost 50 percent* of women in "SET" (Science, Engineering, and Technology) careers will leave because of hostile work environments.[94] Corporate environments that have been referred to as "geek workplace cultures . . . with a super-competitive fraternity of arrogant nerds" prevent women from contributing their full potential at work, though they are equally as prepared—and educated—to do so.[95] Writing in *The People's Platform*, Taylor elegantly sums up the situation:

> The digital is not some realm distinct from real life, which means that the marginalization of women and minorities online cannot be separated from the obstacles they confront offline. Comparatively low rates of digital participation and the discrimination faced by women and minorities within the tech industry matter.[96]

Again, the structural and cultural realms trump occupational changes. As Lantz puts it, "There are no good models for what it looks like when men are actively involved in helping to fix the 'men in tech' problem."[97] There seem to be no good models for what it looks like when men and women address the female advantage in college question either.

In Sum

In 2007 McKinsey & Company baldly acknowledged the absence of a "female advantage" in higher education. In the *Women Matter* report, its authors state: "[U]nless the current rules of [business] are changed, the growth in female graduate numbers will have a very marginal impact on women's representation in governing bodies [at work]."[98] Their analyses of female graduate trajectories from the 1970s, 2000s, and their projections into 2035 are compelling: Even in countries where women are 64 percent of the university graduates in 2005, they predict that no more than 25 percent of these women will have places on business executive committees in 2035. See figure 6.4.

No matter *what* the degree, no matter how *many* degrees, and no matter how many *more* women than men have degrees, it is quite possibly the case that formal education credentials are becoming "something that women do." Ostensibly to gain knowledge, skills, perspectives, and connections, college may be an extra requirement for women to obtain good jobs, while men find new places to create economic and social power. The causal mechanisms for this devaluation are multiple and intersecting, but ultimately not new. One of the primary reasons may be due to casuistry—defined as specious reasoning in the service of justifying questionable behavior, so as to bolster public image as well as to internally rationalize one's decisions.[99] Norton, Vandello, and Darley explored this phenomenon using multiple experimental scenarios that mimicked real life employment decisions, noting that their study participants searched for ways in which to privilege those who were just like themselves. They report:

> Forced to make a decision between members of different social groups, participants quickly search for other cognitions consonant with their eventual choice and, having found them, reify them to the status of dominant criteria to rationalize their decisions—a process that can occur before or after the decision is made.[100]

With particular regard to educational credentials, the researchers noted studies in which male participants inflated the relative value of men's experience over their education credentials when women in the same pool had more education than men. Given the private nature of rationalization, the researchers could only speculate whether the male participants who sought to favor other men consciously inflated the value of the qualification that favored those candidates, or whether the desire to favor one gender actually causes participants to alter their beliefs about which qualifications are more important—ultimately, with the same outcome.

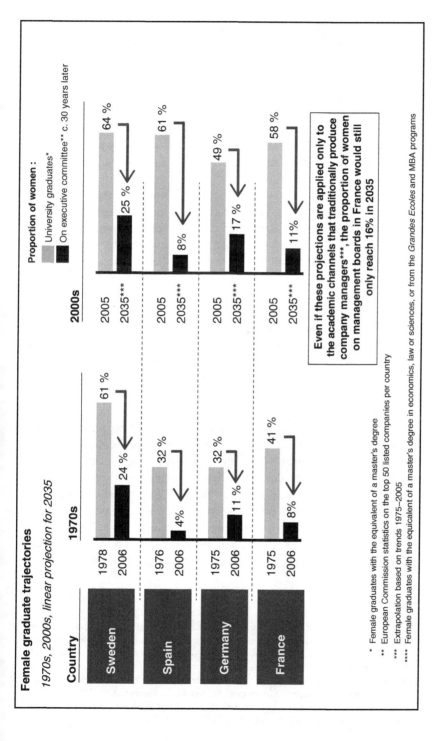

FIGURE 6.4 Female Graduates' Impact on Diversity

Source: OECD; national statistics; Eurostat; European Commission; McKinsey; data from French institutions.

Several other researchers have studied the phenomenon of decision-making involving social categories as they relate to education credentials, all finding that participants inflated the value of whichever qualification their preferred candidate had.[101] None of the researchers made claims about intention; indeed, their studies point to the ways in which public expressions of equal treatment often conflict with a private preference for people who mirror one's socially constructed belief system about who is more qualified for a particular task. The cumulative result, nonetheless, is that entrenched systems of gender and racial dominance influence decision-making, even when the processes of how that occurs are not obvious to others or to ourselves.

Another mechanism likely at work in devaluing women's college credentials as they relate to social equity is the continuance of occupational segregation, combined with men's tendencies to gravitate to masculine-dominant positions. Charles and Grusky argue that extreme sex segregation in the workforce is built deeply into the structure of modern economies, and through their investigation of "occupational ghettos," they explore the question of why sex segregation worldwide is so tenacious, even as other forms of gender inequality have diminished.[102] They take other gender researchers to task for failing to account for the complexity of the processes that comprise gender inequality,[103] and insist that the value of women's education credentials are dependent on economic conditions, traditional gender identities, and political power-sharing. Sadly, they conclude that gender essentialism is still so deeply embedded in micro-level socialization that essentialist ideas will be re-expressed in new forms, even as women gain education credentials.[104] This is exactly the argument for a female disadvantage in higher education.

Ultimately, through the various mechanisms that work to shape gender expectations, women's and men's individual and collective actions are impacted if college is now perceived as more suitable for women. By finding ways in which they can harness the benefits of higher education without participating in its processes, men can reestablish or reinforce their economic, political, and workplace advantages. Higher education may be on its way to becoming a redefined institution—one in which some women wait for men, some gain enough credentials to compete with men, while still others gain more credentials but never more power to change the status that their gender confers. Meanwhile, men have other places to go.

Notes

1. Ringrose, J. (2007). Successful girls? Complicating post-feminist, neoliberal discourses of educational achievement and gender equality. *Gender and Education, 19*(4), p. 481.
2. Covert, B. (2015, April 14). Education alone won't put an end to equal pay days. *The Nation.* Retrieved from www.thenation.com
3. Gerson, K. (2009, December). Changing lives, resistant institutions: A new generation negotiates gender, work, and family change. *Sociological Forum, 24*(4), 735–753.
4. Astin, A. W. (1998). The changing American college student: Thirty-year trends, 1966–96. *The Review of Higher Education, 21*(2), 115–135.

5. Stone, L., & McKee, N. P. (2000). Gendered futures: Student visions of career and family on a college campus. *Anthropology & Education Quarterly*, *31*(1), p. 72.
6. Holland, D. C., & Eisenhart, M. A. (1990). *Educated in romance: Women, achievement, and college culture.* Chicago, IL: University of Chicago Press.
7. See, for example, Grauerholz, E., & Serpe, R. T. (1985). Initiation and response: The dynamics of sexual interaction. *Sex Roles*, *9/10*, 1041–1059; Green, S. K., & Sandos, P. (1983). Perceptions of male and female initiators of relationships. *Sex Roles*, *9*, 849–852; McCormick, A. C. (2003). Swirling and double-dipping: New patterns of student attendance and their implications for higher education. *New Directions for Higher Education*, *2003*(121), 13–24.
8. Holland & Eisenhart 1990.
9. Ibid., p. 63.
10. Wang, W. (2015, June 12). Interracial marriage: Who is "marrying out"? *Pew Research Center*. Retrieved from www.pewresearch.org/fact-tank/2015/06/12/interracial-marriage-who-is-marrying-out/
11. Ibid.
12. Fry, R. & Cohn, D. (2010). Women, men and the new economics of marriage. *Pew Research Center*. Retrieved from www.pewsocialtrends.org/files/2010/11/new-economics-of-marriage.pdf
13. In a separate paper on the same study. Eisenhart, M. A. (1990). Learning to romance: Cultural acquisition in college. *Anthropology & Education Quarterly*, *21*(1), 19–40.
14. Park, L. E., Young, A. F., Troisi, J. D., & Pinkus, R. T. (2011). Effects of everyday romantic goal pursuit on women's attitudes toward math and science. *Personality and Social Psychology Bulletin*, *37*(9), p. 1271.
15. Niemi, N. S. (2005). The emperor has no clothes: Examining the impossible relationship between gendered and academic identities in middle school students. *Gender and Education*, *17*(5), 483–497.
16. Park et al., 2011, p. 1272.
17. Rudman, L. A., & Heppen, J. B. (2003). Implicit romantic fantasies and women's interest in personal power: A glass slipper effect? *Personality and Social Psychology Bulletin*, *29*(11), 1357–1370; Nosek, B. A., Banaji, M. R., & Greenwald, A. G. (2002). Math = male, me = female, therefore math ≠ me. *Journal of Personality and Social Psychology*, *83*(1), 44–59.
18. Park et al., 2011, p. 1271.
19. Armstrong, E. A., & Hamilton, L. T. (2013). *Paying for the party: How college maintains inequality.* Cambridge, MA: Harvard University Press.
20. Ibid., pp. 70, 215.
21. Ibid., p. 70.
22. Ibid., p. 215.
23. DiMaggio, P., & Mohr, J. (1985). Cultural capital, educational attainment, and marital selection. *American Journal of Sociology*, *90*(6), 1231–1261.
24. Armstrong, E. A. & Hamilton, L. T. (2013).
25. Fry, R. & Cohen, D., 2010.
26. Wang, W. (2014, February 12). Record share of wives are more educated than their husbands. *Pew Research Center*. Retrieved from www.pewresearch.org
27. Aliaga, O. A., Kotamraju, P., & Dickinson, E. (2011, November). *Career and technical education course-taking patterns of high school graduates: Exploring the participation in the most frequent sets of occupational areas.* Paper presented at the annual convention of the Association for Career and Technical Education, St. Louis, MO. Podcast of NRC Report, December 16.
28. Galambos, N., Petersen, A. C., Richards, M., & Gitelson, I. B. (1985). The Attitudes Toward Women Scale for Adolescents (AWSA): A study of reliability and validity. *Sex Roles*, *13*, 343–356.

29. Hegewisch, A., & Hartmann, H. (2014). *The Gender Wage Gap: 2014.* Retrieved from www.iwpr.org/publications/pubs/the-gender-wage-gap-2014#sthash.OWFBn Gmq.dpuf

30. Poelmans, S. (2012). The "Triple-N" Model: Changing normative beliefs about parenting and career success. *Journal of Social Issues, 68*(4), 838–847.

31. Goldberg, W. A. et al. (2012). The more things change, the more they stay the same: Gender, culture, and college students' views about work and family. *Journal of Social Issues, 68*(4), p. 830.

32. Goldberg, W. A., & Lucas-Thompson, R. G. (2014). College women miss the mark when estimating the impact of full-time maternal employment on children's achievement and behavior. *Psychology of Women Quarterly, 38*(4), 490–502.

33. Weinshenker, M. N. (2006). Adolescents' expectations about mothers' employment: Life course patterns and parental influence. *Sex Roles, 54*(11/12), 845–857.

34. Goldin, C. D. (2004). The long road to the fast track: Career and family. *The Annals of the American Academy of Political and Social Science, 596*(1), p. 34.

35. Hochschild, A. (1989). *The second shift: Working families and the revolution at home.* New York, NY: Viking.

36. Thébaud, S., & Pedulla, D. S. (2016). Masculinity and the stalled revolution: How gender ideologies and norms shape young men's responses to work–family policies. *Gender & Society, 30*(4), 590–617.

37. Ibid., p. 611.

38. Williams, J. C. (2010). *Reshaping the work–family debate: Why men and class matter* (the William E. Massey Sr. lectures in the history of American civilization). Cambridge, MA: Harvard University Press, p. 80.

39. Fuegen, K., Biernat, M., Haines, E., & Deaux, K. (2004). Mothers and fathers in the workplace: How gender and parental status influence judgments of job-related competence. *Journal of Social Issues, 60*(4), p. 749.

40. Williams, J. C. (2010), p. 81.

41. Jacobs, J. A., & Gerson, K. (2004). *The time divide: Work, family, and gender inequality.* Cambridge, MA: Harvard University Press, p. 73.

42. Gerson, 2009, p. 743.

43. Avishai, O. (2007). Managing the lactating body: The Breast-Feeding Project and privileged motherhood. *Qualitative Sociology, 30*(2), 135–152.

44. Douglas, S. J., & Michaels, M. W. (2004). *The mommy myth: The idealization of motherhood and how it has undermined all women.* New York, NY: Free Press, p. 4.

45. Lowry, R. (2001). Nasty, brutish, and short: Children in day care—and the mothers who put them there. *National Review, 28*, 36–42.

46. Webster Jr., B. H., & Bishaw, A. (2007). Income, Earnings, and Poverty Data from the 2006 American Community Survey. U.S. Census Bureau, U.S. Department of Commerce.

47. Gerson, 2009, p. 738.

48. Christopher, K. (2012). Extensive mothering employed mothers' constructions of the good mother. *Gender & Society, 26*(1), 73–96.

49. Gerson, K. (1985). *Hard choices: How women decide about work, career and motherhood.* Berkeley, CA: University of California Press.

50. Schiebinger, L., & Gilmartin, S. K. (2010). Housework is an academic issue: How to keep talented women scientists in the lab, where they belong. *Academe, 91*(1), 39–44.

51. Ibid.

52. Gerson, 2009, p. 745.

53. Heymann, J., Earle, A., & Hayes, J. (2005). *The work, family and equity index: How does the United States measure up?* Boston, MA: The Project on Global Working Families and the Institute for Health and Social Policy.

54. Williams, J. C. (2010), p. 36.

55. Ibid., p. 39.

56. Collins, C., Kenway, J., & McLeod, J. (2000). Gender debates we still have to have. *The Australian Educational Researcher, 27*(3), 37–48.
57. Philyaw, D. (2016, February 23). Ain't I a mommy? Bookstores brim with motherhood memoirs: Why are so few of them penned by women of color? *Bitch,* (70), 40–52.
58. Christopher, K. (2012). Extensive mothering employed mothers' constructions of the good mother. *Gender & Society, 26*(1), 73–96.
59. Barnes, R.J.D. (2008). Black women have always worked: Is there a work-family conflict among the Black middle class? In E. Rudd & L. Descartes (Eds.), *The changing landscape of work and family in the American middle class.* New York, NY: Lexington Books, pp. 189–210.
60. Gerson, 2009, p. 742.
61. Covert, B. (2014, May 19). In the real world, the so-called "boy-crisis" disappears. *The Nation.* Retrieved from www.thenation.com
62. *On pay gap, millennial women near parity—for now.* (2013, December 11). Retrieved from www.pewsocialtrends.org/2013/12/11/on-pay-gap-millennial-women-near-parity-for-now/
63. Ibid.
64. Corbett, C., & Hill, C. (2012). *Graduating to a pay gap: The earnings of women and men one year after college graduation.* Washington, DC: American Association of University Women.
65. Budig, M. J. (2014). *The fatherhood bonus & the motherhood penalty: Parenthood and the gender gap in pay.* Washington, DC: Third Way, p. 12.
66. Ibid., p. 13.
67. Ibid.
68. American Association of University Professors (AAUP). (2011). *Statement on professional ethics.* Retrieved from www.aaup.org/AAUP/pubsres/policydocs/contents/statementonprofessionalethics.htm
69. Antecol, H., Bedard, K., & Stearns, J. (2016). *Equal but inequitable: Who benefits from gender-neutral tenure clock stopping policies?* (No. 9904). Bonn, Germany: Institute for the Study of Labor (IZA).
70. Ibid., p. 24.
71. Belkin, L. (2003, October 26). The opt-out revolution. *The New York Times Magazine.* Retrieved from www.nytimes.com
72. Williams, J. C. (2010), pp. 13–14.
73. Cohn, D., Livingston, G., & Wang, W. (2014, April). *After decades of decline, a rise in stay-at-home mothers.* Washington, DC: Pew Research Center's Social & Demographic Trends Project.
74. Etaugh, C., & Study, G. (1989). Perceptions of mothers: Effects of employment status, marital status, and age of child. *Sex Roles, 20,* 59–70.
75. Burgess, N. (2013). *The motherhood penalty: How gender and parental status influence judgments of job-related competence and organizational commitment.* Kingston, RI: University of Rhode Island. Retrieved from www.uri.edu
76. Bureau of Labor Statistics, U.S. Department of Labor. (2014). *Highlights of women's earnings in 2013.* Report 1051. Retrieved from http://www.bls.gov/opub/reports/cps/highlights-of-womens-earnings-in-2013.pdf
77. See, for example, Irvine, L., & Vermilya, J. R. (2010). Gender work in a feminized profession: The case of veterinary medicine. *Gender & Society, 24*(1), 56–82; Wingfield, A. H. (2009). Racializing the glass escalator reconsidering men's experiences with women's work. *Gender & Society, 23*(1), 5–26. Also Bobbitt-Zeher, D. (2007). The gender income gap and the role of education. *Sociology of Education, 80*(1), 1–22.
78. Uhlmann, E. L., & Cohen, G. L. (2005). Constructed criteria redefining merit to justify discrimination. *Psychological Science, 16*(6), 474–480.
79. Levanon, A., England, P., & Allison, P. (2009). Occupational feminization and pay: Assessing causal dynamics using 1950–2000 US census data. *Social Forces, 88*(2), p. 885.

80. Corbett, C., Hill, C., & St. Rose, A. (2008). *Where the girls are: The facts about gender equity in education.* Washington, DC: American Association of University Women Educational Foundation.
81. Kezar, A., Maxey, D., & Badke, L. (2014). The imperative for change: Fostering understanding of the necessity of changing non-tenure-track faculty policies and practices. *Delphi Project on Changing Faculty and Student Success.* Retrieved from www.uscrossier.org/pullias/wp-content/uploads/2014/01/IMPERATIVE-FOR-CHANGE_WEB-2014.pdf (accessed June 6, 2014).
82. Benschop, Y., & Brouns, M. (2003). Crumbling ivory towers: Academic organizing and its after effects. *Gender, Work & Organization, 10*(2), 194–212.
83. Bagilhole, B., & Goode, J. (2001). The contradiction of the myth of individual merit, and the reality of a patriarchal support system in academic careers: A feminist investigation. *European Journal of Women's Studies, 8*(2), 161–180.
84. Masse, M. A., & Hogan, K. J. (2010). *Over ten million served: Gendered service in language and literature workplaces.* Albany, NY: SUNY Press.
85. Blickenstaff, J. C. (2005). Women and science careers: Leaky pipeline or gender filter? *Gender and Education, 17*(4), 369–386.
86. Ibid., pp. 371–372.
87. Brakke-Bayer. (1999). AVMA study: Impact of management practices and business behavior on small animal veterinarian's incomes. Retrieved from www.vbma.biz/files/Brakke%20Study%201999.pdf; Irvine & Vermilya, 2010; American Veterinary Medical Association (AVMA). (2008). *Website for veterinary practice management information.* Retrieved from www.avma.org
88. American Veterinary Medical Association (AVMA). (2007a). *Website for veterinary practice management information.* Retrieved from www.avma.org.
89. See, for instance, teaching (Allan, J. (1993). Male elementary teachers: Experiences and perspectives. In C. L. Williams (Ed.), *Doing "Women's Work": Men in Nontraditional Occupations* (pp. 113–127). Newbury Park, CA: Sage Publications; Cognard-Black, A. J. (2004). Will they stay, or will they go? Sex-atypical work among token men who teach. *Sociological Quarterly,* 113–139). For instance, in 2001, men comprised only 21 percent of primary and secondary public school teachers, but were 56 percent of principals in public primary and secondary schools during the 1999–2000 school year. Snyder, T. D., Tan, A. G., and Hoffman, C. M. (2006). *Digest of Education Statistics 2005* (NCES 2006–030). U.S. Department of Education, National Center for Education Statistics. Washington, DC: U.S. Government Printing Office.
90. Analysis of data from the National Sample Survey of Registered Nurses (1988–2008) by Dr. Ulrike Muench, et al. Published in the *Journal of the American Medical Association.* Also in Buerhaus, P. I., Auerbach, D. I., Staiger, D. O., & Muench, U. (2013). Projections of the long-term growth of the registered nurse workforce: A regional analysis. *Nursing Economics, 31*(1), 13–17.
91. Catalyst Inc. (2015). *Women in law in Canada and the U.S.* New York, NY: Catalyst.
92. American Bar Association Commission on Women in the Profession. (2015). *Goal III Report.* Chicago, IL: ABA. Retrieved from www.americanbar.org/
93. Roth, L. M. (2004). Engendering inequality: Processes of sex-segregation on Wall Street. *Sociological Forum, 19*(2), pp. 204, 206.
94. Hewlett, S. A. (2014, March 13). What's holding women back in science and technology industries? *Harvard Business Review,* pp. 1–2.
95. Ibid., p. 2.
96. Taylor, A. (2014). *The people's platform: Taking back power and culture in the digital age.* New York, NY: Harper Collins, p. 4.
97. Lantz, J. (2016, January 31). *Let's talk about the men in tech problem.* Retrieved from https://medium.com/@janessalantz/let-s-talk-about-the-men-in-tech-problem-443e31dece19#.3j6ygduib

98. Desvaux, G., Devillard-Hoellinger, S., & Baumgarten, P. (2007). *Women matter: Gender diversity, a corporate performance driver.* Paris, France: McKinsey, p. 6.

99. Norton, M., Vandello, J., & Darley, J. (2004). Casuistry and social bias. *Journal of Personality and Social Psychology, 87*(6), 817–831.

100. Ibid., p. 819.

101. Hodson, G., Dovidio, J. F., & Gaertner, S. L. (2002). Processes in racial discrimination: Differential weighting of conflicting information. *Personality and Social Psychology Bulletin, 28,* 460–471.

102. Charles, M., & Grusky, D. B. (2004). *Occupational ghettos: The worldwide segregation of women and men* (Vol. 200). Stanford, CA: Stanford University Press, p. 3.

103. Ibid., p. 12.

104. Ibid., p. 316.

7

A DREAM DETERRED?

The rules and rewards of a college education seem clear: learn solid skills (particularly marketable ones), get good grades (high GPAs look good to employers), make professional contacts (the more people you know, the more opportunities you will be exposed to), earn credentials (the more you have, the more money you will make). Americans have understood that earning degrees means increased chances of having more successful and perhaps more fulfilling lives, and they have invested their time, their money, and their dreams in the power that higher education promises. Women, in particular, have placed their dreams of gender equity in the authority that has traditionally been conferred with higher education's credentials. If that authority is diminishing, if the promised rewards are *still* not enough to gain equal control over their professional and personal lives, where do women turn?

It is not that academia has been wholly devalued. Most of the evidence suggests that higher education still offers many women and men opportunities for expanded thinking, better incomes, and in general, a higher quality of life. But it may be the case that as women's academic stars have shined brightly onto a landscape where masculinity feels dimmed, the reflection made possible by a college education is openly questioned, its value proposition slowly eroding. Much like the strategy one uses to catch a lizard—distract it from the front and grab its tail—it is possible that the female advantage argument serves as a cultural distraction for a shifting American male power base.

It is odd to liken schooling to a distraction in a country where the universal right to schooling has been akin to religion. Yet consider the extremes that are currently in the forefront of the American conversations about higher education. "The belief in 'college for all' . . . is here to stay," writes Carnevale,

> because it is animated by a uniquely American mix of cultural and political biases that go deeper than political divisions. Public support for "college for

all" unifies the aspiring middle class with those who have already arrived but have a fear of falling and a dread of downward mobility for their children.[1]

On the other hand, there are numerous counterarguments suggesting that higher education is broken, and that college as we know it is dying. Drucker, for example, predicted the institution's end by 2027:

> Higher education is in deep crisis. It took more than 200 years for the printed book to create the modern school. It won't take nearly that long for the [next] big change. The unsuccessful misfit of diversification should be put out of its misery as fast as possible.[2]

Carey sounded equally apocryphal in his recent book, *The End of College*, stating that "the story of higher education's future is a tale of ancient institutions in their last days of decadence, creating seeds of a new world to come,"[3] while Congressman Dave Brat (R-VA) suggested during a recent House Education and Workforce Committee proceeding that in order to learn, we revert to deep thought while sitting on boulders: "Socrates trained Plato on a rock and then Plato trained on Aristotle roughly speaking on a rock. So, huge funding is not necessary to achieve the greatest minds and the greatest intellects in history."[4]

Carey and Brat reflect at least a portion of the population's long-simmering fears, which are less about funding, and more about the proximity and access to powerful people, two entrées that higher education have traditionally delivered. Questions such as who attends which college, how much it costs the State, who has the opportunity to learn newly valued knowledge and skills, and now, how much wealth a "new world" of education may generate for those who control it: These are the quiet thoughts that underscore the words of those who predict higher education's end. How the answers to these questions affect women, and particularly women of color and lower social class, are central to understanding whether success in higher education still has a chance to fulfill its promises, real and aspirational, for gender equity in America.

College Viability and Cost

One of the driving forces behind the question of college viability for most people is its rate of return: Is the economic rate of return over an individual's lifetime of earnings worth her/his investment in a college degree? "Practically everyone seems to know a well-educated young person who is working in a bar or a mundane clerical job, because he or she can't find anything better," writes Cassidy.[5] The increased supply of college graduates worldwide, in addition to international outsourcing of many jobs, has made it easier for companies to find labor, and harder for individuals to find jobs that correspond to one's degree. Many people with college degrees are over-credentialed, or at least differently credentialed for the jobs in which they are currently employed. Others repeat the mantra that many of college students' future jobs have not even been invented yet, making it feel counterproductive to earn a degree.

Others cite the startling increase in the cost of education as a factor in the question of the worth of college, particularly at public comprehensive universities (PCUs), where many working adults and first-generation students attend. Seventy percent of the undergraduate students at PCUs are female, black, Hispanic, Asian American, Pacific Islander, or Native American, and 80 percent of the graduate students at PCUs fall into these categories. Since 2007 alone, these universities have seen a 28 percent cut in public funding per student.[6] The Center for American Progress reports that over the past 30 years, average tuition for a four-year college has increased more than 250 percent, even as the average family income has risen minimally over the same time period.[7] The very institutions designed to be accessible to students who need more support are the ones that are receiving less state aid; facing deficits, these institutions in turn charge higher tuition and offer less help to the students they were designed to serve. As such, students take out massive loans—in 2012 this amounted to an average debt of $29,400 per student per year[8]—and still too often drop out or, anticipating great debt, opt out of going altogether.

One of the most telling signs of a female disadvantage in higher education is women's share of college loan burden. Since many more women are attending college, they now carry a greater share of the U.S. college debt; subsequently, a much greater percentage of women than men contribute money to student loan payments post-graduation, even as the gender pay gap remains.[9]

Figure 7.1 shows the share of 2001 and 2009 bachelor's degree recipients who are working full time and paying at least some portion of their student loans one year after graduation. Corbett and Hill note that their analysis does not capture the full magnitude of the problem, as it only considers those who have been lucky enough to find full-time employment, and it does not fully take the gender pay gap into account. Taken together, women's overall greater student loan debt and the gender pay gap combine to disadvantage women: Higher education exacts a financial penalty just for being female. Without a degree, women are, on average, going to make less money over their lifetimes than men with similar or even less education; with one, they have some chance to make more money, but are subsequently burdened with higher student debt than men and still experience inequality in pay. If, as Carnevale claims, women are better off getting higher degrees than men in order to compensate for gendered pay disparities, are we not turning college credentials into an educational gender tax?

More Suspect, Less Respect?

Growing questions about the value of something, from whale oil to diamonds, have historically been indicators that the object's inherent value is in question. With heightened attention to the cost of college, questions of its worth follow

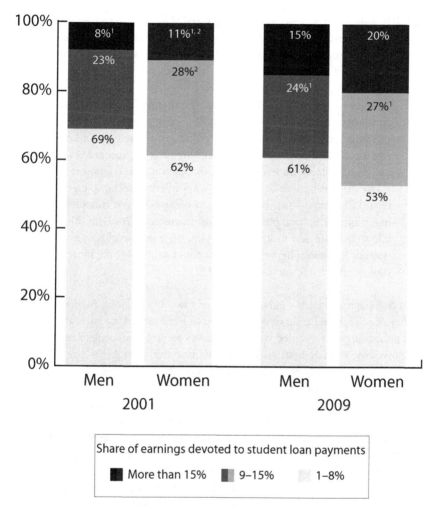

FIGURE 7.1 Student Loan Debt Burden One Year After College Graduation, by Year and Gender

Notes: Student loan debt burden is the percentage of earnings devoted to student loan payments. This chart shows student loan debt burden among 1999–2000 and 2007–08 bachelor's degree recipients who were making non-zero payments on their student loans and were employed full time one year after graduation. This analysis excludes graduates older than age 35 at bachelor's degree completion. Percentages may not add up to 100 because of rounding.

Source: Authors' analysis of U.S. Department of Education, National Center for Education Statistics, *2000–01* and *2008–09 Baccalaureate and Beyond Longitudinal Study* data.

[1] Percentages are not significantly different for men and women ($p < 0.05$, two-tailed t-test).
[2] Before rounding, these numbers add up to 38 percent.

suit. The relationship between Americans and their long-standing belief in the power and promise of higher education seems to be fraying. Yankelovich thinks that "we are living through a particularly difficult chapter of the ancient town-gown struggle." He continues:

> In higher education, the liberal arts, philosophy, and the humanities, the nonscientific ways of truth-seeking have been put on the defensive. While still valued as high culture, they have lost ground as ways of knowing and finding truth. But in our popular culture, it is science that is suspect, and its "probabilities" are less respected than among the cognoscenti.
>
> Americans hunger for religious ways of truth seeking, especially with regard to moral values. By seeming to oppose or even ridicule that yearning, higher education pits itself against mainstream America. Unless it takes a less cocksure and more open-minded approach to the issue of multiple ways of knowing, higher education could easily become more embattled, more isolated, and more politicized.[10]

An aging population, less rigid sequencing of schooling and jobs, American vulnerability in science and technology, the need to learn other languages and cultures, and public support for varied ways of gaining knowledge all contribute, according to Yankelovich's analysis, to a less respected institution of higher education, even as more people than ever enroll in it. Such a perspective may help explain, in part, the increased focus on college and its relationship to marketable skills. When college was a place for people who already had a place in the world, the proof of marketability was not as necessary. Now, however, college cannot be considered by many as a place to hone social connections without worry about employment. For most people, attending college must result in a credential that offers highly probable assurances of getting a job. This holds true even through gendered lenses.

In contrast to Yankelovich, Frank T. Rhodes, President Emeritus of Cornell University, sees the growth of colleges as a "remarkable national commitment to higher education."[11] In addition to the fourfold increase in female enrollment compared to male enrollment, Rhodes cites the doubling of black student enrollment between 1996 and 2006, the 16 percent rise in Hispanic college enrollments, as well as the doubling of Native Americans' college attendance in the past 30 years as evidence of higher education's great health.[12] Clearly, higher education of the 21st century is an increasingly important source of access to knowledge and higher status occupations to those who have been previously underrepresented at these institutions. Populations that have been barred from past participation have now embraced the institution that needs their tuition dollars, as well as their own willingness to learn and gain credentials that they hope will help their futures and families.

These shifting higher education populations are accompanied by suspicion of certain kinds of learning—that is, the kind that does not lead directly to a job or career. This suspicion may be an indication of the tension that new college students feel between the promise of obtaining a college education, and their concern over abandoning their families roots. Becoming educated frequently brings changes in beliefs and values, and these changes subsequently alienate college graduates from their families. "The injuries of class," Williams writes, "are like sunburn so painful that the slightest touch makes you pull away, wincing."[13] As such, greater enrollment by the working class and underrepresented minorities in higher education is largely focused on better economic credentials, not necessarily better intellectual ones. In this way, college students can focus on bringing financial stability to their families, rather than focusing on the learning that might lead to their intellectual and experiential distance from them.

Understanding how college credentials may be understood by generations previously kept from such degrees may help explain the love/hate relationship and lesser completion rates of low-income and racial and ethnic minority students. Americans in general have greater respect for wealth than they do for education. If college credentials are perceived to be a necessary evil on the pathway to wealth, it becomes clear that institutions might garner higher enrollments, even as the surrounding culture holds less esteem for the degree holders themselves.

Changes in Enrollment Drive Changes in Higher Education Structure and Function

The U.S. Department of Education 2006 report, *A Test of Leadership: Charting the Future of U.S. Higher Education*, called for increased college accessibility, affordability, accountability, and quality, particularly for minority students. "For close to a century now," the authors wrote, "access to higher education has been a principal—some would say the principal—means of achieving social mobility [in America]."[14] Much of America's future competitiveness in the global marketplace, they argued, depended on the country's ability to restructure its college system. The recommendations of what became known as *The Spellings Report* consequently underscored the need for:

1. Every student in the nation to have the opportunity to pursue postsecondary education, and that the United States commit to "an unprecedented effort to expand higher education access and success," . . . providing significant increases in aid to low-income students;
2. Restructuring the student financial aid system;
3. A "robust culture" of transparency and accountability;
4. Universities and colleges to develop a culture of innovation through new pedagogies, curricula, and technologies;
5. Higher education to develop strategies for lifelong learning of Americans; and
6. Universities to pay particular attention to the development of professionals in knowledge-intensive professions such as the STEM fields, teaching, nursing, and biomedicine.[15]

These recommendations echo the American cultural and economic themes of the last decade, supporting many other public and academic calls for increased participation and quality in higher education. The Spellings report argued that other countries are now graduating more of their citizens to more advanced levels, and that the United States is losing its competitive world advantage: "Our collective prosperity," the authors stated, "is being threatened."[16] However, nowhere in this report do the authors address the increasingly female population in higher education. This lack of attention to or even mention of gender as an analytic unit is striking.

If attaining college credentials is a waning strategy for male advancement and power, it makes sense to advocate for others to take men's places in colleges so that the *business* of higher education thrives, even as the economic, social, and political power once associated with a college credential seeks new places to reside. *Not* discussing women's increased college enrollment, completion, and success may be a strategy, at least at the federal level, designed to take away the stigma apparently associated with too-many-women. Making more money is at the heart of American success stories, and it makes citizens feel good to be part of an endeavor in which everyone has their individual chance to climb the ladder, even if the realities of doing so are expensive and obscured.

Proponents of college innovation support this line of reasoning, even as they struggle with the financial premises on which public higher education is built. College leaders state it plainly, with variations on the message:

> If college governing boards want more money, they are going to have to deal with people they've never seen in college before: people who do not look like them, sound like them, or have the goals or aspirations that they do.[17]

Arthur Levine, former president of Columbia University, refers to these new students as "the new majority": students who do not attend school full time; have adult financial responsibilities; live off campus with family; need remedial coursework; and are not white, native English speakers, or even American citizens.[18] In short, colleges need new customers.

And customer service, in college as well as in any other business, means giving people what they want. Enter the new ways in which higher education is being shaped: four-year degrees in three years, year-round classes, online courses, digital degrees, learning outcomes tied to business standards, and changing federal financial aid policies among many others.[19] Amidst these changes, it makes sense that one very big change could happen: colleges that operate like for-profit enterprises.

Affluent citizens, major foundations, venture capitalists, and educational entrepreneurs are all rethinking mass education as a rich source of business, and "it is around the issue of cost reduction that interests converge," note Armstrong and Hamilton in *Paying for the Party*.[20] Certainly with the dam of not-for-profit status that once protected institutions of higher education now broken if not shattered, college-as-business analogies proliferate, as well, of course, do businesses that *are* colleges: every for-profit university. With higher education now framed not only *as* business, but also tied *to* business—in the form of credentials offered as job force training—then higher education reform is much more willing and able to create credentials that tie directly to the economic needs of the country.

The educational bar keeps rising; credentialism allows employers to demand workers with more and higher markers of knowledge attainment even though many jobs do not require the level of credentials attained by those who are employed.[21] As long as community colleges, for-profits, public branch campuses, four-year public universities, and less selective private institutions hitch their fiscal well-being to businesses, there may be ways out of the financial crises in which all-but-Ivies and research-intensive universities find themselves.

Of Mind, Men, and Power

If Americans equate college credentials to "women's credentials," those credentials will be tied into a pinkish view of higher education, just as the emerging market of college attendees is growing: Hispanics, blacks, Latinos, working class whites, and virtually everyone who changes jobs. At least this may be what the shapers of the American higher education business community are afraid of. With most institutions of higher education now acknowledging that they are indeed businesses, colleges literally cannot afford to be dismissed as an advantage to females. The survival of the American Dream, and of the thousands of U.S. college-businesses, depends on that not being the case.

"Female advantage" and "boy crisis" arguments ultimately circumvent the greatest underlying issue in higher education: schooling does not meet the learning needs of many women and men, even though decades of scholarship on women and men's college completion offers evidence of its positive societal implications. "Never mind college degrees," writes Krugman. "[A]ll the big gains [in life] are going to a tiny group of individuals holding positions in corporate suites or astride the crossroads of finance. Rising inequality isn't about who has the knowledge—it's about who has the power."[22] Women's overall enrollment and achievement in higher education notwithstanding, on virtually every major dimension of social status, financial well-being, and physical safety, women still fare worse than men because they have less power than men to control these aspects of their lives.[23] The causal connection between success in obtaining higher education credentials and social power outside education is not a given.

The ability to translate a degree into a job, or into any rise in social equity, rests on a host of factors beyond the skills themselves. Many who have investigated the ways in which women have gained some measure of gender equity through formal education have come to the same uncomfortable conclusion.

Spencer, Porsche, and Tolman write about one school's sincere and prolonged efforts to improve gender equity:

> [Our work] has led us to conclude that the current conception of gender equity as equal rights, equal access, and fairness, though having served the crucial purpose of providing equal opportunities for girls and boys, may be too limited. . . . Without explicit attention to gender ideology, current gender equity efforts may not only fail to ameliorate gender differences, they may in some cases have the unintended consequence of intensifying aspects of them. Without revealing and challenging gender as socially constructed, gender equity efforts may be unwittingly undermined for many students.[24]

Ringrose comes to a similar conclusion: "[P]ost-feminist presumptions of gender equality obscure on-going issues of sexual difference and sexism that girls experience in the classroom and beyond."[25] Ultimately, the Dream narrative is one that privileges individual achievement while hiding structural barriers that prevent such achievement from occurring for all but those who have the cultural tools to dismantle them. Those who start their lives at the top of the hierarchy do not need the Dream in the first place.

The American masculine cultural toolkit has always prized money before brains; money is masculinity, and it is power. Being rich marks a man as manly; being intellectual makes him a "wuss."[26] Americans have made this connection many times before, and are in the process of making it again, which is why the "college has no value/college has great value" dichotomy reflects an underlying, painful reality: Americans are ambivalent about female equity, much less a female *advantage*, in anything except perhaps motherhood. Feminism, defined simply as the belief that women of all races and classes are as valuable, as powerful, and as intelligent as men—and should be treated that way, is threatening. In the supremely contested spaces of schooling, women have proven capable of out-performing men, and patriarchy is pushing back.

Gilborn discusses how "gap talk in education" works as a way to divide and conquer marginalized groups as they compete for educational resources. By pitting groups against one another, those with financial power work amidst the cracks in the groups, shaping realities even as those with less power are distracted by the fight for contested financial resources. Connell notes that the statistical gaps researchers have so clearly identified in the back-and-forth about who is doing better and worse in schooling operate to "reduce our imaginations" about what a relevant gender issue can be in schools.[27] With such reduced and self-imposed options, we do not have to argue about the ways in which black boys are systematically disenfranchised or about Hispanic girls who are expected to succeed in school and then return home to take care of their families. The logic of individualized competition makes proponents of school reform argue amongst themselves.

Beyond the Binary

Is it possible to move to a place where college credentials are powerful mechanisms for women and men to contribute to social equity for all? Can having more and better college credentials ever offer enough compensation to women to equal men's social, political, and economic power? The answer is not promising for at least two major reasons.

First, the connection between capitalism and higher education has likely sealed the trajectory for the wholesale auction of intellectual capital. That is, public universities and less-elite private colleges, in order to survive, will want to attract affluent out-of-state and international students and families, and therefore will continue to provide them with what they want: Greek life, beautiful buildings, "easy majors" like sports communication and hospitality, high-profile sports teams, and parties. The "country clubization" of the American university, with luxury residence halls complete with special amenities and private accommodations, will stratify students even further, and make up, to some degree, the status that is lost for those who cannot get admitted to more prestigious schools. Armstrong and Hamilton note this trend, stating that "on four-year residential campuses around the country, increases in student spending for student services—including recreation and athletics—have surpassed those for academic instruction and financial aid."[28] Students who cannot afford this idealistic vision of college, they argue, "are not blocked from higher education altogether," but will be increasingly directed to mass-produced options like online courses and virtual degree programs.

Second, the equity that women still need—all women, in spite of social class, race, and other differences—is not delivered by a college credential alone. Indeed, it may be hubris to suggest that more credentials will ameliorate the injustices women face in employment and economic security; family, sex, and reproductive justice; and sexual freedom, among many others. It is hard to believe that educational attainment acts as a powerful lever for women, for example, when attending college is no longer even an option for women who need to remain on welfare; either women on welfare work at a job and maintain benefits, or they can attend college, and lose them.[29] Complex relational struggles and politics surround sex and power, and they have a way of finding new hiding places in contemporary debates. The female advantage narrative has formed a gendered education discourse in popular political consciousness and, in doing so, issues of academic achievement are now separate from issues of gender equality. This severing of academic achievement from issues of power has diverted Americans' cultural attention from issues of equity to a zero-sum game of the sex wars: Who has it better in school?

Through Disequilibrium?

nericans today do not think that men have more advantages than women.[30] With a nod to Betty Friedan, many Americans feel that with regard to women and schooling, we found a name for the nameless problem—many boys were advantaged—and now we have solved it so well that it is girls who are advantaged in education. The problem, for women, apparently no longer exists.

Neither all women nor all men have educational advantages as we have seen throughout this book; the high school dropout rates for black and Hispanic males are abysmal and the college completion rate for first-time college enrollees is less than 50 percent after six years.[31] Persistent and deep systemic disparities continue to communicate powerful messages about who in this country is valued, and who is not. In the face of these realities, what might we do? I offer 10 suggestions:

1. Acknowledge that college should be hard—for everyone. Completing college is difficult and any college degree or credential that is worthwhile is worth hard work. Males often underestimate that serious commitment to school work is needed continuously, and females need to understand that their effort in college will not be sufficient to overtake their gendered disadvantages outside of school.

2. As we transition from higher education as liberal arts for the privileged few to higher education as optional grades 13–17, we need to admit that we are extending high school. Doing so will allow us to view college as an extension of learning, thereby offering students whose high school educations were inadequate another chance at foundational literacy and numeracy, at the very least.

3. As college becomes more aligned to the workplace, we need to bring in gender equity lessons and challenges from the workplace back to the Academy. As colleges and workplaces resemble each other, they will also resemble their most sexist characteristics—which means that we need to stop thinking of academic institutions as protected places, and more as places where reform is needed.

4. Engage in college advising that directly addresses the inequities that most women face. Advisors and parents need to ask young women what they are going to do with their credentials, and they need to help them see how life changes in the future may be softened or made more difficult by their current college choices. We need to remind women that academic success does not mean perfect performance, but substantive learning that leads to new knowledge and skills.

5. Create college cultures that make all who work in higher education accountable for the ways in which women and men are sexually respected on campus.

6. Resist writing stories that glorify men, at the expense of women, who achieve power by eschewing formal education.

7. Continue to recognize the need for collective identities in studies of women's development. This is hard to do when women have different needs, and most women do not see how movements working toward gender equity

would benefit them personally. Divisions across age, race, class, and ideology complicate efforts to establish priorities, but do not prevent women from creating priorities that benefit more of us.

8. Create and support new feminist movements in order to influence public policy and educational reform. The women's movement is now less visible because it has been institutionalized by churches, educational structures, the military, and workplaces. We need to once again make feminist movements positive forces if they are to impact conversations and action regarding equity.

9. Encourage political and academic leaders to have the courage to speak about the dynamics of power and privilege that continue to shape women's lives.

10. Challenge the gender stereotypes that devalue women's competence and that penalize assertiveness of women; doing so will always point to the ways and places in which power hides.

Ultimately, we need to stop pretending that education serves as the great equalizer of American society. Formal education is and has been one of the most valuable human rights, nationally and throughout the world. American women have fought hard to be included in the privileges of higher education, and without this access, millions of women and their country would be diminished in countless ways. But in America, the idea that women's attainment of formal higher education credentials will permanently create gender equity is simply untrue. Men, with college credentials or without, in "masculine" places old and new, still have power to shape the fabric of our lives. Until gender equity stops looking like male diminishment, women will remain at a disadvantage. Acknowledging these realities may be the biggest recommendation of all.

Notes

1. Carnevale, A. P. (2008, January/February). College for all? *Change*, p. 23.
2. Lenzer, R., & Johnson, S. S. (1997, March 3). Seeing things as they really are. [An interview with Peter Drucker]. *Forbes*. Retrieved from www.forbes.com/
3. Carey, K. (2015). *The end of college: Creating the future of learning and the university of everywhere*. New York, NY: Riverhead Books, p. 1.
4. Ragland, W. (2014). Congressman says we don't need education funding because "Socrates trained Plato on a rock." *Think progress.org*. Retrieved from https://think progress.org/congressman-says-we-dont-need-education-funding-because-socrates-trained-plato-on-a-rock-22521dd2f53e#.bntqip8bv
5. Cassidy, J. (2015, September 7). College calculus: What is college worth? *The New Yorker*. Retrieved from www.newyorker.com/magazine/2015/09/07/college-calculus
6. Oliff, P., Palacios, V., Johnson, I., & Leachman, M. (2013). *Recent deep state higher education cuts may harm students and the economy for years to come*. Washington, DC: Center on Budget and Policy Priorities.
7. J. Erickson & M. Ettlinger (Eds.). (2013). *300 million engines of growth*. Retrieved from www.americanprogress.org/wp-content/uploads/2013/06/ProgressiveGrowth-1.pdf
8. Reed M., & Cochrane, D. (2014, November). Student debt and the class of 2013. *The Institute for College Access and Success*. Retrieved from http://ticas.org/sites/default/files/legacy/fckfiles/pub/classof2013.pdf

9. Corbett, C., & Hill, C. (2012). *Graduating to a pay gap: The earning of women and men one year after college graduation*. Washington, DC: American Association of University Women. Retrieved from www.aauw.org

10. Yankelovich, D. (2005). Ferment and change: Higher education in 2015. *The Chronicle of Higher Education, 52*(14), B6–B9. Retrieved from http://www.chronicle.com/article/FermentChange-Higher/14934

11. Rhodes, F. (2006, October 20). Sustainability: The ultimate liberal art. *Chronicle of Higher Education*, p. A8. Retrieved from http://www.chronicle.com/article/After-40-Years-of-Growth-and/9929

12. Fry, R., & Lopez, H. (2011). *Hispanic student enrollments reach new highs, in 2011*. Washington, DC: Pew Research Center.

13. Williams, J. C. (2010). *Reshaping the work–family debate: Why men and class matter.* (The William E. Massey Sr. lectures in the history of American civilization). Cambridge, MA: Harvard University Press, p. 190.

14. United States Department of Education. (2006). *A test of leadership: Charting the future of U.S. higher education.* A report of the commission appointed by Secretary of Education Margaret Spellings. ED-06-C0–0013.

15. Ibid, p. 12.

16. Ibid.

17. Fischer, K. (2011, December 12). At forum on the future, leaders dissect what ails higher education today. *Chronicle of Higher Education*. Retrieved from http://chronicle.com/article/At-Forum-on-the-Future/130087/

18. Hersh, R. H., & Merrow, J. (Eds.). (2005). *Declining by degrees: Higher education at risk.* New York, NY: Palgrave Macmillan.

19. Fischer, 2011.

20. Armstrong, E. A., & Hamilton, L. T. (2013). *Paying for the party: How college maintains inequality.* Cambridge, MA: Harvard University Press, p. 246.

21. Lowe, in Cruikshank, J. (2007). Lifelong learning and the new economy: Rhetoric or reality? *Education Canada, 47*(2), 32–36.

22. Hersh & Merrow, 2005, p. A19.

23. Rhode, D. L. (2014). *What women want: An agenda for the women's movement.* Oxford, UK: Oxford University Press.

24. Spencer, R., Porche, M., & Tolman, D. (2003). We've come a long way—maybe: New challenges for gender equity in education. *The Teachers College Record, 105*(9), p. 1802.

25. Ringrose, J. (2013). *Postfeminist education? Girls and the sexual politics of schooling.* London, UK: Routledge, p. 138.

26. Williams, J. C. (2010).

27. Connell, R. W. (2010). Kartini's children: On the need for thinking gender and education together on a world scale. *Gender and Education, 22*(6), 603–616.

28. Armstrong & Hamilton, 2013.

29. Rhode, 2014.

30. Ibid.

31. Schott Foundation. (2015). *Black lives matter: The Schott Foundation 50 state report on public education and black males.* Retrieved from www.blackboys.org; National Center for Education Statistics (NCES). (2014). *The condition of education.* Retrieved from https://nces.ed.gov/

BIBLIOGRAPHY

Abidansky, H. (2009). *Organized crime*. Belmont, CA: Cengage Learning.

Achieve, Inc. (2005). *Rising to the challenge: Are high school graduates prepared for college and work? A study of recent high school graduates, college instructors, and employers*. Washington, DC: Peter D. Hart Research Associates/Public Opinion Strategies.

Adams, J. (2008, October). Conference panel. *History matters: Patriarchy and the challenge of feminism*. Social Science History Association, Miami, FL.

Agars, M. D. (2004). Reconsidering the impact of gender stereotypes on the advancement of women in organizations. *Psychology of Women Quarterly, 28*, 103–111.

Ainsworth, J. W., & Roscigno, V. J. (2005). Stratification, school-work linkages and vocational education. *Social Forces, 84*(1), 257–284. DOI: 10.1353/sof.2005.0087.

Aliaga, O. A., Kotamraju, P., & Dickinson, E. (2011, November). *Career and technical education course-taking patterns of high school graduates: Exploring the participation in the most frequent sets of occupational areas*. Paper presented at the annual convention of the Association for Career and Technical Education, St. Louis, MO.

Allan, J. (1993). Male elementary teachers: Experiences and perspectives. In C. L. Williams (Ed.), *Doing "women's work": Men in nontraditional occupations* (pp. 113–127). Newbury Park, CA: Sage Publications.

Alper, J. (1993). The pipeline is leaking women all the way. *Science, 260*, 409–411.

Altucher, J. (2010, August). Seven reasons not to send your kids to college. Retrieved from https://collegerealitychat.wordpress.com/dont-go-to-college/saying-no/james-altucher/

American Association of University Professors. (2001). *Statement of principles on family responsibilities and academic work*. Retrieved from www.aaup.org/statements/REPORTS/re01fam.htm#7

American Bar Association Commission on Women in the Profession. (2015). *Goal III report*. Chicago, IL: ABA. Retrieved from www.americanbar.org/

American Psychological Association. (2013). *Gun violence: Prediction, prevention, and policy*. Retrieved from www.apa.org/pubs/info/reports/gun-violence-prevention.aspx

American Society of Plastic Surgeons. (2013). *2013 plastic surgery statistics report.* Retrieved from www.plasticsurgery.org/Documents/news-resources/statistics/2013-statistics/plastic-surgery-statistics-full-report-2013.pdf

American Veterinary Medical Association (AVMA). (2007a, 2008). *Website for veterinary practice management information.* Retrieved from www.avma.org

Angrist, J., Lang, D., & Oreopoulos, P. (2006). *Lead them to water and pay them to drink: An experiment with services and incentives for college achievement* (Working Paper No. w12790), pp 1–61. Cambridge, MA: National Bureau of Economic Research. Retrieved from www.nber.org/papers/w12790

Antecol, H., Bedard, K., & Stearns, J. (2016). *Equal but inequitable: Who benefits from gender-neutral tenure clock stopping policies?* (Report No. 9904). Bonn, Germany: Institute for the Study of Labor (IZA).

Appiah, K. A. (2015, September 13). The college crossroads: The dream and the crisis of higher education. *The New York Times Magazine,* pp. 17–20.

Armstrong, E. A., & Hamilton, L. T. (2013). *Paying for the party: How college maintains inequality.* Cambridge, MA: Harvard University Press.

Armstrong, J. E. (1910). The advantages of limited sex segregation in the high school. *School Review, 18,* 337–338.

Aronson, P. (2008). The markers and meanings of growing up: Contemporary young women's transition from adolescence to adulthood. *Gender and Society, 22*(1), 56–82.

Ashcraft, C., & Blithe, S. (2009). *Women in IT: The facts.* Boulder, CO: National Center for Women in Information Technology.

Ashcraft, C., Eger, E., & Friend, M. (2012). *Girls in IT: The facts.* Boulder, CO: National Center for Women & Technology.

Ashcraft, C., McLain, B., & Eger, E. (2016, Update). *Women in tech: The facts.* Boulder, CO: National Center for Women & Technology.

Ashmore, R. D., Deaux, K., & McLaughlin-Volpe, T. (2004). An organizing framework for collective identity: Articulation and significance of multidimensionality. *Psychological Bulletin, 130,* 80–114.

Astin, A. W. (1998). The changing American college student: Thirty-year trends, 1966–96. *The Review of Higher Education, 21*(2), 115–135.

Astin, A. W., & Oseguera, L. (2004). The declining "equity" of American higher education. *The Review of Higher Education, 27*(3), 321–341.

Autor, D. (2010). *The polarization of job opportunities in the U.S. labor market: Implications for employment and earnings.* Washington, DC: Center for American Progress and The Hamilton Project.

Autor, D., & Wasserman, M. (2013). *Wayward sons: The emerging gender gap in labor markets and education.* Washington, DC: Third Way.

Avishai, O. (2007). Managing the lactating body: The Breast-Feeding Project and privileged motherhood. *Qualitative Sociology, 30*(2), 135–152.

Bae, Y., Choy, S., Geddes, C., Sable, J., & Snyder, T. (2000). *Trends in educational equity of girls & women.* Washington, DC: U.S. Department of Education, National Center for Education Statistics.

Baenninger, M. (2011, October 2). For women on campuses, access doesn't equal success. *Chronicle of Higher Education.* Retrieved from www.chronicle.com/article/for-women-on-campuses-access/129242

Bagilhole, B., & Goode, J. (2001). The contradiction of the myth of individual merit, and the reality of a patriarchal support system in academic careers: A feminist investigation. *European Journal of Women's Studies, 8*(2), 161–180.

Bailey, M. J., & Dynarski, S. M. (2011). *Gains and gaps: Changing inequality in US college entry and completion* (Working Paper No. w17633). Cambridge, MA: National Bureau of Economic Research. Retrieved from www.nber.org

Bailyn, L. (2003). Academic careers and gender equity: Lessons learned from MIT. *Gender, Work & Organization, 10*(2), 137–153.

Baker, D. P. (2011). Forward and backward, horizontal and vertical: Transformation of occupational credentialing in the schooled society. *Research in Social Stratification and Mobility, 29*, 5–29.

Baker, J. (2008). The ideology of choice. Overstating progress and hiding injustice in the lives of young women: Findings from a study in North Queensland, Australia. *Women's Studies International Forum, 31*(1), 53–64.

Baker, J. (2010). Great expectations and post-feminist accountability: Young women living up to the "successful girls" discourse. *Gender and Education, 22*(1), 1–15.

Baker, L. A., & Emery, R. E. (1993). When every relationship is above average: Perceptions and expectations of divorce at the time of marriage. *Law and Human Behavior, 17*(4), 439–450.

Barnes, R. J. D. (2008). Black women have always worked: Is there a work-family conflict among the Black middle class? In E. Rudd & L. Descartes (Eds.), *The changing landscape of work and family in the American middle class* (pp. 189–209). New York, NY: Lexington Books.

Barnett, R. C., & Hyde, J. S. (2001). Women, men, work and family: An expansionist theory. *American Psychologist, 56*(10), 781–796.

Baron, J. N., Hannan, M. T., Hsu, G., & Kocak, O. (2002). Gender and the organization-building process in young, high-tech firms. In M. F. Guillen, R. Collins, P. England, & M. Meyer (Eds.), *The new economic sociology: Developments in an emerging field* (pp. 245–273). New York: Russell Sage Foundation.

Bartlett, T. (2009, November 22). The puzzle of boys. *The Chronicle of Higher Education.* Retrieved from http://chronicle.com

Baum, S., & Goodstein, E. (2005). Gender imbalance in college applications: Does it lead to a preference for men in the admissions process? *Economics of Education Review, 24*, 665–675.

Beaudry, P., & Lewis, E. (2012). *Do male-female wage differentials reflect differences in return to skill?* (NBER Working Paper No. 18159). Cambridge, MA: National Bureau of Economic Research. Retrieved from www.nber.org/papers/w18159

Beede, D., Julian, T., Langdon, D., McKittrick, G., Khan, B., & Doms, M. (2011, August). *Women in STEM: A gender gap to innovation* (ESA Issue Brief #04–11). Washington, DC: Office of the Chief Economist, U.S. Department of Commerce.

Belkin, L. (2003, October 26). The opt-out revolution. *The New York Times Magazine.* Retrieved from www.nytimes.com

Belkin, L. (2008, June 15). When mom and dad share it all. *The New York Times Magazine*, pp. 44–51, 74, 78.

Bellah, R., Madsen, R., Sullivan, W., Swindler, A., & Tipton, S. (1985). *Habits of the heart: Individualism and commitment in American life.* Berkeley and Los Angeles, CA: University of California Press.

Bennett, J. M. (1997). Confronting continuity. *Journal of Women's History, 9*(3), 73–94.

Bennhold, K. (2010, January 24). German woman cast off a taboo on the way to work. *The New York Times*, p. 6N.

Bennhold, K. (2010, October 11). Where having it all doesn't mean having equality. *The New York Times.* Retrieved from www.nytimes.com/2010/10/12/world/europe/12iht-ffffrance.html

Benschop, Y., & Brouns, M. (2003). Crumbling ivory towers: Academic organizing and its after effects. *Gender, Work & Organization, 10*(2), 194–212.

Benson, A., Esteva, R., & Levy, F. S. (2015, January 26). *Is college worth it? The economic return to college under realistic assumptions*. Available at SSRN: https://ssrn.com/abstract=2325657 or http://dx.doi.org/10.2139/ssrn.2325657

Bertaux, N. E., & Anderson, M. C. (2001). An emerging tradition of educational achievement: African American women in college and the professions, 1920–1950. *Equity and Excellence in Education, 34*(2), 16–21.

Bertrand, M., Goldin, C., & Katz, L. F. (2010). Dynamics of the gender gap for young professionals in the financial and corporate sectors. *American Economic Journal: Applied Economics, 2*(3), 228–255.

Bettie, J. (2003). *Women without class: Girls, race, and identity*. Berkeley, CA: University of California Press.

Bielby, R., Posselt, J. R., Jaquette, O., & Bastedo, M. N. (2014). Why are women underrepresented in elite colleges and universities? A non-linear decomposition analysis. *Research in Higher Education, 55*(8), 735–760.

Bielby, W. T., & Bielby, D. D. (1992). I will follow him: Family ties, gender-role beliefs, and reluctance to relocate for a better job. *American Journal of Sociology, 97*(5), 1241–1267.

Bird, S., Wang, Y., & Litt, J. S. (2004). Creating status of women reports: Institutional housekeeping as "women's work." *NWSA Journal, 16*(1), 194–206.

Blair-Loy, M. (2001). It's not just what you know, it's who you know: Technical knowledge, rainmaking, and gender among finance executives. *Research in the Sociology of Work, 10*, 51–83.

Blair-Loy, M. (2009). *Competing devotions: Career and family among women executives*. Cambridge, MA: Harvard University Press.

Blair-Loy, M., & Wharton, A. S. (2002). Employees' use of work-family policies and the workplace social context. *Social Forces, 80*(3), 813–845.

Blau, F. D. (1998). Trends in the well-being of American women 1970–1995. *Journal of Economic Literature, 36*(1), 112–165.

Blau, F. D., Brinton, M. C., & Grusky, D. B. (Eds.). (2006). *The declining significance of gender*. New York: Russell Sage Foundation.

Blau, F. D., Brummund, P., & Liu, A. (2013). Trends in occupational segregation by gender 1970–2009: Adjusting for the impact of changes in the occupational coding system. *Demography, 50*, 471. DOI:10.1007/s13524-012-0151-7

Blau, F. D., & Kahn, L. M. (2016). *The gender wage gap: Extent, trends, and explanations* (Discussion Paper No. 9656). Bonn, Germany: The Institute for the Study of Labor.

Blickenstaff, J. C. (2005). Women and science careers: Leaky pipeline or gender filter? *Gender and Education, 17*(4), 369–386.

Bobbitt-Zeher, D. (2007). The gender income gap and the role of education. *Sociology of Education, 80*(1), 1–22.

Bobbitt-Zeher, D. (2011). Gender discrimination at work connecting gender stereotypes, institutional policies, and gender composition of workplace. *Gender & Society, 25*(6), 764–786.

Bolton, S., & Muzio, D. (2008). The paradoxical processes of feminization in the professions: The case of established, aspiring and semi-professions. *Work, Employment & Society, 22*(2), 281–299.

Boris, E. (2009). Politicizing women's history, engendering policy history. *The Journal of Policy History, 21*(4), 431–438. DOI: 10.1017/S0898030609990169.

Boushey, H. (2005). *Are women opting out? Debunking the myth.* Washington, DC: Center for Economic and Policy Research.

Boushey, H. (2008). "Opting out?" The effect of children on women's employment in the United States. *Feminist Economics, 14*(1), 1–36.

Boushey, H., Baker, D., & Rosnick, D. (2005). *Gender bias in the current economic recovery? Declining employment rates for women in the 21st century* (CEPR No. 2005–24). Washington, DC: Center for Economic and Policy Research.

Bowen, W. G., Bok, D. C., & Shulman, J. L. (1998). *The shape of the river: Long-term consequences of considering race in college and university admissions.* Princeton, NJ: Princeton University Press.

Bowman, N. A., & Bastedo, M. N. (2009). Getting on the front page: Organizational reputation, status signals, and the impact of "U.S. News and World Report" on student decisions. *Research in Higher Education, 50*(5), 415–436.

Boyd-Franklin, N. B., & Franklin, A. J. (2000). *Boys into men: Raising our African American teenage sons.* New York, NY: E. P. Dutton.

Bradley, K. (2000). The incorporation of women in higher education: Paradoxical outcomes? *Sociology of Education, 73*(1), 1–18.

Brickhouse, N. W., & Potter, J. T. (2001). Young women's scientific identity formation in an urban context. *Journal of Research in Science Teaching, 38*(8), 965–980.

Britton, D. M. (2000). The epistemology of the gendered organization. *Gender & Society, 14*(3), 418–434.

Brock, T. (2010). Young adults and higher education: Barriers and breakthroughs to success. *The Future of Children, 20*(10), 109–132.

Brooks, D. (2012, September 10). Why men fail. *The New York Times,* p. A23.

Brown, B. L. (2001). Women and minorities in high-tech careers. *ERIC Digest, 226.*

Brown, D. K. (2001). The social sources of educational credentialism: Status cultures, labor markets, and organizations. *Sociology of Education, 74,* 19–34.

Brown, J. (2007). From cult of masculinity to smart macho: Gender perspectives on police occupational culture. *Sociology of Crime, Law and Deviance, 8,* 205–226.

Brown, L. M., Chesney-Lind, M., & Stein, N. (2006). What about the boys? *Education Week, 25*(39), 35.

Brown, S. W. (2008). The gender differences: Hispanic females and males majoring in science or engineering. *Journal of Women and Minorities in Science and Engineering, 14*(2), 205–223.

Bruder, A. (2012). *Determination and resistance in women's higher education.* Retrieved from http://greenfield.brynmawr.edu/items/show/50

Bryant, Erica. (2008, October 26). Helping boys catch up means livelier classes. Rochester (NY) *Democrat and Chronicle,* pp. 1A, 13A.

Buchmann, C. (2009). Gender inequalities in the transition to college. *Teachers College Record, 111*(10), 2320–2351.

Buchmann, C., & Dalton, B. (2002). Interpersonal influences and educational aspirations in 12 countries: The importance of institutional context. *Sociology of Education, 75*(2), 99–122.

Buchmann, C., & DiPrete, T. A. (2006). The growing female advantage in college completion: The role of family background and academic achievement. *American Sociological Review, 71*(4), 515–541.

Buchmann, C., DiPrete, T. A., & McDaniel, A. (2008). Gender inequalities in education. *Annual Review of Sociology, 34,* 319–337.

Buchmann, C., DiPrete, T. A., & Powell, T. A. (2004). *The growing female advantage in American higher education: Do family processes explain the trend?* Paper presented at colloquium series of the Center for Advanced Social Science Research at New York University, September.

Budig, M. J. (2002). Male advantage and the gender composition of jobs: Who rides the glass escalator? *Social Problems, 49,* 258–277.

Budig, M. J. (2014). *The fatherhood bonus & the motherhood penalty: Parenthood and the gender gap in pay.* Washington, DC: Third Way.

Budig, M. J., & England, P. (2001). The wage penalty for motherhood. *American Sociological Review, 66,* 204–225.

Buerhaus, P. I., Auerbach, D. I., Staiger, D. O., & Muench, U. (2013). Projections of the long-term growth of the registered nurse workforce: A regional analysis. *Nursing Economics, 31*(1), 13–17.

Bureau of Labor Statistics, U.S. Department of Labor. (2004, September 30). *Fatal occupational injuries by industry.* Retrieved from www.bls.gov

Bureau of Labor Statistics, U.S. Department of Labor. (2005, March 30). Recent high school graduates in college and in the work force. *The Economics Daily.* Retrieved from www.bls.gov

Bureau of Labor Statistics, U.S. Department of Labor. (2011). *Labor force statistics from the current population survey: Household data annual averages, 11: Employed persons by detailed occupation, sex, race, and Hispanic or Latino ethnicity.* Retrieved from www.bls.gov/cps/aa2011/cpsaat11.htm

Bureau of Labor Statistics, U.S. Department of Labor. (2012). *Education and training outlook for occupations 2012–2022.* Retrieved from www.bls.gov

Bureau of Labor Statistics, U.S. Department of Labor. (2014a). *Career outlook: Education level and jobs: Opportunities by state.* Retrieved from www.bls.gov/careeroutlook/2014/article/education-level-and-jobs.htm

Bureau of Labor Statistics, U.S. Department of Labor. (2014b). *Highlights of women's earnings in 2013* (Report No. 1051). Retrieved from www.bls.gov/opub/reports/cps/highlights-of-womens-earnings-in-2013.pdf

Bureau of Labor Statistics, U.S. Department of Labor. (2015). *Employment projections, 2014–2024* (Report No. USDL-15-2327). Retrieved from www.bls.gov/news.release/pdf/ecopro.pdf

Bureau of Labor Statistics, U.S. Department of Labor. (2015, July). *Rising to the challenge of a 21st century workforce.* Retrieved from www.bls.gov/opub/mlr/2015/article/rising-to-the-challenge-of-a-21st-century-workforce.htm

Burgess, N. (2013). *The motherhood penalty: How gender and parental status influence judgments of job-related competence and organizational commitment.* Kingston, RI: University of Rhode Island. Retrieved from www.uri.edu

Burrows, L. (2013, January 27). Women remain outsiders in video game industry. *The Boston Globe.* Retrieved from www.bostonglobe.com/business/2013/01/27/women-remain-outsiders-video-game-industry/275JKqy3rFylT7TxgPmO3K/story.html

Bushweller, K. (2001). The new networkers: The path to hot IT jobs begins in high school. *American School Board Journal, 188*(1), 16–19.

Caldwell, C. (2007, February 25). The way we live now: What a college education buys. *The New York Times Magazine,* pp. 15–16.

Cammorata, J. (2008). The gendered and racialized pathways of Latina and Latino youth: Different struggles, different resistances in the urban context. *Anthropology and Education Quarterly, 35*(1), 53–74.

Cantor, M., & Laurie, B. (Eds.). (1977). *Sex, class, and the woman worker.* Westport, CT: Greenwood Press.

Carey, K. (2015). *The end of college: Creating the future of learning and the university of everywhere.* New York, NY: Riverhead Books.

Carnevale, A. P. (2008, January/February). College for all? *Change,* pp. 23–29.

Carnevale, A. P., Jayasundera, T., & Hanson, A. R. (2012). *Career and technical education: Five ways that pay along the way to a B.A.* Washington, DC: Georgetown Public Policy Institute, Center for Education and the Workforce.

Carnevale, A. P., Rose, S. J., & Hanson, A. R. (2012). *Certificates: Gateway to gainful employment and college degrees.* Washington, DC: Georgetown University Center on Education and the Workforce. Retrieved from http://cew.georgetown.edu/certificates/

Carnevale, A. P., Smith, N., Stone, J. R. III, Kotamraju, P., Steuernagel, B., & Green, K. (2011). *Career clusters: Forecasting demand for high school through college jobs, 2008–2018.* Washington, DC: Georgetown University Center on Education and the Workforce.

Cassidy, J. (2015, September 7). College calculus: What is college worth? *The New Yorker.* Retrieved from www.newyorker.com/magazine/2015/09/07/college-calculus

Catalyst, Inc. (2015). *Women in law in Canada and the U.S.* New York, NY: Catalyst.

Catalyst, Inc., & General Motors Corporation. (2005). *Women "take care," men "take charge": Stereotyping of US business leaders exposed.* New York, NY: Catalyst.

Cech, E. A., & Blair-Loy, M. (2010). Perceiving glass ceilings? Meritocratic versus structural explanations of gender inequality among women in science and technology. *Social Problems, 57*(3), 371–397.

Ceci, S. J., & Williams, W. M. (Eds.). (2007). *Why aren't more women in science: Top researchers debate the evidence.* Washington, DC: American Psychological Association.

Ceci, S. J., & Williams, W. M. (2009). *The mathematics of sex: How biology and society conspire to limit talented women and girls.* New York: Oxford University Press.

Ceci, S. J., & Williams, W. M. (2010). Sex differences in math-intensive fields. *Current Directions in Psychological Science, 19*(5), 275–279.

Ceci, S. J., Williams, W. M., Sumner, R. A., & DeFraine, W. C. (2011). Do subtle cues about belongingness constrain women's career choices? *Psychological Inquiry, 22*(4), 255–258.

Cha, Y. (2010). Reinforcing separate spheres: The effect of spousal overwork on men's and women's employment in dual-earner households. *American Sociological Review, 75*(2), 303–329.

Charles, K. K., & Luoh. M. C. (2003). Gender differences in completed schooling. *Review of Economics and Statistics, 85*(3), 559–577.

Charles, M., & Bradley, K. (2002). Equal but separate? A cross-national study of sex segregation in higher education. *American Sociological Review, 67*(4), 573–599.

Charles, M., & Bradley, K. (2009). Indulging our gendered selves? Sex segregation by field of study in 44 countries. *American Journal of Sociology, 114*(4), 924–976.

Charles, M., & Grusky, D. B. (2004). *Occupational ghettos: The worldwide segregation of women and men* (Vol. 200). Redwood City, CA: Stanford University Press.

Cheryan, S., Plaut, V., Handron, C., & Hudson, L. (2013). The stereotypical computer scientist: Gendered media representations as a barrier to inclusion for women. *Sex Roles, 69*(1/2), 58–71.

Chesney-Lind, M., & Jones, N. (Eds.). (2010). *Fighting for girls: New perspectives on gender and violence.* Albany, NY: State University of New York Press.

Chesney-Lind, M., & Pasko, L. J. (2003). *The female offender: Girls, women and crime.* Thousand Oaks, CA: Sage.

Chiappori, P. A., Iyigun, M., & Weiss, Y. (2009). Investment in schooling and the marriage market. *The American Economic Review, 99*(5), 1689–1713.

Child Trends Databank. (2012). *Young adults in jail or prison*. Retrieved from www. childtrends.org

Cho, D. (2007). The role of high school performance in explaining women's rising college enrollment. *Economics of Education Review, 26*(4), 450–462.

Choo, H. Y., & Ferree, M. M. (2010). Practicing intersectionality in sociological research: A critical analysis of inclusions, interactions, and institutions in the study of inequalities. *Sociological Theory, 28*(2), 129–149.

Christensen, G., Steinmetz, A., Alcorn, B., Bennett, A., Woods, D., & Emanuel, E. J. (2013, November 6). *The MOOC phenomenon: Who takes massive open online courses and why?* Retrieved from SSRN: http://ssrn.com/abstract=2350964 or http://dx.doi.org/10.2139/ssrn.2350964

Christian-Smith, L. K. (1990). *Becoming a woman through romance.* New York, NY: Routledge.

Christopher, K. (2012). Extensive mothering: Employed mothers' constructions of the good mother. *Gender & Society, 26*(1), 73–96.

Chugh, D., & Brief, A. P. (2008). 1964 was not that long ago: A story of gateways and pathways. In A. P. Brief (Ed.), *Diversity at work* (pp. 318–340). Cambridge, UK: Cambridge University Press.

Clarke, E. H. (1875). *Sex in education: Or, a fair chance for girls.* Boston, MA: James R. Osgood and Company.

The Clinton Foundation and the Bill and Melinda Gates Foundation. (2015, March). *No ceilings: The full participation report.* Retrieved from www.noceilings.org

Clynes, T. (2016, June 5). Peter Thiel's dropout army. *The New York Times*, p. A5.

Cobb, R., & Sennett, R. (1974). *The hidden injuries of class.* New York, NY: Knopf.

Cockburn, C. (1988). *Machinery of dominance: Women, men, and technical know-how.* Boston: Northeastern University Press.

Cognard-Black, A. J. (2004). Will they stay, or will they go? Sex-atypical work among token men who teach. *Sociological Quarterly 45*(1), 113–139.

Cohn, D., Livingston, G., & Wang, W. (2014, April). *After decades of decline, a rise in stay-at-home mothers.* Washington, DC: Pew Research Center's Social & Demographic Trends project.

Cohoon, J. (2007, April). *The state of research on girls and IT.* Retrieved from www.ncwit.org/stateofgirls

Colavecchio-Van Sickler, S. (2007, April 2). Lawmakers look to schools to fill high-tech skills gap: Programs would smooth path from school to work. *St. Petersburg Times*, pp. A1, A14.

Cole, J. R., & Zuckerman, H. (1987). Marriage, motherhood, and research performance in science. In H. Zuckerman, J. R. Cole, & J. T. Bruer (Eds.), *The outer circle women in the scientific community* (pp. 157–170). New York, NY: W. W. Norton & Company.

Coley, R. J. (2001). *Differences in the gender gap: Comparisons across racial/ethnic groups in education and work.* Princeton, NJ: Educational Testing Service.

The College Board: Advocacy & Policy Center. (2013). *The educational experience of young men of color.* Retrieved from http://youngmenofcolor.collegeboard.org

Collins, A., & Halverson, R. (2009). *Rethinking education in the age of technology: The digital revolution and the schools.* New York, NY: Teachers College Press.

Collins, C. W., Kenway, J., & McLeod, J. (2000). Gender debates we still have to have. *The Australian Educational Researcher, 27*(3), 37–48.

Collins, C. W., McLeod, J., & Kenway, J. (2000). *Factors influencing the educational performance of males and females in school and their initial destinations after leaving school.* Canberra, Australia: Commonwealth Department of Education, Training and Youth Affairs.

Collins, G. (2009). *When everything changed: The amazing journey of American women from 1960 to the present.* New York: Little, Brown and Company.

Collins, R. (1979). *The credential society: An historical sociology of education and stratification.* New York, NY: Academic Press.

Collins, R., Chafetz, J. S., Blumberg, R. L., Coltrane, S., & Turner, J. H. (1993). Toward an integrated theory of gender stratification. *Sociological Perspectives, 36*(3), 185–216.

Collinson, D. L. (2003). Identities and insecurities: Selves at work. *Organization, 10*(3), 527–547.

Coltrane, S. (2004). Elite careers and family commitment: It's (still) about gender. *Annals of the American Academy of Political and Social Science, 596*(1), 214–220.

Committee on Women Faculty. (1999). *A study on the status of women faculty in science at MIT.* Boston: Massachusetts Institute of Technology.

Connell, R. W. (1995, 2005). *Masculinities.* Berkeley, CA: University of California Press.

Connell, R. W. (2000). *The men and the boys.* Berkeley, CA: University of California Press.

Connell, R. W. (2010). Kartini's children: On the need for thinking gender and education together on a world scale. *Gender and Education, 22*(6), 603–616.

Contreras, F. (2011). *Achieving equity for Latino students: Expanding the pathway to higher education through public policy.* New York: Teachers College Press.

Cook, B. W. (Ed.). (1978). *Women and revolution.* New York, NY: Oxford University Press.

Coontz, S. (1992). *The way we never were: American families and the nostalgia trap.* New York: Basic Books.

Coontz, S. (2005). *Marriage, a history: From obedience to intimacy, or how love conquered marriage.* New York: Viking.

Coontz, S. (2012, September 30). The myth of male decline. *New York Times, Sunday Review,* pp. 1, 4–5.

Corbett, C., & Hill, C. (2012). *Graduating to a pay gap: The earnings of women and men one year after college graduation.* Washington, DC: American Association of University Women.

Corbett, C., Hill, C., & St. Rose, A. (2008). *Where the girls are: The facts about gender equity in education.* Washington, DC: American Association of University Women Educational Foundation.

Correll, S. J., Benard, S., & Paik, I. (2007). Getting a job: Is there a motherhood penalty? *American Journal of Sociology, 112*(5), 1297–1339.

Covert, B. (2014, May 19). In the real world, the so-called "boy-crisis" disappears. *The Nation.* Retrieved from www.thenation.com

Covert, B. (2015, April 14). Education alone won't put an end to equal pay days. *The Nation.* Retrieved from www.thenation.com

Cox, T. (2007, December 14). Blacks using military to get ahead. *National Public Radio* [Audio Broadcast]. Retrieved from www.npr.org/templates/story/story.php?storyId= 17259797

Crocco, M. S., & Waite, C. L. (2007). Education and marginality: Race and gender in higher education, 1940–1955. *History of Education Quarterly, 47*(1), 69–91.

Cron, W. L., Slocum Jr, J. V., Goodnight, D. B., & Volk, J. O. (2000). Impact of management practices and business behaviors on small animal veterinarians' incomes. *JAVMA*

Executive summary. Retrieved from http://s3.amazonaws.com/academia.edu.documents/ 31930277/Brakke_Study_1999_vet_management_.pdf?AWSAccessKeyId=AKIAI WOWYYGZ2Y53UL3A&Expires=1488487092&Signature=vUQU7gJScx1e37zd 9CG4oSe%2FMOM%3D&response-content-disposition=inline%3B%20filename %3DBrakke_Study_1999_vet_management.pdf

Cross, T., & Slater, R. B. (2000). The alarming decline in the academic performance of African-American men. *Journal of Blacks in Higher Education, 27,* 82–87.

Cruikshank, J. (2007). Lifelong learning and the new economy: Rhetoric or reality? *Education Canada, 47*(2), 32–36.

Cuban, L., & Shipps, D. (Eds.). (2000). *Reconstructing the common good in education: Coping with intractable American dilemmas.* Redwood City, CA: Stanford University Press.

Cuyjet, M. J., & Associates (Eds.). (2006). *African American men in college.* San Francisco, CA: Jossey-Bass.

Dance, L. J. (2002). *Tough fronts: The impact of street culture on schooling.* New York: Routledge Falmer.

David, M. E., Ball, S. J., Davies, J., & Reay, D. (2003). Gender issues in parental involvement in student choices of higher education. *Gender and Education, 15*(1), 21–36.

Davidson, A. L. (1996). *Making and molding identity in schools: Student narratives on race, gender, and academic engagement.* Albany, NY: State University of New York Press.

Davies, B., Dormer, S., Gannon, S., Laws, C., Rocco, S., Taguchi, H. L., & McCann, H. (2001). Becoming schoolgirls: The ambivalent project of subjectification. *Gender and Education, 13*(2), 167–182.

Davis, J. A., Smith, T. W., & Marsden, P. V. (2009). *General Social Surveys, 1972–2008* [Cumulative File]. Ann Arbor, MI: Inter-University Consortium for Political and Social Research.

Davis, J. E. (2003). Early schooling and academic achievement of African American males. *Urban Education, 38*(5), 515–537.

Davis, S. N., & Greenstein, T. N. (2009). Gender ideology: Components, predictors, and consequences. *Annual Review of Sociology, 35,* 87–105.

Dempster, S. (2009). Having the balls, having it all? Sport and constructions of undergraduate laddishness. *Gender and Education, 21*(5), 481–500.

Dempster, S. (2010). "I drink, therefore I'm man": Gender discourses, alcohol and the construction of British undergraduate masculinities. *Gender and Education, 23*(5), 635–653.

Desvaux, G., Devillard-Hoellinger, S., & Baumgarten, P. (2007). *Women matter: Gender diversity, a corporate performance driver.* Paris, France: McKinsey.

Dewan, S., & Gebeloff, R. (2012, May 20). More men enter fields dominated by women. *The New York Times.* Retrieved from www.nytimes.com

De Welde, K., & Laursen, S. (2011). The glass obstacle course: Informal and formal barriers for women Ph. D. students in STEM fields. *International Journal of Gender, Science and Technology, 3*(3), 571–595.

Dey, J. G., & Hill, C. (2007). *Behind the pay gap.* Washington, DC: American Association of University Women Educational Foundation.

Dickson, L. (2010). Race and gender differences in college major choice. *The Annals of the American Academy of Political and Social Science, 627*(1), 108–124.

Diekman, A. B., Brown, E. R., Johnston, A. M., & Clark, E. K. (2010). Seeking congruity between goals and roles a new look at why women opt out of science, technology, engineering, and mathematics careers. *Psychological Science, 21*(8), 1051–1057.

DiMaggio, P., & Mohr, J. (1985). Cultural capital, educational attainment, and marital selection. *American Journal of Sociology, 90,* 1231–1261.

DiPrete, T. A., & Buchmann, C. (2006). Gender-specific trends in the value of education and the emerging gender gap in college completion. *Demography, 43*(1), 1–24.

DiPrete, T. A., & Buchmann, C. (2013). *The rise of women: The growing gender gap in education and what it means for American schools.* New York, NY: Russell Sage Foundation.

DiPrete, T. A., & Jennings, J. L. (2012). Social and behavioral skills and the gender gap in early educational achievement. *Social Science Research, 41*(1), 1–15.

Douglas, S. J., & Michaels, M. W. (2004). *The mommy myth: The idealization of motherhood and how it has undermined all women.* New York, NY: Free Press.

Duckworth, A. L., & Seligman, M. E. (2006). Self-discipline gives girls the edge: Gender in self-discipline, grades, and achievement test scores. *Journal of Educational Psychology, 98*(1), 198.

Dude Ranchers' Association. (1926). Retrieved from www.duderanch.org

Dwyer, R. E., Hodson, R., & McCloud, L. (2013). Gender, debt, and dropping out of college. *Gender & Society, 27*(1), 30–55.

Dyer, S. K. (Ed.). (2001). *Beyond "gender wars": A conversation about girls, boys, and education.* Washington, DC: American Association of University Women Educational Foundation.

Dynarski, S. (2007). *Cradle to college: The puzzle of gender differences in educational outcomes.* Unpublished manuscript, Harvard University, Kennedy School of Government & National Bureau of Economic Research, Cambridge, MA.

Eaton, J. (1997). The evolution of access policy: 1965–1990. In L. F. Goodchild, C. D. Lovell, E. R. Hines, & J. I. Gill (Eds.), *Public policy in higher education* (pp. 237–246). Needham Heights, MA: Pearson Custom Publishing.

Eckholm, E. (2008, June 26). Career programs stress college, too, and give students a leg up, study says. *The New York Times.* Retrieved from www.nytimes.com

Egan, J. (2012, March 8). *One out of every ten Black girls suspended from school.* Retrieved from the National Women's Law Center www.nwlc.org

Eisenhart, M. A. (1990). Learning to romance: Cultural acquisition in college. *Anthropology & Education Quarterly, 21*(1), 19–40.

Eisenhart, M. A., & Finkel, E. (1998). *Women's science: Learning and succeeding from the margins.* Chicago, IL: The University of Chicago Press.

Eisenhart, M. A., & Holland, D. C. (1983). Learning gender from peers: The role of peer groups in the cultural transmission of gender. *Human Organization, 42*(4), 321–332.

Eisenhart, M. A., & Lawrence, N. R. (1994). Anita Hill, Clarence Thomas, and the culture of romance. In A. Kibbey, K. Short, & A. Farmanfarmaian (Eds.), *Sexual artifice: Persons, images, and politics* (pp. 94–121). New York: New York University Press.

Eisenmann, L. (2006). *Higher education for women in Postwar America, 1945–1965.* Baltimore, MD: Johns Hopkins University Press.

Elliott, J. R., & Smith, R. A. (2004). Race, gender, and workplace power. *American Sociological Review, 69*(3), 365–386.

Ely, R., & Meyerson, D. (2006). *Unmasking manly men: The organizational reconstruction of men's identity.* Academy of Management Proceedings 1, J1–J6.

Emerson, M. O., Smith, C., & Sikkink, D. (1999). Equal in Christ, but not in the world: White conservative protestants and explanations of black-white inequality. *Social Problems, 46*(3), 398–417.

EMS Workforce for the Twenty-First Century: A National Assessment. (2008). *National highway traffic safety administration.* Hauppauge, NY: Nova Science.

England, P. (2006). Toward gender equality: Progress and bottlenecks. In F. D. Blau, M. C. Brinton, & D. B. Grusky (Eds.), *The declining significance of gender?* (pp. 245–264). New York: Russell Sage Foundation.

England, P. (2010). The gender revolution uneven and stalled. *Gender & Society, 24*(2), 149–166.

England, P., Allison, P., Li, S., Mark, N., Thompson, J., Budig, M. J., & Sun, H. (2007). Why are some academic fields tipping toward female? The sex composition of US fields of doctoral degree receipt, 1971–2002. *Sociology of Education, 80*(1), 23–42.

England, P., & Farkas, G. (1986). *Households, employment, and gender: A social, economic, and demographic view.* Hawthorne, NY: Aldine Publishing.

England, P., Herbert, M. S., Kilbourne, B. S., Reid, L. L., & Megdal, L. M. (1994). The gendered valuation of occupations and skills: Earnings in 1980 census occupations. *Social Forces, 73*(1), 65–100.

England, P., & Li, S. (2006). Desegregation stalled the changing gender composition of college majors, 1971–2002. *Gender & Society, 20*(5), 657–677.

England, P., Shafer, E. F., & Fogarty, A. C. (2007). Hooking up and forming romantic relationships on today's college campuses. In M. Kimmel & A. Aronson (Eds.), *The gendered society reader* (3rd Ed., pp. 531–547). New York: Oxford University Press.

Epstein, C. F. (1970). *Woman's place: Options and limits in professional careers.* Berkeley, CA: University of California Press.

Erchull, M. J., Liss, M., Axelson, S. J., Staebell, S. E., & Askari, S. F. (2010). Well . . . she wants it more: Perceptions of social norms about desires for marriage and children and anticipated chore participation. *Psychology of Women Quarterly, 34*(2), 253–260.

Erickson, J., & Ettlinger, M. (2013). *300 million engines of growth: A middle-out plan for jobs, business, and a growing economy.* Washington, DC: Center for American Progress.

Espenshade, T. J., Hale, L. E., & Chung, C. Y. (2005). The frog pond revisited: High school academic context, class rank, and elite college admission. *Sociology of Education, 78*(4), 269–293.

Espinosa, L. L. (2011). Pipelines and pathways: Women of color in undergraduate STEM majors and the college experiences that contribute to persistence. *Harvard Educational Review, 81*(2), 209–241.

Etaugh, C., & Study, G. (1989). Perceptions of mothers: Effects of employment status, marital status, and age of child. *Sex Roles, 20,* 59–70.

Ewert, S., & Kominski, R. (2014, January). *Measuring alternative educational credentials: 2012: Household economic studies* (U.S. Census Bureau Report No. P70–138). Retrieved from www.census.gov

Executive Office of the President, & President's Council of Advisors on Science and Technology (PCAST). (2012). *Engage to excel: Producing one million additional college graduates with degrees in science, technology, engineering, and mathematics.* Washington, DC: PCAST.

Fain, P. L. (2012, June 6). Certificates are misunderstood credentials that pay off mostly for men. *Inside Higher Ed.* Retrieved from www.insidehighered.com/

Fan, P. L., & Marini, M. M. (2000). Influences on gender-role attitudes during the transition to adulthood. *Social Science Research, 29*(2), 258–283.

Farrell, C. (2001, March 16). Men are falling behind in the degree race. *Business Week Online.* Retrieved from www.businessweek.com

Fennell, S., & Arnot, M. (Eds.). (2007). *Gender education & equality in a global context: Conceptual frameworks and policy perspectives.* London, UK: Routledge.

Fertig, J. (2011, August). Success without college. *Academic Questions, 24,* 291–299.

Fewer mothers prefer full-time work: From 1997–2007. (2007, July 12). *Pew Research Center.* Retrieved from http://pewresearch.org

Fields, G. (2008, October 21). The high school dropout's economic ripple effect. *The Wall Street Journal.* Retrieved from http://wsj.com

Fine, C. (2010). *Delusions of gender: How our minds, society, and neurosexism create difference.* New York: W. W. Norton & Company.

Fischer, K. (2011, December 12). At forum on the future, leaders dissect what ails higher education today. *Chronicle of Higher Education.* Retrieved from http://chronicle.com/article/At-Forum-on-the-Future/130087/

Fiske, E. B. (2000, February 14). US Colleges attempt to redress gender balance: Men go missing on campus. *The New York Times.* Retrieved from www.nytimes.com

Flexner, E., & Fitzpatrick, E. (1996). *Century of struggle: The women's rights movement in the United States* (Expanded Ed.). Cambridge, MA: Harvard University Press, pp. 208–217.

Folbre, N. (2014, October 15). Should you go to college? In Geier, K., Folbre, N., Clark, A. and Feiner, S. *The Nation.* Retrieved from www.thenation.com/article/should-you-go-college/

Foster, V. (2000). Is female educational "success" destabilizing the male learner citizen? In M. Arnot & J. A. Dillaough (Eds.), *Challenging democracy, international perspectives on gender, education and citizenship* (pp. 203–215). London, UK: Routledge-Falmer.

Fox, J. (2015, September 25). Keep digging to find the gig economy. *Bloomberg View.* Retrieved from www.bloombergview.com/articles/2015-09-25/keep-digging-to-find-the-size-of-the-gig-economy

Francis, A. M., & Tannuri-Pianto, M. (2012). The redistributive equity of affirmative action: Exploring the role of race, socioeconomic status, and gender in college admissions. *Economics of Education Review, 31*(1), 45–55.

Francis, B., & Skelton, C. (2005). *Reassessing gender and achievement: Questioning contemporary key debates.* London, UK: Routledge.

Francis, D. R. (2006). *Why do women outnumber men in college?* (NBER Working Paper No. 12139). Washington, DC: National Bureau of Economic Research.

Frank, T. (2014, May 8). Congratulations, class of 2014: You're totally screwed. *Salon.com.* Retrieved from www.salon.com/2014/05/18/congratulations_class_of_2014_youre_totally_screwed/

Franklin, E. B. (2006, January 28). African American boys: The cries of a crisis. *The Kansas City Star.* Retrieved from www.kansascity.com

Fraser, N. (2009). Feminism, capitalism and the cunning of history. *New Left Review, 56,* 97–117.

Freeman, C. E. (2004). *Trends in educational equity of girls and women: 2004* (Report No. NCES 2005–016). Washington, DC: National Center for Educational Statistics & Institute of Education Sciences.

Frehill, L. M. (2000). Race, class, gender, and college completion: The 1980 high school senior cohort. *Race, Gender & Class, 7,* 81–107.

Friedman, T. (2014, February 16). Start-up America: Our best hope. *The New York Times,* p. SR1.

Frontline World. (2002). *Kids' eye view: Looking through the hole in the wall.* Retrieved from www.pbs.org/frontlineworld/stories/india/kids.html

Froschl, M., & Sprung, B. (2005). *Raising and educating healthy boys: A report on the growing crisis in boys' education.* New York: Educational Equity Center at The Academy for Educational Development.

Fuegen, K., Biernat, M., Haines, E., & Deaux, K. (2004). Mothers and fathers in the workplace: How gender and parental status influence judgments of job-related competence. *Journal of Social Issues, 60*(4), 737–754.

Gabriel, P. E., & Schmitz, S. (2007, June). Gender differences in occupational distributions among workers. *Monthly Labor Review,* pp. 19–24.

Gaines, K. (1996). *Uplifting the race: Black leadership, politics and culture in the twentieth century.* Chapel Hill, NC: University of North Carolina Press.

Galambos, N., Petersen, A. C., Richards, M., & Gitelson, I. B. (1985). The Attitudes toward Women Scale for Adolescents (AWSA): A study of reliability and validity. *Sex Roles, 13,* 343–356.

Gandel, C. (2013, September 10). Discover 11 hot college majors that lead to jobs. *U.S. News & World Report.* Retrieved from www.usnews.com/education/best-colleges/articles/2013/09/10/discover-11-hot-college-majors-that-lead-to-jobs

Garibaldi, A. M. (1986). Sustaining Black educational progress: Challenges for the 1990s. *The Journal of Negro Education, 55,* 386–396.

Garibaldi, A. M. (2014). The expanding gender and racial gap in American higher education. *The Journal of Negro Education, 83*(3), 371–384.

Gatta, M. L., & Roos, P. A. (2005). Rethinking occupational integration. *Sociological Forum, 20*(3), 369–402.

Gee, J. P. (2000). Identity as an analytic lens for research in education. *Review of Research in Education, 25,* 99–125.

Gerarda Power, N., & Baqee, S. (2010). Constructing a "culture of safety": An examination of the assumptions embedded in occupational safety and health curricula delivered to high school students and fish harvesters in Newfoundland and Labrador, Canada. *Policy and Practice in Health and Safety, 8*(1), 5–23.

Gerson, K. (1985). *Hard choices: How women decide about work, career and motherhood.* Berkeley, CA: University of California Press.

Gerson, K. (2009, December). Changing lives, resistant institutions: A new generation negotiates gender, work, and family change. *Sociological Forum, 24*(4), 735–753.

Gerson, K. (2010). *The unfinished revolution: How a new generation is reshaping family, work, and gender in America.* New York, NY: Oxford University Press.

Ghaill, M.M.A. (1994). *The making of men: Masculinities, sexualities, and schooling.* Buckingham, England: Open University Press.

Ghaill, M.M.A. (1996). "What about the boys?": Schooling, class and crisis masculinity. *Sociological Review, 44*(3), 381–397.

Gibbs, A. (2009, January 4). After layoffs, couples wrestle with role reversal. *WE News.* Retrieved from www.womensenews.org

Gibbs, N. (2009, October 14). What women want now: The state of the American woman. *Time.* Retrieved from www.time.com

Gilborn, D. (2008). *Racism and education: Coincidence or conspiracy.* London, UK: Routledge.

Gilder, G. (2005). The idea of the (feminized) university. *National Review, 57*(24), 26–28.

Gittell, R. (2009). Constrained choices and persistent gender inequity the economic status of working women in a high-income, low-poverty state. *American Behavioral Scientist, 53*(2), 170–192.

Glenn, D. (2001, December 3). The war on campus: Will academic freedom survive? *The Nation,* pp. 11–14.

Goldberg, W. A., Kelly, E., Matthews, N. L., Kang, H., Li, W., & Sumaroka, M. (2012). The more things change, the more they stay the same: Gender, culture, and college students' views about work and family. *Journal of Social Issues, 68*(4), 814–837.

Goldberg, W. A., & Lucas-Thompson, R. G. (2014). College women miss the mark when estimating the impact of full-time maternal employment on children's achievement and behavior. *Psychology of Women Quarterly, 38*(4), 490–502.

Goldin, C. D. (1990). *Understanding the gender gap: The economic history of American women.* New York: Oxford University Press.

Goldin, C. D. (1991). The role of World War II in the rise of women's employment. *The American Economic Review, 81*(4), 741–756.

Goldin, C. D. (1992). *The meaning of college in the lives of American women: The past one-hundred years* (Working Paper No. w4099). Chicago, IL: National Bureau of Economic Research.

Goldin, C. D. (1995). *Career and family: College women look to the past* (Working Paper No. w5188). Chicago, IL: National Bureau of Economic Research.

Goldin, C. D. (1998). America's graduation from high school: The evolution and spread of secondary schooling in the twentieth century. *Journal of Economic History, 58*(2), 345–374.

Goldin, C. D. (2004). The long road to the fast track: Career and family. *The Annals of the American Academy of Political and Social Science, 596*(1), 20–35.

Goldin, C. D., & Katz, L. F. (2002). The power of the pill: Oral contraceptives and women's career and marriage decisions. *Journal of Political Economy, 110*(4), 730–770.

Goldin, C. D., Katz, L. F., & Kuziemko, I. (2006). The homecoming of American college women: The reversal of the college gender gap. *The Journal of Economic Perspectives, 20*(4), 133–156.

Gorman, E. H. (2005). Gender stereotypes, same-gender preferences, and organizational variation in the hiring of women: Evidence from law firms. *American Sociological Review, 70*(4), 702–728.

Gose, B. (1997). Liberal-arts colleges ask: Where have the men gone? *Chronicle of Higher Education, 43*(39), A35–A36.

Goyette, K. A. (2008). College for some to college for all: Social background, occupational expectations, and educational expectations over time. *Social Science Research, 37*(2), 461–484.

Goyette, K. A., & Mullen, A. L. (2006). Who studies the arts and sciences? Social background and the choice and consequences of undergraduate field of study. *Journal of Higher Education, 77*(3), 497–538.

Granieri, R. J. (2010). The worst of both worlds: The crisis in American higher education. *Quarterly Review, 4*(3), 32–37.

Grauerholz, E., & Serpe, R. T. (1985). Initiation and response: The dynamics of sexual interaction. *Sex Roles, 9/10*, 1041–1059.

Green, S. K., & Sandos, P. (1983). Perceptions of male and female initiators of relationships. *Sex Roles, 9*, 849–852.

Greene, H., & Greene, M. (2004). The widening gender gap: Shifting student demographics will have significant impact on college admissions. *University Business, 7*(9), 27–29.

Greene, J. P., & Winters, M. A. (2005). *Public high school graduation and college-readiness rates: 1991–2002* (Education Working Paper No. 8). New York: Center for Civic Innovation.

Greene, J. P., & Winters, M. A. (2006). *Leaving boys behind: Public high school graduation rates* (Civic Report No. 48). New York: Center for Civic Innovation.

Greenhouse, S. (2015, December 7). Uber: On the road to nowhere. *The American Prospect.* Retrieved from http://prospect.org/article/road-nowhere-3

Gurian, M. (1996). *The wonder of boys: What parents, mentors, and educators can do to raise boys into exceptional men.* New York, NY: Tarcher/Putnam.

Gurian, M. (2005, December 4). Disappearing act. *The Washington Post.* Retrieved from www.washingtonpost.com/wpdyn/content/article/2005/12/02/AR2005120201334.html

Gurian, M., & Stevens, K. (2005, May 2). What is happening with boys in school? *Teachers College Record.* Retrieved from www.tcrecord.org ID Number: 11854

Gushue, G. V., & Whitson, M. L. (2006). The relationship of ethnic identity and gender role attitudes to the development of career choice goals among black and Latina girls. *Journal of Counseling Psychology, 53*(3), 379–385.

Hacker, S. L. (1989). *Pleasure, power and technology: Some tales of gender, engineering, and the cooperative workplace.* Boston: Unwin Hyman.

Hacker, S. L. (1990). *Doing it the hard way: Investigation of gender and technology.* Winchester, MA: Unwin Hyman.

Hafner, K. (2012, April 2). Giving women the access code. *The New York Times.* Retrieved from www.nytimes.com

Hagan, J. (1990). The gender stratification of income inequality among lawyers. *Social Forces, 68*(3), 835–855.

Haines, L. (2004). *Why are there so few women in games?* Manchester, UK: Media Training Northwest.

Hall, E. J., & Rodriguez, M. S. (2003). The myth of postfeminism. *Gender & Society, 17*(6), 878–902.

Hall, G. S. (1904, 1916). Adolescence: Its psychology and its relations to physiology, anthropology, sociology, sex, crime, religion, and education. 2 vols. New York, NY: D. Appleton & Company.

Hamilton, L., Geist, C., & Powell, B. (2011). Marital name change as a window into gender attitudes. *Gender & Society, 25*(2), 145–175.

Hanauer, N., & Rolf, D. (2015, Summer). Shared security, shared growth. *Democracy Journal, 37.* Retrieved from www.democracyjournal.org/37/shared-security-shared-growth.php

Harper, S. R., & Harris, F. III. (2010). *College men and masculinities: Theory, research, and implications for practice.* San Francisco, CA: John Wiley & Sons.

Harris, A. P. (2000). *Gender, violence, race, and criminal justice.* Retrieved from www.nccd-crc.org/nccd/pubs/2007jan_justice_for_some.pdf (accessed April 10, 2008).

Harris, A. P. (2004). *Future girl: Young women in the twenty-first century.* New York: Routledge.

Harris, A. P. (Ed.). (2004). *All about the girl: Culture, power, and identity.* New York: Routledge.

Haywood, C., & Mac an Ghaill, M. (2012). What next for masculinity? Reflexive directions for theory and research on masculinity and education. *Gender and Education, 24*(6), 577–592.

Hennessey, S. (2008, June 29). Grads still see a gender-based pay gap. *Businessweek.* Retrieved from www.businessweek.com/archive/news

Hersh, R., & Merrow, J. (Eds.). (2005). *Declining by degrees: Higher education at risk.* New York, NY: Palgrave MacMillan.

Hewitt, V. L. (2015). *A challenge to excel: Creating a new image for elite women's colleges in the 1970s.* Unpublished dissertation, University of Pennsylvania, Philadelphia, PA.

Hewlett, S. A. (2014, March 13). What's holding women back in science and technology industries? *Harvard Business Review,* pp. 1–2.

Hewlett, S. A., & Luce, C. B. (2005). Off-ramps and on-ramps: Keeping talented women on the road to success. *Harvard Business Review, 83*(3), 43–54.

Hewlett, S. A., Luce, C. B., & Servon, L. J. (2008). Stopping the exodus of women in science. *Harvard Business Review, 86*(6), 22–24.

Heymann, J., Earle, A., & Hayes, J. (2005). *The work, family and equity index: How does the United States measure up?* Boston, MA: The Project on Global Working Families and The Institute for Health and Social Policy.

Higginbotham, E., & Weber, L. (1992). Moving up with kin and community: Upward social mobility for black and white women. *Gender & Society, 6*(3), 416–440.

Higginson, J. H. (1974). Dame schools. *British Journal of Educational Studies, 22,* 167.

Higher Education Research Institute, & Cooperative Institutional Research Program. (2010, January). *Degrees of success: Bachelor's degree completion rates among initial STEM majors.* Retrieved from www.heri.ucla.edu

Hill, C., Corbett, C., & St Rose, A. (2010). *Why so few? Women in science, technology, engineering, and mathematics.* Washington, DC: American Association of University Women.

Hindman, M. (2008). *The myth of digital democracy.* Princeton, NJ: Princeton University Press.

History of athletics in U.S. colleges and universities. (n.d.) Retrieved from http://education. stateuniversity.com/pages/1846/College-Athletics

Hochschild, A. R. (1989). *The second shift: Working families and the revolution at home.* New York: Viking.

Hochschild, A. R. (1997). Time in the balance. *The Nation, 264*(20), 11–15.

Hodgson, D. (2007). Towards a more telling way of understanding early school leaving. *Issues in Educational Research, 17*(1), 40–61.

Hodson, G., Dovidio, J. F., & Gaertner, S. L. (2002). Processes in racial discrimination: Differential weighting of conflicting information. *Personality and Social Psychology Bulletin, 28,* 460–471.

Hoff Sommers, C. (2013, February 3). The boys at the back. *The New York Times,* Sunday Review, pp. 1, 6.

Holland, D. C., & Eisenhart, M. A. (1981). *Women's peer groups and choice of career* (Final Report No. NIE-G-79-0108). Washington, DC: National Institute of Education (NIE).

Holland, D. C., & Eisenhart, M. A. (1990). *Educated in romance: Women, achievement, and college culture.* Chicago, IL: University of Chicago Press.

Holland, D. C., & Skinner, D. (1987). Prestige and intimacy: The cultural models behind Americans' talk about gender types. In D. Holland & N. Quinn (Eds.), *Cultural models in language and thought* (pp. 78–111). Cambridge, UK: Cambridge University Press.

Hossfeld, K. J. (1990). "Their logic against them": Contradictions in sex, race, and class in Silicon Valley. In K. B. Ward (Ed.), *Women workers and global restructuring* (pp. 149–178). Ithaca, NY: ILR Press, Cornell University.

Houston, M. (2006, November 27). The truth about boys. *The Age.* Retrieved from www. theage.com.au

Hu, W. (2007, January 14). Equal cheers for boys and girls draw some boos. *The New York Times,* pp. A1, A35.

Huerta, A. H. (2015). "I didn't want my life to be like that": Gangs, college, or the military for Latino male high school students. *Journal of Latino/Latin American Studies, 7*(2), 119–132.

Hulett, D. A., Bendick, M., Thomas, S. Y., & Moccio, F. (2008). *National report card on women in firefighting: Institute for women and work, school of Industrial and Labor Relations (ILR).* Ithaca, NY: Cornell University.

Hultin, M. (2003). Some take the glass escalator, some hit the glass ceiling? Career consequences of occupational sex segregation. *Work and Occupations, 30*(1), 30–61.

Hurt, H. III. (2007, June 17). Oh, to be 19 and an entrepreneur. *The New York Times,* p. 7.

Hyde, J. S. (2005). The gender similarities hypothesis. *American Psychologist, 60*(6), 581–592.

Institute for Women's Policy Research (IWPR). (2015). *The status of women in the United States: 2015: Employment and earnings.* Washington, DC. Retrieved from http://statu sofwomendata.org/app/uploads/2015/02/EE-CHAPTER-FINAL.pdf

Irvine, L., & Vermilya, J. R. (2010). Gender work in a feminized profession: The case of veterinary medicine. *Gender & Society*, *24*(1), 56–82.

Jackson, C., Dempster, S., & Pollard, L. (2015). "They just don't seem to really care, they just think it's cool to sit there and talk": Laddism in university teaching learning contexts. *Educational Review*, *67*(3), 300–314, DOI: 10.1080/00131911.2014.910178.

Jacob, B. A. (2002). Where the boys aren't: Non-cognitive skills, returns to school and the gender gap in higher education. *Economics of Education Review*, *21*(6), 589–598.

Jacobs, J. A. (1995). Gender and academic specialties: Trends among recipients of college degrees in the 1980s. *Sociology of Education*, *68*(2), 81–98.

Jacobs, J. A. (1996). Gender inequality and higher education. *Annual Review of Sociology*, *22*(1), 153–185.

Jacobs, J. A. (2003). Detours on the road to equality: Women, work and higher education. *Contexts*, *2*(1), 32–41.

Jacobs, J. A., & Gerson, K. (2004). *The time divide: Work, family, and gender inequality.* Cambridge, MA: Harvard University Press.

Jacobs, J. A., & King, R. B. (2002). Age and college completion: A life-history analysis of women aged 15–44. *Sociology of Education*, *75*(3), 211–230.

Jaschik, S. (2008, September 22). New question on women, academe and careers. *Inside Higher Ed*. Retrieved from www.insidehighered.com

Jha, J., & Kelleher, F. (2006). *Boys' underachievement in education: An exploration in selected commonwealth countries*. London, UK: Commonwealth Secretaria, Commonwealth of Learning.

Johnson, J. P. (1982). Can computers close the educational equity gap? *Civil Rights Quarterly Perspectives*, *14*(3), 20–25.

Johnston, D. D., & Swanson, D. H. (2007). Cognitive acrobatics in the construction of worker–mother identity. *Sex Roles*, *57*(5–6), 447–459.

Johnston, T. (2005, February 9). No evidence of innate gender difference in math and science, scholars assert. *Stanford Report*. Retrieved from http://news.stanford.edu

Jones, S. (2009). Dynamic social norms and the unexpected transformation of women's higher education, 1965–1975. *Social Science History*, *33*(3), 248–291.

Jordan-Young, R. M. (2010). *Brainstorm: The flaws in the science of sex differences*. Cambridge, MA: Harvard University Press.

Joy, L. (2003). Salaries of recent male and female college graduates: Educational and labor market effects. *Industrial & Labor Relations Review*, *56*(4), 606–621.

Kaledin, E. (1984). *Mothers and more: American women in the 1950s*. Boston, MA: Twayne.

Kamenetz, A. (2010). *DIY U: Edupunks, edupreneurs, and the coming transformation of higher education*. White River Junction, Vermont: Chelsea Green Publishing.

Keddie, A. (2006). Negotiating and enabling spaces for gender justice. *Issues in Educational Research*, *16*(1), 21–37.

Keddie, A., & Mills, M. (2007). Teaching for gender justice. *Australian Journal of Education*, *51*(2), 205–219.

Kelly, C. (2012, September 16). Drop out, dive in, start up. *The New York Times*, pp. BU1, 8–9.

Kenway, J. (Ed.). (1997). *Will boys be boys? Boys' education in the context of gender reform*. Deakin West, Australia: Australian Curriculum Studies Association.

Kerr, B. (1999, March 5). When dreams differ: Male-female relations on campuses. *The Chronicle of Higher Education*, pp. B7, B8.

Kessler-Harris, A. (2003). *Out to work: A history of wage-earning women in the United States*. New York: Oxford University Press.

Kezar, A., Maxey, D., & Badke, B. (2014). The imperative for change: Fostering understanding of the necessity of changing non-tenure track policies and practices. *The Delphi Project on the Changing Faculty and Student.* Retrieved from www.thechangingfaculty.org

Kimmel, M. (Ed.). (1995). *The politics of manhood: Profeminist men respond to the mythopoetic men's movement (and the mythopoetic leaders answer).* Philadelphia, PA: Temple University Press.

Kimmel, M. (2002). Gender, class and terrorism. *The Chronicle of Higher Education, 48*(22), 8.

Kimmel, M. (2006). A war against boys? *Dissent, 53*(4), 65–70.

Kimmel, M. (2008). *Guyland: The perilous world where boys become men.* New York, NY: Harper Collins.

Kimmel, M. (2010). *Boys and school: A background paper on the "boy crisis."* Stockholm: Swedish Government Report SOU 2010:53.

Kimmel, M. (2011). Mapping "guyland" in college. In J. A. Laker & T. David (Eds.), *Masculinities in higher education: Theoretical and practical considerations* (pp. 3–15). New York, NY: Taylor and Francis.

Kimmel, M. S., & Holler, J. Z. (2000). *The gendered society.* New York: Oxford University Press.

Kimmel, M. S., & Mahler, M. (2003). Adolescent masculinity, homophobia, and violence: Random school shootings, 1982–2001. *American Behavioral Scientist, 46,* 1439–1458. DOI: 10.1177/0002764203046010010.

Kimura, D. (2002, April). Sex differences in the brain. *Scientific American.* Retrieved from www.scientificamerican.com

Kindlon, D. (2006). *Alpha girls: Understanding the new American girl and how she is changing the world.* New York: Rodale.

Kindlon, D., & Thompson, M. (2000). *Protecting the emotional life of boys.* New York, NY: Random House.

King, J. E. (2000). *Gender equity in higher education: Are male students at a disadvantage?* Washington, DC: American Council on Education.

King, J. E. (2006). *Gender equity in higher education: 2006.* Washington, DC: American Council on Education.

King, M. L. Jr. (1947). The purpose of education. *The Maroon Tiger* (Morehouse College Newspaper). Retrieved from http://kingencyclopedia.stanford.edu/encyclopedia/documentsentry/doc_470200_000.1.html

Kinser, K. (2005). A profile of regionally accredited for-profit institutions of higher education. *New Directions for Higher Education, 2005*(129), 69–83.

Kleemans, E. R., & de Poot, C. J. (2008). Criminal careers in organized crime and social opportunity structure. *European Journal of Criminology, 5*(1), 69–98.

Klein, J. (2004). Who is most responsible for gender differences in scholastic achievements: Pupils or teachers? *Educational Research, 46*(2), 183–193.

Klein, S. S., Richardson, B., Grayson, D. A., Fox, L. H., Kramarae, C., Pollard, D. S., & Dwyer, C. A. (Eds.). (2007). *Handbook for achieving gender equity through education* (2nd Ed.). Mahwah, NJ: Lawrence Erlbaum Associates.

Kleykamp, M. A. (2006). College, jobs, or the military? Enlistment during a time of war. *Social Science Quarterly, 87*(2), 272–290.

Koerner, B. I., Hardigg, V., Lackaff, D., Morrow, J., Wildavsky, B., & Lord, M. (1999). Where the boys aren't. (Cover story). *U.S. News & World Report, 126*(5), 46.

Kramarae, C. (2003). Gender equity online, when there is no door to knock on. In M. Moore & W. Anderson (Eds.), *Handbook of Distance Education* (pp. 261–272). Mahwah, NJ: Erlbaum.

Krefting, L. A. (2003). Intertwined discourses of merit and gender: Evidence from academic employment in the USA. Gender. *Work & Organization, 10*(2), 260–278.

Kristof, N. D. (2008, February 10). When women rule. *The New York Times,* p. A13.

Kristof, N. D. (2010, March 27). The boys have fallen behind. *The New York Times.* Retrieved from www.nytimes.com

Kristof, N. D. (2014, May 10). What's so scary about smart girls? *The New York Times.* Retrieved from www.newyorktimes.com

Krugman, P. (2015, February 23). Knowledge isn't power. *The New York Times,* p. A19.

Kunin, M. (2012). *The new feminist agenda: Defining the next revolution for women, work, and family.* White River Junction, VT: Chelsea Green Publishing.

Lahelma, E. (2005). School grades and other resources: The "failing boys" discourse revisited. *Nordic Journal of Women's Studies, 13*(2), 78–89.

Langton, L. (2010). *Women in law enforcement, 1987–2008* (U.S. Department of Justice Report, NCJ 230521), Washington, DC.

Latty, Y. (2004). *We were there: Voices of African American veterans, from World War II to the war in Iraq.* New York, NY: Harper Collins/Amistad.

Lay, S. (2014, September). Ku Klux Klan in the twentieth century. *New Georgia Encyclopedia.* Retrieved from www.georgiaencyclopedia.org

Lee, J. D. (2002). More than ability: Gender and personal relationships influence science and technology involvement. *Sociology of Education, 75*(4), 349–73.

Lee, S. (2012, August 9). The for-profit higher education industry, by the numbers. *Pro Publica.* Retrieved from www.propublica.org/

Lee, Y. J., & Roth, W. M. (2004, January). Making a scientist: Discursive "doing" of identity and self-presentation during research interviews. *Forum: Qualitative Social Research, 5*(1). Retrieved from http://nbn-resolving.de/urn:nbn:de:0114-fqs0401123

Lent, R. W. (2013). Social cognitive career theory. In S. D. Brown & R. W. Lent (Eds.), *Career development & counseling: Putting theory and research to work* (2nd Ed., pp. 115–146). New York, NY: Wiley.

Lenzer, R., & Johnson, S. S. (1997, March 3). Seeing things as they really are. [An interview with Peter Drucker]. *Forbes.* Retrieved from www.forbes.com/

Leonard, D. K., & Jiang, J. (1999). Gender bias and the college predictions of the SATs: A cry of despair. *Research in Higher Education, 40*(4), 375–407.

Leonhardt, D. (2006, December 24). Gender pay gap, once narrowing, is stuck in place. *The New York Times,* pp. 1, 16.

Lerner, S. (2007, March 4). The motherhood experiment. *The New York Times Magazine,* p. 20.

Lesko, N. (Ed.). (1999). *Masculinities at school.* Thousand Oaks, CA: Sage Publications.

Levanon, A., England, P., & Allison, P. (2009). Occupational feminization and pay: Assessing causal dynamics using 1950–2000 US census data. *Social Forces, 88*(2), 865–891.

Levinson, B. A., Foley, D. E., & Holland, D. C. (Eds.). (1996). *The cultural production of the educated person: Critical ethnographies of schooling and local practice.* Albany, NY: State University of New York Press.

Lewin, T. (2006, July 9). At colleges, women are leaving men in the dust. *The New York Times,* pp. A1, A16.

Lewin, T. (2010, March 22). Bias called persistent hurdle for women in sciences. *The New York Times.* Retrieved from www.nytimes.com

Lewis, S. K., & Oppenheimer, V. K. (2000). Educational assortative mating across marriage markets: Non-hispanic whites in the United States. *Demography, 37*(1), 29–40.

Light, A. (2004). Gender differences in the marriage and cohabitation income premium. *Demography, 41*(2), 263–284.

Light, A., & Strayer, W. (2002). From Bakke to Hopwood: Does race affect college attendance and completion? *Review of Economics and Statistics, 84*(1), 34–44.

Lincoln, A. E. (2010). The shifting supply of men and women to occupations: Feminization in veterinary education. *Social Forces, 88*(5), 1969–1998.

Lingard, B. (2003). Where to in gender policy in education after recuperative masculinity politics? *International Journal of Inclusive Education, 7*(1), 33–56.

Lingard, B., Martino, W., & Mills, M. (2009). *Boys and schooling: Beyond structural reform.* New York: Palgrave Macmillan.

Lipka, S. (2010, March 9). To get more men to volunteer, colleges must make an extra effort. *The Chronicle of Higher Education.* Retrieved from www.chronicle.com

Lips, H. M. (2000). College students' visions of power and possibility as moderated by gender. *Psychology of Women Quarterly, 24*(1), 39–43.

Lips, H. M. (2001). Envisioning positions of leadership: The expectations of university students in Virginia and Puerto Rico. *Journal of Social Issues, 57*(4), 799–813.

Lips, H. M. (2004). The gender gap in possible selves: Divergence of academic self-views among high school and university students. *Sex Roles, 50*(5–6), 357–371.

Lips, H. M. (2007). Gender and possible selves. *New Directions for Adult and Continuing Education, 2007*(114), 51–59.

Lorber, J. (1994). *Paradoxes of gender.* New Haven, CT: Yale University Press.

Lowry, R. (2001). Nasty, brutish, and short: Children in day care—and the mothers who put them there. *National Review, 28*, 36–42.

Lyman, M. D., & Potter, G. W. (2000). *Organized crime.* Upper Saddle River, NJ: Prentice Hall.

MacLean, A. (2005). Lessons from the Cold War: Military service and college education. *Sociology of Education, 78*(3), 250–266.

MacLean, A., & Elder Jr, G. H. (2007). Military service in the life course. *Annual Review of Sociology, 33*(1), 175–196.

Mainiero, L. A., & Sullivan, S. E. (2005). Kaleidoscope careers: An alternate explanation for the "opt-out" revolution. *The Academy of Management Executive, 19*(1), 106–123.

Margolis, J., & Fisher, A. (2002). *Unlocking the clubhouse: Women in computing.* Cambridge, MA: MIT Press.

Marsden, J. (1998). *Secret men's business.* Sydney, Australia: Pan MacMillan Australia.

Martin, P. Y. (2003). "Said and done" versus "saying and doing" gendering practices, practicing gender at work. *Gender & Society, 17*(3), 342–366.

Martin, P. Y. (2004). Gender as social institution. *Social Forces, 82*(4), 1249–1273.

Martin, P. Y. (2006). Practicing gender at work: Further thoughts on reflexivity. *Gender, Work & Organization, 13*(3), 254–276.

Martino, W., & Berrill, D. (2003). Boys, schooling and masculinities: Interrogating the "right" way to educate boys. *Educational Review, 55*(2), 99–117.

Martino, W., Kehler, M. D., & Weaver-Hightower, M. B. (Eds.). (2009). *The problem with boys' education: Beyond the backlash.* New York: Routledge.

Martino, W., Lingard, B., & Mills, M. (2004). Issues in boys' education: A question of teacher threshold knowledges. *Gender and Education, 16*(4), 435–454.

Martino, W., & Pallotta-Chiarolli, M. (2003). *So what's a boy? Addressing issues of masculinity and schooling.* Philadelphia, PA: Open University Press.

Masse, M. A., & Hogan, K. J. (2010). *Over ten million served: Gendered service in language and literature workplaces.* Albany, NY: SUNY Press.

Massey, D. S. (2007). *Categorically unequal: The American stratification system*. New York: Russell Sage Foundation.

Mathieu, C. (2009). Practising gender in organizations: The critical gap between practical and discursive consciousness. *Management Learning, 40*(2), 177–193.

May, A. M. (2006, October). "Sweeping the heavens for a comet": Women, the language of political economy, and higher education in the United States. *Feminist Economics, 12*(4), 625–640. DOI: 10.1080/13545700600885321.

McCarthy, B., & Gartner, R. (2014, August). Five facts about women's involvement in organized crime. *OUP Blog*. Retrieved from www.blog.oup.com

McCormick, A. C. (2003). Swirling and double-dipping: New patterns of student attendance and their implications for higher education. *New Directions for Higher Education, 2003*(121), 13–24.

McCormick, N. B., & Jesser, C. J. (1983). The courtship game: Power in the sexual encounter. In E. R. Allgeier & N. B. McCormick (Eds.), *Changing boundaries: Gender roles and sexual behavior* (pp. 64–86). Palo Alto, CA: Mayfield.

McDonough, P. M. (1997). *Choosing colleges: How social class and schools structure opportunity*. Albany, NY: State University of New York Press.

McHugh, M. C., & Frieze, I. H. (1997). The measurement of gender-role attitudes: A review and commentary. *Psychology of Women Quarterly, 21*(1), 1–16.

Mead, S. (2006). *The truth about boys and girls*. Washington, DC: Education Sector.

Melin, J. (2016). Desperate choices: Why black women join the US military at higher rates than men and all other racial and ethnic groups. *New England Journal of Public Policy, 28*(2), 8.

Mendez, J. B., & Wolf, D. L. (2001). Where feminist theory meets feminist practice: Border-crossing in a transnational academic feminist organization. *Organization, 8*(4), 723–750.

Messing, K., Punnett, L., Bond, M., Alexanderson, K., Pyle, J., Zahm, S., Wegman, D., Stock, S. R., & de Grosbois, S. (2003). Be the fairest of them all: Challenges and recommendations for the treatment of gender in occupational health research. *American Journal of Industrial Medicine, 43*(6), 618–629.

Meyer, J. (2000). Reflections on education as transcendence. In L. Cuban & D. Shipps (Eds.), *Reconstructing the common good in education* (pp. 206–222). Redwood City, CA: Stanford University Press.

Meyerson, D., & Tompkins, M. (2007). Tempered radicals as institutional change agents: The case of advancing gender equity at the University of Michigan. *Harvard Journal of Law and Gender, 30*, 303–320.

Milkman, K., Akinola, M., & Chugh, C. (2014). A field experiment exploring how pay and representation differentially shape bias on the pathway into organizations: Working paper. *Social Science Research Network*. Retrieved from http://ssrn.com/abstract=2063742

Miller, C. C. (2010, April 17). Out of the loop in Silicon Valley. *The New York Times*, pp. BU1, 8–9.

Miller, C. C. (2016, March 18). As women take over a male-dominated field, the pay drops. *The New York Times*. Retrieved from www.nytimes.com/2016/03/20/upshot/as-women-take-over-a-male-dominated-field-the-pay-drops.html

Misa, T. J. (Ed.). (2011). *Gender codes: Why women are leaving computing*. San Francisco, CA: John Wiley & Sons.

Moehling, C. M. (2001). Women's work and men's unemployment. *The Journal of Economic History, 61*(04), 926–949.

Monaghan, L. (2002). Hard men, shop boys and others: Embodying competence in a masculinist occupation. *Sociological Review, 50*(3), 334–355.

Montgomery, L. M. (2004). "It's just what I like": Explaining persistent patterns of gender stratification in the life choices of college students. *International Journal of Qualitative Studies in Education, 17*(6), 785–802.

Mortenson, T. (1995). *The Mortenson research letter on public policy analysis of opportunity for postsecondary education.* Retrieved from www.postsecondary.org/

Mortenson, T. (1999, November 15–16). *The changing gender balance: An overview. Fewer men on campus a puzzle for liberal arts colleges and universities.* Postsecondary Education Opportunity. Goucher College, Baltimore, Maryland.

Mortenson, T. (2003). *The Mortenson research letter on public policy analysis of opportunity for postsecondary education.* Retrieved from www.postsecondary.org/

Moskos, C., & Butler, J. S. (1996). *All that we can be: Black leadership and racial integration the army way.* New York, NY: Basic Books.

Moss-Racusin, C. A., Dovidio, J. F., Brescoll, V. L., Graham, M. J., & Handelsman, J. (2012). Science faculty's subtle gender biases favor male students. *Proceedings of the National Academy of Sciences, 109*(41), 16474–16479.

Mullen, A. L. (2010). *Degrees of inequality: Culture, class, and gender in American higher education.* Baltimore, MD: Johns Hopkins University Press.

Mullen, A. L. (2014). Gender, social background, and the choice of college major in a liberal arts context. *Gender & Society, 28*(2), 289–312.

Musick, K., Brand, J. E., & Davis, D. (2012). Variation in the relationship between education and marriage: Marriage market mismatch? *Journal of Marriage and Family, 74*(1), 53–69.

Myers, K. (2004). Ladies first: Race, class, and the contradictions of a powerful femininity. *Sociological Spectrum, 24*(1), 11–41.

Nash, M. A., & Romero, L. S. (2012). "Citizenship for the college girl": Challenges and opportunities in higher education for women in the United States in the 1930s. *Teachers College Record, 114*, 1–35.

National Academy of Sciences, National Academy of Engineering, & Institute of Medicine. (2007). *Rising above the gathering storm: Energizing and employing America for a brighter future.* Washington, DC: National Academy Press.

National Association of Women Lawyers (NAWL). (2008). *Report of the third annual national survey of retention and promotion of women in law firms.* Chicago, IL: NAWL Foundation.

National Center for Education Statistics (NCES). (2000). *The condition of education.* Retrieved From https://nces.ed.gov/

National Center for Education Statistics (NCES). (2012). *The condition of education.* Retrieved from https://nces.ed.gov/

National Center for Education Statistics (NCES). (2013). *The condition of education.* Retrieved from https://nces.ed.gov/

National Center for Education Statistics (NCES). (2014). *The condition of education.* Retrieved from https://nces.ed.gov/

National Center for Education Statistics (NCES). (2015). *The condition of education.* Retrieved from https://nces.ed.gov/

National Center for Education Statistics (NCES). (2016). *The condition of education.* Retrieved from https://nces.ed.gov/

National Center for Women & Information Technology (NCWIT). (2016). *By the Numbers.* Retrieved from www.ncwit.org/sites/default/files/resources/btn_03092016_web.pdf

National Coalition for Women and Girls in Education (NCWGE). (2012). *Title IX at 40: Working to ensure gender equity in education.* Washington, DC: NCWGE.

National Law Enforcement Officers Memorial Fund. (2014). Retrieved from www.nleomf.org/facts/enforcement/

National Longitudinal Surveys & U.S. Bureau of Labor Statistics. (1979). *National Longitudinal Survey of Youth* (Report No. NLSY79). Retrieved from www.nlsinfo.org

National Longitudinal Surveys & U.S. Bureau of Labor Statistics. (2000). *Number of jobs held by individuals from age 18 to age 36 in 1978–2000 by educational attainment, sex, race, Hispanic ethnicity, and age* (Report No. NLSY79 Round 19). Retrieved from www.bls.gov

National Public Radio. (2013). *Do women have a responsibility when men misbehave?* Original broadcast date: July 31. Transcript retrieved from http://www.npr.org/templates/transcript/transcript.php?storyId=207292641

National Science Board. (2003). *The science and engineering workforce: Realizing America's potential* (Document No. NSB 03–69). Retrieved from www.nsf.gov

National Science Foundation. (2003, 2004, 2006). *New formulas for America's workforce: Girls in science and engineering* (Document No. NSF 03207). Retrieved from www.nsf.gov

National Science Foundation. (2006). *New tools for America's workforce 2: Girls in science and engineering* (Document No. NSF 06–60). Retrieved from www.nsf.gov

National Science Foundation. (2007, August 27). *Back to school: Five myths about girls and science* (Press release 07–108). Retrieved from www.nsf.gov

National Science Foundation & Division of Science Resources Statistics. (2004). *Women, minorities, and persons with disabilities in science and engineering* (NSF 04–317). Arlington, VA: National Science Foundation.

National Women's Law Center. (2013). *Insecure and unequal: Poverty and income among women and families, 2000–2012.* Retrieved from www.nwlc.org/sites/default/files/pdfs/final_2013_nwlc_povertyreport.pdf

Newkirk, T. (2002). *Misreading masculinity: Boys, literacy, and popular culture.* Portsmouth, NH: Heinemann.

Newsome, Y. D., & Dodoo, F.N.A. (2002). Reversal of fortune explaining the decline in black women's earnings. *Gender & Society, 16*(4), 442–464.

Niemi, N. S. (2005). The emperor has no clothes: Examining the impossible relationship between gendered and academic identities in middle school students. *Gender and Education, 17*(5), 483–497.

Noguera, P. A. (2009). *The trouble with black boys: And other reflections on race, equity, and the future of public education.* San Francisco, CA: John Wiley & Sons.

Norton, M., Vandello, J., & Darley, J. (2004). Casuistry and social bias. *Journal of Personality and Social Psychology, 87*(6), 817–831.

Nosek, B. A., Banaji, M. R., & Greenwald, A. G. (2002). Math = male, me = female, therefore math ≠ me. *Journal of Personality and Social Psychology, 83*(1), 44–59.

Obama, B. (2009, July 14). *The 2020 American graduation initiative.* Speech given in Warren, Michigan. Retrieved from www.whitehouse.gov

O'Brien, T. L. (2006, March 19). Why do so few women reach the top of big law firms? *The New York Times.* Retrieved from www.nytimes.com

Ochs, E. (1988). *Culture and language development.* Cambridge, UK: Cambridge University Press.

Ogbu, J. U. (2003). *Black American students in an affluent suburb: A study of academic disengagement.* Mahwah, NJ: Lawrence Erlbaum Associates.

Ojalvo, H. E. (2012, February 2). Why go to college at all? *The New York Times.* Retrieved from www.nytimes.com

Oliff, P., Palacios, V., Johnson, I., & Leachman, M. (2013). *Recent deep state higher education cuts may harm students and the economy for years to come.* Washington, DC: Center on Budget and Policy Priorities.

Ono, H., & Zavodny, M. (2003). Gender and the Internet. *Social Science Quarterly, 84*(1), 111–121.

Ono, H., & Zavodny, M. (2007). Digital inequality: A five-country comparison using microdata. *Social Science Research, 36*, 1135–1155.

Pacholok, S. (2013). *Into the fire: Disaster and the remaking of gender.* Toronto, Canada: University of Toronto Press.

Park, L. E., DiRaddo, A. M., & Calogero, R. M. (2009). Sociocultural influence and appearance-based rejection sensitivity among college students. *Psychology of Women Quarterly, 33*(1), 108–119.

Park, L. E., Young, A. F., Troisi, J. D., & Pinkus, R. T. (2011). Effects of everyday romantic goal pursuit on women's attitudes toward math and science. *Personality and Social Psychology Bulletin, 37*(9), 1259–1273.

Parshall, G. (1992). The Great Panic of '93. *U.S. News & World Report, 113*(17), 70.

Patten, E., & Parker, K. (2011). Women in the military: Growing share, distinctive profile. *Pew Social & Demographic Trends.* Retrieved from http://pewsocialtrends.org

Patton, S. (2013, March 29). Advice for the young women of Princeton: The daughters I never had. *The Daily Princetonian.* Retrieved from https://thedailyprincetonian.wordpress.com/2013/03/29/opinion-letter-to-the-editor-march-29-2013/

Paul, A. M. (2014). The MOOC gender gap. *The Hechinger Report.* Retrieved from www.slate.com or www.slate.com/articles/technology/future_tense/2014/09/mooc_gender_gap_how_to_get_more_women_into_online_stem_classes.html

Persell, C. H., Catsambis, S., & Cookson, P. W. (1992). Differential asset conversion: Class and gendered pathways to selective colleges. *Sociology of Education, 65*(3), 208–225.

Peter, K., & Horn, L. (2005). Gender differences in participation and completion of undergraduate education and how they have changed over time. *Postsecondary education descriptive analysis reports* (NCES 2005–169). Washington, DC: U.S. Department of Education.

Pew Research Center. (2014). Retrieved from www.pewresearch.org/fact-tank/2014/04/24/more-hispanics-blacks-enrolling-in-college

Philyaw, D. (2008, Summer). Ain't I a mommy? Bookstores brim with motherhood memoirs: Why are so few of them penned by women of color? *Bitch* (40), 40–52.

Pimentel, A. (2004). *Supporting boys' resilience: A dialogue with researchers, practitioners, and the media.* New York: Ms. Foundation for Women.

Pixley, J. E. (2008). Life course patterns of career-prioritizing decisions and occupational attainment in dual-earner couples. *Work and Occupations, 35*(2), 127–163.

Pizzini-Gambetta, V. (2014). Organized crime: The gender constraints of illegal markets. In R. Gartner & B. McCarthy (Eds.), *The Oxford handbook of gender, sex, and crime* (pp. 448–467). Oxford, UK: Oxford University Press.

Poelmans, S. (2012). The "Triple-N" Model: Changing normative beliefs about parenting and career success. *Journal of Social Issues, 68*(4), 838–847.

Pollack, W. (1999). *Real boys: Rescuing our sons from the myths of boyhood.* New York: Random House.

Pollitt, K. (1999, December 27). Subject to debate: Affirmative action for men? *The Nation, 269*(22), 10.

Pollitt, K. (2003, November 17). Subject to debate: There they go again. *The Nation*, *277*(16), 9.

Pollitt, K. (2005, November 14). Subject to debate: Madam President, madam President. *The Nation*, *281*(16), 10.

Pollitt, K. (2006, December 18). Subject to debate: Double, double, toil and trouble. *The Nation*, *283*(21), 14.

Pomerantz, S., & Raby, R. (2011). "Oh, she's so smart": Girls' complex engagements with post/feminist narratives of academic success. *Gender and Education*, *23*(5), 549–564.

Porter, E. (2013, November 13). Rethinking the rise of inequality. *The New York Times*. Retrieved from www.nytimes.com/2013/11/13/business/rethinking-the-income-gap-and-a-college-education.html

Pratto, F., & Stewart, A. L. (2012). Group dominance and the half-blindness of privilege. *Journal of Social Issues*, *68*(1), 28–45.

Prentice, D. A., & Carranza, E. (2002). What women and men should be, shouldn't be, are allowed to be, and don't have to be: The contents of prescriptive gender stereotypes. *Psychology of Women Quarterly*, *26*(4), 269–281.

Prentice, D. A., & Carranza, E. (2004). Sustaining cultural beliefs in the face of their violation: The case of gender stereotypes. In M. Schaller & C. S. Crandall (Eds.), *The psychological foundations of culture* (pp. 259–280). Mahwah, NJ: Lawrence Erlbaum.

Prokos, A., & Padavic, I. (2002). "There oughtta be a law against bitches": Masculinity lessons in police academy training. *Gender, Work & Organization*, *9*(4), 439–459.

Public Agenda.org. (2016, September 12). *Public opinion on higher education*. Retrieved from www.publicagenda.org/pages/public-opinion-higher-education-2016

Rahbari, L. (2014, March 4–5). *Are educated women ugly? Stigmatizing women in higher education*. Proceedings of the Global Summit on Education GSE 2014 (E- ISBN 978-967-11768-5-6), Kuala Lumpur, Malaysia.

Reay, D., Ball, S., & David, M. (2002). "It's taking me a long time but I'll get there in the end": Mature students on access courses and higher education choice. *British Educational Research Journal*, *28*(1), 5–19.

Reay, D., Davies, J., David, M., & Ball, S. J. (2001). Choices of degree or degrees of choice? Class, "race" and the higher education choice process. *Sociology*, *35*(04), 855–874.

Reskin, B. (1993). Sex segregation in the workplace. *Annual Review of Sociology*, *19*(1), 241–270.

Reskin, B. F., & Roos, P. A. (Eds.). (1990). *Job queues, gender queues: Explaining women's inroads into male occupations*. Philadelphia, PA: Temple University Press.

Reynolds, J. R., & Burge, S. W. (2008). Educational expectations and the rise in women's post-secondary attainments. *Social Science Research*, *37*(2), 485–499.

Rhode, D. L. (1997). *Speaking of sex: The denial of gender inequality*. Cambridge, MA: Harvard University Press.

Rhode, D. L. (2014). *What women want: An agenda for the women's movement*. Oxford, UK: Oxford University Press.

Rhodes, F. (2006, October 20). Sustainability: The ultimate liberal art. *Chronicle of Higher Education*, p. A8.

Richtel, M. (2014, March 8). The youngest Technorati. *The New York Times*, BU1.

Ridgeway, C. L. (1997). Interaction and the conservation of gender inequality: Considering employment. *American Sociological Review*, *62*(2), 218–235.

Ridgeway, C. L., & Correll, S. J. (2004). Motherhood as a status characteristic. *Journal of Social Issues*, *60*(4), 683–700.

Ridgeway, C. L., & Kricheli-Katz, T. (2013). Intersecting cultural beliefs in social relations gender, race, and class binds and freedoms. *Gender & Society, 27*(3), 294–318.

Riegle-Crumb, C. (2010). More girls go to college: Exploring the social and academic factors behind the female postsecondary advantage among Hispanic and White students. *Research in Higher Education, 51*(6), 573–593.

Riesman, D. (1965). Two generations. In R. J. Lifton (Ed.), *The American woman* (pp. 72–97). Boston, MA: Houghton-Mifflin.

Ringrose, J. (2007). Successful girls? Complicating post-feminist, neoliberal discourses of educational achievement and gender equality. *Gender and Education, 19*(4), 471–489.

Ringrose, J. (2013). *Postfeminist education? Girls and the sexual politics of schooling.* London, UK: Routledge.

Riordan, C. (2003). Failing in school? Yes; victims of war? No. *Sociology of Education, 76*(4), 369–372.

Rios, V. M. (2009). The consequences of the criminal justice pipeline on black and Latino masculinity. *The ANNALS of the American Academy of Political and Social Science, 623*(1), 150–162.

Rivers, C., & Barnett, R. C. (2006, April 9). The myth of "the boy crisis." *The Washington Post.* Retrieved from www.washingtonpost.com

Roksa, J. (2005). Double disadvantage or blessing in disguise? Understanding the relationship between college major and employment sector. *Sociology of Education, 78*(3), 207–232.

Roman, L. G., & Eyre, L. (Eds.). (1997). *Dangerous territories: Struggles for difference and equality in education.* New York: Routledge.

Rose, S., & Frieze, I. H. (1993). Young singles' contemporary dating scripts. *Sex Roles, 28*(9–10), 499–509.

Rosin, H. (2010, June 8). The end of men. *The Atlantic.* Retrieved from www.theatlantic.com/magazine/archive/2010/07/the-end-of-men/308135/

Rosin, H. (2012, August 30). Who wears the pants in this economy? *The New York Times Magazine.* Retrieved from www.nytimes.com

Roth, L. M. (2004). Engendering inequality: Processes of sex-segregation on Wall Street. *Sociological Forum, 19*(2), 203–228.

Rothschild, M. (1981). To scout or to guide? The girl scout-boy scout controversy, 1912–1941. *Frontiers: A Journal of Women Studies, 6*(3), 115–121. Retrieved from www.jstor.org/stable/3346224. DOI:10.2307/3346224

Ruch, R. (2001). *Higher ed. Inc.: The rise of the for-profit university.* Baltimore, MD: The Johns Hopkins University Press.

Rudman, L. A., & Glick, P. (2001). Prescriptive gender stereotypes and backlash toward agentic women. *Journal of Social Issues, 57*(4), 743–762.

Rudman, L. A., & Glick, P. (2008). *The social psychology of gender: How power and intimacy shape gender relations.* New York: Guilford Press.

Rudman, L. A., & Heppen, J. B. (2003). Implicit romantic fantasies and women's interest in personal power: A glass slipper effect? *Personality and Social Psychology Bulletin, 29*(11), 1357–1370.

Rudman, L. A., Moss-Racusin, C. A., Phelan, J. E., & Nauts, S. (2012). Status incongruity and backlash effects: Defending the gender hierarchy motivates prejudice against female leaders. *Journal of Experimental Social Psychology, 48*(1), 165–179.

Rudolph, F. (1962). *The American college and university: A history.* New York, NY: Alfred A. Knopf.

Rury, J. (2013). *Education and social change: Contours in the history of American schooling* (4th Ed.). New York: Routledge.

Russell, W. (2001). An examination of flow state occurrence in college athletes. *Journal of Sport Behaviour, 24*(1), 83–107.

Sabol, W., West, H., & Cooper, M. (2008). Prisoners in 2008 (revised 2010). *Bureau of Justice Statistics Bulletin.* U.S. Department of Justice. NCJ 228417.

Said, C. (2007, April 1). No degree required: Technical courses gain favor for those interested in finding new career path. *The San Francisco Chronicle.* Retrieved from www.sfgate.com

Samuelson, R. J. (2012, May 27). It's time to drop the college-for-all crusade. *The Washington Post.* Retrieved from www.washingtonpost.com/opinions/its-time-to-drop-the-college-for-all crusade/2012/05/27/gJQAzcUGvU_story.html

Sandberg, S., & Grant, A. (2015, January 12). Speaking while female. *The New York Times.* Retrieved from www.nytimes.com/2015/01/11/opinion/sunday/speaking-while-female.html

Sax, L. J. (1996). The dynamics of "tokenism": How college students are affected by the proportion of women in their major. *Research in Higher Education, 37*(4), 389–425.

Sax, L. J. (2006). *Why gender matters: What parents and teachers need to know about the emerging science of sex differences.* New York, NY: Broadway Books.

Sax, L. J. (2007). *Boys adrift: The five factors driving the growing epidemic of unmotivated boys and underachieving young men.* New York, NY: Basic Books.

Sax, L. J. (2008). *The gender gap in college: Maximizing the developmental potential of women and men.* San Francisco, CA: Jossey-Bass.

Schiebinger, L., & Gilmartin, S. K. (2010). Housework is an academic issue: How to keep talented women scientists in the lab, where they belong. *Academe, 91*(1), 39–44.

Schmitt, J., & Boushey, H. (2010). The college conundrum: Why the benefits of a college education May not be so clear, especially to men. *Center for American Progress.* Retrieved from www.americanprogress.org/wp-content/uploads/issues/2010/12/pdf/college_conundrum.pdf

Schmitt, M. T., Spoor, J. R., Danaher, K., & Branscombe, N. R. (2009). Rose-colored glasses: How tokenism and comparisons with the past reduce the visibility of gender inequality. In M. E. Barreto, M. K. Ryan, & M. T. Schmitt (Eds.), *The glass ceiling in the 21st century: Understanding barriers to gender equality* (pp. 49–71). Washington, DC: American Psychological Association.

Schneider, C. G. (2005). Making excellence inclusive: Liberal education & America's promise. *Liberal Education, 91*(2). Retrieved from www.aacu.org

Schott Foundation. (2015). *Black lives matter: The Schott Foundation 50 state report on public education and black males.* Retrieved from www.blackboys.org

Schwartz, C. R., & Mare, R. D. (2005). Trends in educational assortative marriage from 1940 to 2003. *Demography, 42*(4), 621–646.

Sharp, E. H., Coatsworth, J. D., Darling, N., Cumsille, P., & Ranieri, S. (2007). Gender differences in the self-defining activities and identity experiences of adolescents and emerging adults. *Journal of Adolescence, 30*(2), 251–269.

Shields, S. A. (2005). The politics of emotion in everyday life: "Appropriate" emotion and claims on identity. *Review of General Psychology, 9*(1), 3.

Shields, S. A. (2008). Gender: An intersectionality perspective. *Sex Roles, 59*(5–6), 301–311.

Shih, J. (2006). Circumventing discrimination gender and ethnic strategies in Silicon Valley. *Gender & Society, 20*(2), 177–206.

Silverstone, R., & Hirsch, E. (Eds.). (1992). *Consuming technologies: Media and information in domestic spaces.* London, UK: Routledge.

Skelton, C. (2010). Gender and achievement: Are girls the "success stories" of restructured education systems? *Educational Review, 62*(2), 131–142.

Skelton, C., & Francis, B. (2009). *Feminism and "the schooling scandal."* New York: Routledge.

Sklansky, D. A. (2006). Not your father's police department: Making sense of the new demographics of law enforcement. *The Journal of Criminal Law and Criminology (1973), 96*(3), 1209–1243.

Smith, H. (2013). Why men are avoiding college. *Minding the Campus: Reforming our Universities.* Retrieved from www.mindingthecampus.org/2013/05/why_men_are_avoiding_college/

Smith, J. A. (2009). *The daddy shift: How stay-at-home dads, breadwinning moms, and shared parenting are transforming the American family.* Boston: Beacon Press.

Smith, W., & Bender, T. (2008). Introduction. In W. Smith & T. Bender (Eds.). *American higher education transformed: 1940–2005* (pp. 1–11). Baltimore, MD: Johns Hopkins University Press.

Snyder, K. A., & Green, A. I. (2008). Revisiting the glass escalator: The case of gender segregation in a female dominated occupation. *Social Problems, 55*(2), 271–299.

Snyder, T. D., & Dillow, S. A. (2011). *Digest of education statistics 2010* (NCES 2011–015). Washington, DC: U.S. Department of Education, Institute of Education Sciences. National Center for Education Statistics.

Snyder, T. D., Dillow, S. A., & Hoffman, C. M. (2007). *Digest of education statistics 2006* (NCES 2007–017). Washington, DC: U.S. Department of Education, Institute of Education Sciences. National Center for Education Statistics.

Solomon, B. M. (1985). *In the company of educated women: A history of women and higher education in America.* New Haven, CT: Yale University Press.

Sommers, C. H. (2001). *The war against boys: How misguided feminism is harming our young men.* New York: Simon & Schuster Paperbacks.

Spencer, R., Porche, M., & Tolman, D. (2003). We've come a long way—maybe: New challenges for gender equity in education. *The Teachers College Record, 105*(9), 1774–1807.

Srinivas, A. (2013, February 21). Penn has male, female student balance, despite national difference. *The Daily Pennsylvanian,* p. 1. Retrieved from http://www.thedp.com/article/2013/02/penn-has-male-female-student-balance-despite-national-difference

Stacey, J. (1995). Disloyal to the disciplines: A feminist trajectory in the borderlands. In D. Standton & A. J. Stewart (Eds.), *Feminisms in the academy* (pp. 311–329). Ann Arbor: University of Michigan Press.

Statistical Abstract of the United States. (1974). Prepared under the direction of William Lerner. Washington, DC: GPO.

STEM Workforce Data Project. (2004). *Twenty years of scientific and technical employment (Report No. 1).* Washington, DC: Commission on Professionals in Science and Technology.

Stephens, D. J. (2013, March 7). Do you really have to go to college? *The New York Times.* Retrieved from http://thechoice.blogs.nytimes.com/2013/03/07/do-you-really-have-to-go-to-college/comment-page-4/?_r=0

Stevens, M. L. (2009). *Creating a class: College admissions and the education of elites.* Cambridge, MA: Harvard University Press.

St. George, D. (2007, March 20). Despite "mommy guilt," time with kids increasing. *The Washington Post.* Retrieved from www.washingtonpost.com

Stone, L., & McKee, N. P. (2000). Gendered futures: Student visions of career and family on a college campus. *Anthropology & Education Quarterly, 31*(1), 67–89.

Stone, P. (2007). *Opting out? Why women really quit careers and head home.* Berkeley, CA: University of California Press.

Story, L. (2005, September 20). Many women at elite colleges set career path to motherhood. *The New York Times.* Retrieved from www.nytimes.com/2005/09/20/us/many-women-at-elite-colleges-set-career-path-to-motherhood.html

Straumheim, C. (2013, September 3). Masculine open online courses. *Inside Higher Ed.* Retrieved from www.insidehighered.com/news/2013/09/03/more-female-professors-experiment-moocs-men-still-dominate

Streitfeld, D. (2015, March 27). Ellen Pao Loses Silicon Valley bias case against Kleiner Perkins. *The New York Times.* Retrieved from www.nytimes.com/2015/03/28/technology/ellen-pao-kleiner-perkins-case-decision.html

Sue, D. W., (2013, November). Race talk: The psychology of racial dialogues. *American Psychologist, 68*(8), 663–671.

Suggs, D. W. (2009). *Selective college admissions and the gender gap: The implications of institutional decision-making.* Unpublished dissertation, University of Georgia, Athens, GA.

Sullivan, L., Meschede, T., Dietrich, L., Shapiro, T., Traub, A., Ruetschlin, C., & Draut, T. (2015). *The racial wealth gap: Why policy matters.* Boston, MA & New York, NY: Institute for Assets and Social Policy & Demos.

Sum, A., Fogg, N., Harrington, P., Khatiwada, I., Palma, S., Pond, N., & Tobar, P. (2003). *The growing gender gaps in college enrollment and degree attainment in the US and their potential economic and social consequences.* Boston: Center for Labor Market Studies, Northeastern University.

Summers, L. H. (2005). *Remarks at NBER conference on diversifying the science & engineering workforce.* Cambridge, MA: Harvard University Office of the President.

Syrett, N. (2009). *The company he keeps: A history of white college fraternities.* Chapel Hill, NC: University of North Carolina Press.

Szeman, I. (2015). Entrepreneurship as the new common sense. *South Atlantic Quarterly, 114*(3), 471–490.

Taylor, A. (2014). *The people's platform: Taking back power and culture in the digital age.* New York, NY: Harper Collins.

Taylor, K. (2014). The difference between a solopreneur and a side-gigger (Infographic). *Enterpreneur.com.* Retrieved from www.entrepreneur.com/article/239522

Taylor, P., Fry, R., Cohn, D., Wang, W., Velasco, G., & Dockterman, D. (2010). Women, men and the new economics of marriage (pp. 1–18). *Pew Research Center.* Retrieved from http://www.pewsocialtrends.org/files/2010/11/new-economics-of-marriage.pdf

Testi, A. (1995). The gender of reform politics: Theodore Roosevelt and the culture of masculinity. *The Journal of American History, 81*(4), 1509–1533.

Thébaud, S., & Pedulla, D. S. (2016). Masculinity and the stalled revolution: How gender ideologies and norms shape young men's responses to work–family policies. *Gender & Society, 30*(4), 590–617. DOI: 10.1177/0891243216649946.

Thurnell-Read, T., & Parker, A. (2008). Men, masculinities and firefighting: Occupational identity, shop-floor culture and organisational change. *Emotion, Space and Society, 1*(2), 127–134.

Tolman, D. L. (2002). *Dilemmas of desire: Teenage girls talk about sexuality.* Cambridge, MA: Harvard University Press.

Tomlinson, M. (2008). "The degree is not enough": Students' perceptions of the role of higher education credentials for graduate work and employability. *British Journal of Sociology of Education, 29*(1), 49–61.

Tone, A. (2001). *Devices and desires: A history of contraceptives in America.* New York, NY: Hill and Wang.

Tonso, K. L. (1996a). Student learning and gender. *Journal of Engineering Education, 85*(2), 143–150.

Tonso, K. L. (1996b). The impact of cultural norms on women. *Journal of Engineering Education, 85*(3), 217–225.

Tonso, K. L. (1999). Engineering gender: Gendering engineering: A cultural model for belonging. *Journal of Women and Minorities in Science and Engineering, 5*(4), 365–405.

Tonso, K. L. (2001). Plotting something dastardly: Hiding a gender curriculum in engineering. In E. Margolis (Ed.), *The hidden curriculum in higher education* (pp. 154–174). New York: Routledge.

Tonso, K. L. (2006a). Student engineers and engineer identity: Campus engineer identities as figured world. *Cultural Studies of Science Education, 1*(2), 273–307.

Tonso, K. L. (2006b). Teams that work: Campus culture, engineer identity, and social interactions. *Journal of Engineering Education, 95*(1), 25–37.

Tonso, K. L. (2007). *On the outskirts of engineering: Learning identity, gender, and power via engineering practice.* Rotterdam, The Netherlands: Sense Publishers.

Tracy, S. J., Myers, K. K., & Scott, C. W. (2006). Cracking jokes and crafting selves: Sensemaking and identity management among human service workers. *Communication Monographs, 73*(3), 283–308.

Tracy, S. J., & Trethewey, A. (2005). Fracturing the real-self↔ fake-self dichotomy: Moving toward "crystallized" organizational discourses and identities. *Communication Theory, 15*(2), 168–195.

Tsolidis, G. (2006). Strategic encounters: Choosing school subcultures that facilitate imagined futures. *British Journal of Sociology of Education, 27*(5), 603–616.

Turkle, S. (1988). Computational reticence: Why women fear the intimate machine. In C. Kramerae (Ed.), *Technology and women's voices: Keeping in touch* (pp. 41–61). New York, NY and London, UK: Routledge and Kegan Paul.

Turner, S. (2004). Going to college and finishing college: Explaining different educational outcomes. In C. Hoxby (Ed.), *College choices: The economics of where to go, when to go, and how to pay for it* (pp. 13–62). Chicago, IL: University of Chicago Press.

Turner, S. E., & Bowen, W. G. (1999). Choice of major: The changing (unchanging) gender gap. *Industrial & Labor Relations Review, 52*(2), 289–313.

Tyack, D. (1966). The kingdom of God and the common school. *Harvard Educational Review, 26*(4), 447–469.

Tyack, D. (1974). *The one best system: A history of American urban education.* Cambridge, MA: Harvard University Press.

Tyack, D., & Hansot, E. (1992). *Learning together: A history of coeducation in American public schools.* New York: Russell Sage Foundation.

Tyre, P. (2009). *The trouble with boys: A surprising report card on our sons, their problems at school, and what parents and educators must do.* New York: Three Rivers Press.

Uhlmann, E. L., & Cohen, G. L. (2005). Constructed criteria redefining merit to justify discrimination. *Psychological Science, 16*(6), 474–480.

United States Agency International Development (USAID). (2008). *Gender equality framework.* Washington, DC: USAID.

United States Bureau of Education. (1918–1920). *Biennial survey of education, 1918–20.* Washington, DC: GPO, 1923, p. 497.

United States Department of Education. (2006). *A test of leadership: Charting the future of U.S. Higher Education: A report of the commission appointed by Secretary of Education Margaret Spellings.* ED-06-C0–0013. Washington, DC.

United States Secret Service & United States Department of Education. (2002). *The final report and findings of the safe school initiative.* Washington, DC.

United States Senate. (2012). *For profit higher education: The failure to safeguard the federal investment and ensure student success.* Retrieved from www.help.senate.gov/imo/media/ for_profit_report/Contents.pdf

U.S. Department of Commerce, Economics and Statistics Administration and Executive Office of the President, Office of Management and Budget. (2011). *Women in America: Indicators of social and economic well being.* Retrieved from www.esa.doc.gov/

U.S. Department of Defense. (2014). 2014 demographics: Profile of the military community. *Office of the deputy assistant secretary of defense* (Military Community and Family Policy) Retrieved from http://download.militaryonesource.mil/12038/MOS/ Reports/2014-Demographics-Report.pdf

U.S. Department of Labor. (2005). *College enrollment and work activity of 2004 high school graduates.* Washington, DC: U.S. Bureau of Labor Statistics.

U.S. Department of Labor. (2007). *American time use survey—2006 results.* Washington, DC: U.S. Bureau of Labor Statistics.

Waite, L. J., Bachrach, C., Hindin, M. J., Thomson, E., & Thornton, A. (Eds.). (2000). *The ties that bind: Perspectives on marriage and cohabitation.* Hawthorne, NY: Walter de Gruyter, Inc.

Walkerdine, V. (1990). *Schoolgirl fictions.* London, UK: Verso Books.

Wang, W. (2014, February 12). Record share of wives are more educated than their husbands. *Pew Research Center.* Retrieved from www.pewresearch.org/fact-tank/2014/02/12/ record-share-of-wives-are-more-educated-than-their-husbands/

Wang, W. (2015, June 12). Interracial marriage: Who is "marrying out"? *Pew Research Center.* Retrieved from www.pewresearch.org/fact-tank/2015/06/12/interracial-marriage-who-is-marrying-out/

Watters, A. (2013). *Hacking at education: TED, Technology entrepreneurship, uncollege, and the hole in the wall.* Retrieved from http://hackeducation.com/2013/03/03/ hacking-your-education-stephens-hole-in-the-wall-mitra/

Weaver-Hightower, M. B. (2003a). The "boy turn" in research on gender and education. *Review of Educational Research, 73*(4), 471–498.

Weaver-Hightower, M. B. (2003b). Crossing the divide: Bridging the disjunctures between theoretically oriented and practice-oriented literature about masculinity and boys at school. *Gender and Education, 15*(4), 407–423.

Weaver-Hightower, M. B. (2008). *The politics of policy in boys' education: Getting boys "right."* New York: Palgrave Macmillan.

Weaver-Hightower, M. B. (2010). Where the guys are: Males in higher education. *Change: The Magazine of Higher Learning, 42*(3), 29–35.

Webber, G., & Williams, C. (2008). Mothers in "good" and "bad" part-time jobs different problems, same results. *Gender & Society, 22*(6), 752–777.

Weinshenker, M. N. (2006). Adolescents' expectations about mothers' employment: Life course patterns and parental influence. *Sex Roles, 54*(11–12), 845–857.

Welter, B. (1966). The cult of true womanhood: 1820–1860. *American Quarterly, 18* (2), 151–174. DOI: 10.2307/2711179.

West, C., & Zimmerman, D. H. (1987, June). Doing gender. *Gender and Society, 1*(1), 125–151.

Wexler, P., Crichlow, W., Kern, J., & Matusewicz, R. (1992). *Becoming somebody: Toward a social psychology of school.* London, UK: Falmer Press.

The White House. (2011). *Education blueprint: An economy built to last.* Retrieved from www.whitehouse.gov

Whitmire, R. (2010). *Why boys fail: Saving our sons from an educational system that's leaving them behind*. New York: American Management Association.

Willard, E. (1819). *An address to the public particularly to the members of the legislature of New York proposing a plan for improving female education*. Middlebury, VT: J.W. Copeland.

Williams, A. (2010, February 7). The new math on campus: When women outnumber men at a college, dating culture is skewed. *The New York Times*, pp. ST1, 8.

Williams, A. (2013). The glass escalator, revisited: Gender inequality in neoliberal times. *Gender & Society, 27*, 609–629.

Williams, A. P., Domnick-Pierre, K., Vayda, E., Stevenson, H. M., & Burke, M. (1990). Women in medicine: Practice patterns and attitudes. *Canadian Medical Association Journal, 143*(3), 194–121.

Williams, A. P., Pierre, K. D., & Vayda, E. (1992). Women in medicine: Toward a conceptual understanding of the potential for change. *Journal of the American Medical Women's Association, 48*(4), 115–121.

Williams, C. L., Muller, C., & Kilanski, K. (2012). Gendered organizations in the new economy. *Gender & Society, 26*(4), 549–573.

Williams, J. C. (2007, March). The opt-out revolution revisited. *The American Prospect, 18*(3), A12–A15.

Williams, J. C. (2010). *Reshaping the work–family debate: Why men and class matter* (the William E. Massey Sr. lectures in the history of American civilization). Cambridge, MA: Harvard University Press.

Wingfield, A. H. (2009). Racializing the glass escalator reconsidering men's experiences with women's work. *Gender & Society, 23*(1), 5–26.

Wingfield, N. (2012, September 30). Fostering tech talent in schools. *The New York Times*. Retrieved from www.nytimes.com

Winn, J. (2004). Entrepreneurship: Not an easy path to top management for women. *Women in Management Review, 19*(3), 143–153.

Winn, J., & Heeter, C. (2009). Gaming, gender, and time: Who makes time to play? *Sex Roles, 61*(1–2), 1–13.

Wirt, J., Choy, S., Rooney, P., Provasnik, S., Sen, A., & Tobin, R. (2004). The Condition of Education 2004: U.S. Department of Education. Washington, DC: U.S. Government Printing Office.

Wood, P. (2011). Higher education's precarious hold on consumer confidence. *Academic Questions, 24*(3), 262–281.

Woody, T. (1929). *A history of women's education in the United States*. New York, NY: The Science Press.

Working Mother Research Group. (2011). *What moms choose: The working mother report*. Retrieved from www.workingmother.com

Yankelovich, D. (2005). Ferment and change: Higher education in 2015. *The Chronicle of Higher Education, 52*(14), B6–B9.

Yoder, J. D. (1991). Rethinking tokenism: Looking beyond numbers. *Gender & Society, 5*(2), 178–192.

Yoder, J. D., & Kahn, A. S. (2003). Making gender comparisons more meaningful: A call for more attention to social context. *Psychology of Women Quarterly, 27*(4), 281–290.

Young turks in the corner office. (2007, January 8). *Business Week*, p. 8.

Zyngier, D. (2009). Doing it to (for) boys (again): Do we really need more books telling us there is a problem with boys' underachievement in education? *Gender and Education, 21*(1), 111–118.

INDEX